CA

AUSTRALIA
Law Book Co.
Sydney

CANADA and USA
Carswell
Toronto

HONG KONG
Sweet & Maxwell Asia

NEW ZEALAND
Brookers
Wellington

SINGAPORE and MALAYSIA
Sweet & Maxwell Asia
Singapore and Kuala Lumpur

Effective Legal Research

by

PHILIP A. THOMAS
Professor of Socio Legal Studies, Cardiff Law School, University of Wales, Cardiff

JOHN KNOWLES
Law Librarian, Queen's University Belfast

THOMSON

SWEET & MAXWELL

Published in 2006 by
Sweet & Maxwell Limited of
100 Avenue Road London NW3 3PF
http:/www/sweetandmaxwell.co.uk
Typeset by Servis Filmsetting Limited, Manchester
Printed in England by Ashford Colour Press, Gosport, Hants

A CIP catalogue record for this book is available from the British Library

ISBN 0421 922 702

No natural forests were destroyed to make this product, only farmed timber
was used and re-planted.

Contents

3. Law reports

4. Legislation

5. Journals

6. UK official publications

7. How to find information on a subject

8. European Community law

x   Contents

Acknowledgments

The authors and publishers would like to thank those organisations who have allowed their copyrighted materials to be reproduced as examples throughout this book. All efforts were made to contact the copyright holders and grateful acknowledgment is made to ICLR, TSO, BAILII and Westlaw UK, amongst others for their permissions.

All extracted materials are represented in the format and with the correct content at the time of writing the book and are subject to change.

Preface

A new law student is faced with a potentially bewildering variety of sources of law. A recent case mentioned in a lecture might be found in a database of law reports, a printed report, or a website providing access to recent court judgments. There might be journal articles or newspaper reports that discuss the case. The text of an Act can be found in a number of different ways, using both online sources and editions of statutes found in a law library. It can be difficult to know where to start. This book aims to help you make effective use of the law resources to which you have access. Online sources are placed alongside traditional print sources in each of the chapters of the book and their use explained, in order that you can make the best possible use of both.

In a sense, this book is a labour-saving device. Use it as a reference throughout your time as a student, or indeed thereafter, should you decide to go into legal practice. Though some of the more detailed coverage is most likely to be of use if you are embarking on a legal research module (or a post-graduate qualification), it is not intended to be a textbook associated with a particular course. It is a reference aid to be consulted whenever you have a problem. Consequently, you might use the book selectively, referring to those sections which are useful at a particular point in your studies, or when recommended to look up a case, statute or issue by a member of the teaching staff.

The book concentrates on the law in England and Wales. Detailed coverage is also given of European human rights law and the law of the European Union. A brief appendix covers online sources of Scots and Northern Ireland law.

Most of the coverage of print sources found in *Dane & Thomas: How to Use a Law Library*, 4th edition, 2001, has been retained and revised for the current work. The coverage of online sources has been largely re-written.

1   Making the most of a law library

Introduction

A law library might seem the most traditional of libraries. A university law library contains   **1–1** many shelves of heavy bound volumes of statutes and law reports, along with a wide variety of academic journals and textbooks. Sometimes the law library will be housed in a separate building; more often it will form one area within a larger library.

Imposing as these print collections can be, however, they constitute only one part of what a law library offers. The library is also a gateway to online collections of legal materials. Sometimes the extent of these materials can even surpass what is available in print. To learn how to research the law efficiently and effectively is to learn how to make use of both the online and the print collections of a law library.

The Library Catalogue

The online library catalogue is your guide to the extent of the print and online materials   **1–2** available to you. It will also be supplemented by library web pages which usually provide access to online services. Online catalogues are easy to use and computers dedicated to catalogue access will be available throughout the library building. You can also connect to the catalogue from outside the library using the internet. Find the library catalogue and web pages as soon as you can and familiarise yourself with the way they work. If you are not already well acquainted with the law library, make use of library induction talks and seek out guides provided for you, both in print and on the library website. Remember that librarians are there to support you and so do not be afraid to ask for help, especially at the start of your course.

Books

1–3   The books held in a university library are usually the best starting point for legal research. Making good use of them can save a great deal of wasted effort.

You will find three different kinds of book on the library shelves. Textbooks designed for undergraduates explain the fundamentals of law in a particular area. These are complemented by research texts (sometimes called monographs) which offer detailed descriptions of the law and usually a more advanced level of discussion. These often assume the knowledge set out in undergraduate textbooks. Practitioner texts and loose-leaf updating services, in contrast, aim to provide a detailed, authoritative, statement of the law in a particular area. They are designed first and foremost for the legal profession. All three types of book can be useful to legal research. Check dates of publication, to ensure that you are using the most recent edition.

Books of all kinds are usually grouped on the shelves according to their subject. The subject dealt with in each book is indicated by numbers, or letters and numbers, which are usually printed on the spine of the book. These symbols indicate the exact subject matter of each volume. They are known as the classification number or classmark and bring together, in one area of the library, all books dealing with the same subject, such as torts, criminal law and constitutional law.

There may be a number of separate sequences in the library. Large books (folios and quartos) and very thin books (pamphlets) may be kept in a separate part of the library. Thus, the size of the book may be important in helping you to find it on the shelves. There will normally be some indication on the catalogue entry for a book, if a book is shelved separately.

Searching the library catalogue

1–4   Library catalogues allow you to search for books by the author's name, or the title of the book. It is usually easier and quicker to search by title (ignoring words such as "The" or "A" in the title), or alternatively by a combination of author surname and title. If you do not have the exact title, a "keyword search" enables you to search for words occurring anywhere in the title. Additional searches by subject area or classification are usually also possible (7–29). If the library has the book you want, the catalogue entry will give you its full details (e.g. its publisher, the date of publication and the length of the book in pages) and the location of the book on the shelves.

Author searches should be used with care. Even if you are sure of the author of the book, you may need to check a number of author entries before you find the right one. Suppose you have a reference to a book written by John Jackson. If you use the author search and enter "Jackson, J" you will see index entries that might feature the following variations of the name (among others):

Jackson, J.A., John Archer, 1929–
Jackson, J.D, John Dugland, 1955–
Jackson, J.E., John Ellwood

Jackson, John, 1887–1958
Jackson, John E.

You need to start with "Jackson, J.A." and work
down the list in order to find the right author. In this
case, the second author listed is a writer on legal subjects, but a search using "Jackson, John" would have
missed the correct entry. The index display would
begin with "Jackson, John, 1881–1952".

SEARCH TIP

Use keyword or "keyword in title" searches to
find books in the library catalogue. Combine
keywords with the author surname if known.

Law books often continue to be known by the name of the original author, even though
that author might be dead. This is something you will need to take account of when using
the catalogue. Let us take as an example, *Winfield and Jolowicz on Tort*. This is in its six-
teenth edition. Winfield has not been involved with the work for many years, but it is still
referred to by his name. You will usually find an entry in the author catalogue under
Winfield, but in addition, there will also be an entry under Rogers, W.V.H. who is the author
of the current edition. If you are using a title search you need to search for "Winfield and
Jolowicz on Tort", not "Tort", which was the original title of the book.

Many law books have been written jointly by two or more authors. You may be referred
for example to Craig and de Burca (*EU Law*) or Clayton and Tomlinson (*The Law of Human
Rights*). There will be an entry in the catalogue for both authors, and title searches should
be for "EU Law" or "Law of Human Rights".

Sometimes a book does not have an individual as the author. It is published by an organisation or society and the organisation is, in effect, the author. In this case, you will find an
entry in the catalogue under the name of the body, e.g. Law Commission, Law Society, Legal
Action Group, United Nations.

Finding and borrowing books

The classification number for a book appears prominently in the library catalogue entry. It   **1–5**
is usually combined with letters and numbers based on the author's name which enable you
to trace the precise place the book should appear on the shelves. Remember to check also
for any indication that the book you wish to find may be shelved in a separate sequence
(pamphlets, large-sized books etc).

If the book is on loan to another reader, the library catalogue will give the current return
date for the book. It is usually possible for you to reserve the book using the catalogue, in
which case the book will be recalled from its present borrower.

A book may be mis-shelved or missing, or have been removed by library staff for some
reason, e.g. re-binding. If you have any problems finding a book, ask a member of the library
staff for help.

When you borrow a book from a library issue desk (or self-service issue machine), you
will be given a return date for the book. Remember that the book could be requested before
that date if another reader has reserved it. There will also be fines for late return. These fines
can be expensive if the book has been borrowed from a short-loan, reserve, or consultation
collection.

Law Reports and Journals

1–6   In the course of your legal studies you will often need to look at reports of cases which have been heard in courts, both in the UK and abroad. These reports are published in a number of publications called law reports. Amongst the best known series of law reports are the *All England Law Reports*, the *Weekly Law Reports* and the *Law Reports*. These are examined in more detail in chapter 3. There is a standard form of writing references to law reports, and this is explained in **3–3**.

The bound volumes of law reports found on library shelves are usually held in a separate sequence. These volumes are not for loan. In a well established library, the collections of law reports will be extensive. A single series of these reports, *The Law Reports*, first published in 1864 occupies many metres of shelving in the law library. Although this is the most extensive series, there are many others. In addition to the shelves containing such bound volumes, the library will also have prominently located display shelves for recent, unbound issues of law reports.

Most law reports are also available online and access is provided almost exclusively by the database services such as LexisNexis Professional and Westlaw UK. These are described in **2–2**. It is worth keeping in mind just how much information these services contain. *The Law Reports* are almost certainly available to you online and they form only one part of a single database within LexisNexis Professional and Westlaw UK.

You will find, in addition, that you are referred to articles and case notes in journals (or periodicals). Journals provide commentary on cases and advanced discussion of legal issues. They are published for the most part either weekly, monthly or quarterly (hence the name, periodical). A journal reference should give you the author and title of a journal article, the year, the volume number, an abbreviation for the title of the journal in which the article appeared and the page number of the first page of the article itself, e.g.

J Jackson "The effect of human rights in criminal evidentiary processes" (2005) 68 M.L.R. 737

Law database providers such as LexisNexis Professional and Westlaw UK provide access to the full text of journal articles as well as to law reports, though not all UK journals are available online. Library subscriptions also ensure that the full text of many other journals can be accessed directly from publisher's websites or through intermediary sites.

As is the case with law reports, the bound print volumes of printed journals are usually shelved in a separate sequence in the library. There is usually a display area for recent unbound issues similar to the display area for unbound law reports.

Abbreviations

1–7   The tradition adopted by lecturers and authors of referring to journals and law reports only by an abbreviated form of their full title can present a major difficulty for new students. Instead of writing the name of the journal or law report in full, they are invariably short-ened to such cryptic abbreviations as:

(2005) 68 (5) M.L.R. 737
[2005] 3 W.L.R. 3281

This may make it difficult for you to know whether you are looking for a law report or a journal article. If you are in any doubt as to the nature of a reference, ask a member of the library staff for advice. Many of the references are confusingly similar, e.g. L.R. can be the abbreviation for both "law report" and "law review". The law reports are shelved together, but separately from the law reviews, which are journals. Consequently, if you are looking along the shelves of bound volumes for a publication, you could find yourself looking in the wrong sequence. A common mistake, for instance, is to assume that a reference to a report of a case in "Crim.L.R." means that you must search amongst the law reports for a series entitled the Criminal Law Reports. There is no such series (although there is a series called the *Criminal Appeal Reports*). The reference "Crim.L.R." is the *Criminal Law Review*, which is a journal shelved with the other journals. It contains both articles and reports of cases.

The meaning of abbreviations can be checked both online and in print and key sources are noted in **3–5**.

Tracing journals and law reports

It can be difficult to establish which journals and law reports are available online. The library catalogue and web pages may provide an A-Z list of the journals and law reports you can access. If not, you need to search the journals sections of LexisNexis Professional and Westlaw UK (assuming these are available), in order to establish whether access to the full text of the journal which interests you is provided by either service (see **5–2**). Links to the websites of publishers providing subscription access may also be provided from the library catalogue. To discover if this is the case, search the catalogue as if you were looking for the print volumes of the journal. The full online text of journals is usually only available for journal articles published after the mid 1990s.   **1–8**

To find out if the printed volumes of a journal or law report are available in the library, search the library catalogue using the full title of the journal or report, not its abbreviation. The catalogue should allow you to select a separate journal title search, so that you only search for journal entries.

If you are looking for a journal which includes the name of an organisation in its title, you may by unsure of the precise title to use. Is it the *American Bar Association Journal*, for example, or the *Journal of the American Bar Association*? In these cases it is usually possible to search for the journal by the name of the organisation that produces it. If the publication you wish to find has "Bulletin", "Transactions" or "Proceedings" at the start of its title, retain these words when you make your search or use a "keyword in title" search.

Reference Sources

A number of reference sources are available for legal research, both online and in print. The key legal encyclopaedia is *Halsbury's Laws of England* (**7–3**), accessed online from LexisNexis Butterworths.   **1–9**

Dictionaries

1–10   Lawyers have a language of their own, which is a mixture of Latin, French and English. There are several small single volume dictionaries of law which may be useful for your research. Some may be available in the library reference section. The library may also have subscriptions for online versions. Examples include the Oxford Reference *Dictionary of Law* (2003) and the *Collins Dictionary of Law* (2001), both available online and in print. Check the library catalogue or reference web pages for online access. The library shelves are also likely to contain more substantial multi-volume law dictionaries such as *Strouds Judicial Dictionary of Words and Phrases*. Standard English dictionaries may also be useful. The multi-volume *Oxford English Dictionary* should be available, in many cases in both online and print versions.

Latin phrases and maxims may cause difficulties for students who have no classical languages. Latin phrases appear in most legal dictionaries and a collection of legal maxims appears in H. Broom, *A Selection of Legal Maxims* (2000). If you are carrying out research in legal history, you may need J.H. Baker, *Manual of Law French* (1990).

Tracing people and addresses

1–11   The law library reference collection will contain a number of standard directories which can help you find the addresses of courts, legal firms, professional bodies, etc. Solicitors and barristers can be easily traced from the online listing provided by the directory websites. The Waterlows website (at *www.waterlowlegal.com*) provides access to the lists of solicitors and barristers contained in their *Solicitors' and Barristers' Directory*. QCs, judges, Benchers of the Inns, Recorders and members of the Institute of Legal Executives are also included. If you want to trace a solicitor by area of specialisation this can be done by using the Law Society website (at *www.solicitors-online.com*) which provides access to the listing contained in the Law Society's *Directory of Solicitors*. The sections of the *Bar Directory* covering barristers' chambers by location and barristers in private practice can be searched online (at *www.sweetandmaxwell.co.uk/bardirectory/website*). The Legalease website provides access both to the *Legal 500* (at *www.legal500.com*), a guide to barristers' chambers and solicitors firms for commercial clients, and the online version of *Who's Who in the Law*, which provides professional profiles of barristers and solicitors. Biographical details of prominent members of the legal profession can also be found in *Who's Who*. *Debrett's Correct Form* provides advice on the correct form of address when writing to, or addressing, members of the judiciary and other eminent people. Check the library catalogue for online subscription access to *Who's Who* and *Debrett's*. The addresses of regional legal aid offices are found on the Legal Services Commission website (at *www.legalservices.gov.uk*).

The addresses of many organisations and bodies may be found in the *Directory of British Associations*, and in the companion publication, *Councils, Committees and Boards*. The latter group of organisations in particular can be difficult to trace from general internet searches. The main reference collection in your library will contain many other print sources enabling you to trace people and organisations. Ask library reference staff for advice if you need help.

2 Using online sources of law

Introduction

The last decade has seen a dramatic shift in the scope and availability of information online. **2–1** Finding useful information on the internet using a web search engine such as Google has become second nature for many people. Nevertheless, beware of assuming that a web search engine is the only route to online information, especially when undertaking legal research. A great deal of relatively recent case law and legislation, along with important parliamentary and government publications, can be found using a web search engine. The response will also be gratifyingly quick and apparently comprehensive. However, a great deal of useful source material for research will also be missed.

To make effective use of online sources of law also requires that you learn how to use the database services already noted in chapter 1. Services such as LexisNexis Professional and Westlaw UK are the only sources, for example, that can give you a complete statement of law in force for England and Wales. They, and other subscription services, also contain extensive archives of case law which are not otherwise available online. Just as important, the vast majority of journal articles currently accessible online are only available from database services, or from other subscription websites. All of these information sources—cases, legislation in force and journal articles—are effectively part of the hidden web. This means that unless you have access to subscription sources made available by a library, they will be closed to you.

Searching subscription database services such as LexisNexis Professional and Westlaw UK using keywords and indexes also requires a different approach to that used in searching internet search engines. Key elements of how to search online databases are noted in **2–11**. The coverage of the services themselves is noted from **2–2** onwards.

It would be wrong, however, to suggest that subscription databases services provide the only important source of law online. The BAILII website and OPSI legislation pages provide free public access to primary sources and their use should not be ignored. Further information on these sites is provided in **2–12**.

Understanding the way both subscription and non-subscription law sites work will help you get the best from the online sources available to you. You will find them referred to a great deal in the following chapters. Throughout the book the use of an online resource for legal research is outlined first, followed by an outline of how to use the print alternative, if there is one. Remember, there remain advantages to the use of print sources in your legal research (**2–16**).

Subscription Database Services

2–2   Your university library or law school is likely to have subscriptions to at least two of the services provided by the major commercial database providers. These are services which provide access to a package of case law, legislation, and often either index references to journal articles, or the full text of the articles themselves. Practitioner texts may also be included as online books.

These services are web-based and the home page of the service once found looks much like any other web page on the internet; so too will the search and results pages. One difference is that the web pages you see when you are using one of the online subscription services are part of a live interactive session in which you are sending questions and commands to a database and receiving information in response. There will be some form of logging on and exit procedure to start and finish your online session and you may also be "timed out" if you leave a page for a long period of time and then wish to restart. Because you are logged on to a remote service it is also not advisable to use the "forward" and "back" commands of your web browser, as this can mean that the pages you are using become out of step with the server at the other end of your search session. The logging on procedure will also ensure that you are a valid user of the system. Standard logging on and authentication procedures for UK universities are covered in **2–8**.

The database coverage of each of the major subscription services is outlined in the following sections. Understanding the different coverage and publishing affiliations of the database providers can help you decide where to start your legal research online. LexisNexis Professional and Westlaw UK for example are linked to LexisNexis and Sweet & Maxwell publishing respectively. As a result, journals, law reports and practitioner texts published by Sweet & Maxwell do not appear in the LexisNexis Professional databases. Likewise, LexisNexis (formally Butterworths) publications do not appear as full text publications in Westlaw UK.

LexisNexis Professional

2–3   The LexisNexis Professional service is part of the LexisNexis publishing group which also includes LexisNexis Butterworths (**2–4**). However, LexisNexis Professional is a distinct service which shares its databases with LexisNexis services based in the USA.

UK and EU sources of law are highlighted in the main search menu of LexisNexis Professional. The *UK Cases* database includes over 30 specialist law reports in full text along with the full text of the *All England Law Reports* and the *Law Reports* (from 1864). The *All England Law Reports Reprints* covering 1558 to 1935 were added in 2005. Transcripts of the judgments made in "unreported" cases (see **3–19**) have been included since the mid 1980s. Completing the UK coverage, the *UK Legislation* database provides the full text of law in force for England and Wales. The content of the *EU Case Law* and *EU Legislation* databases corresponds to the EU's EUR-Lex database of primary sources (see **8–3**).

The US-based nature of the service allows LexisNexis Professional users access to substantial databases of US primary law, along with the full text of a large number of North

American law journals. Primary law and some journals from other jurisdictions are also available—for the most part from Commonwealth or former Commonwealth countries. The full range of databases can be viewed from the source directory found under the "Power Search" option on the LexisNexis Professional search page (see figure on p. 10).

Much of the full text coverage is the same as that provided by Westlaw UK. However, coverage of the specialist UK law reports is different, with LexisNexis Professional including reports published by LexisNexis Butterworths, e.g. *Butterworths' Company Law Cases* and the *Education Law Reports*. Many of the full text law journals available from the *UK Journals* database are also LexisNexis Butterworths or Oxford University Press publications, though others are included. Currently over 80 titles can be searched, including the *New Law Journal* and the *Oxford Journal of Legal Studies*. Perhaps confusingly, the *UK Journals* database includes a number of publications which would be found in loose-leaf binders on the library bookshelves, such as *Butterworths Corporate Law Service* and *Butterworths Planning Law Service*.

The news databases provided by LexisNexis Professional can be of particular benefit for legal research. The full text of all UK national newspapers is included, for the most part from the mid 1980s, along with many regional papers. Some universities also subscribe to the companion LexisNexis Executive service which adds coverage of international news sources.

Access to LexisNexis Professional is expected to be integrated more fully with the LexisNexis Butterworths databases from 2006.

LexisNexis Butterworths

The LexisNexis Butterworths service provides access to a range of databases formally provided by Butterworths Direct. Unlike either Westlaw UK or LexisNexis Professional, the range of databases available will vary from library to library as libraries are able to subscribe to databases on a title by title basis. The databases available are grouped under three major headings: Case Law, Legislation and Commentary. Many of the database titles mirror the content of printed law reports and commentaries and libraries are likely to have access, for example, to online versions of the *All England Law Reports* and *Halsbury's Laws of England*. The legislation databases include *UK Parliament Acts and Statutory Instruments* and *Scottish Parliament Acts and Statutory Instruments*. As with LexisNexis Professional, specialist titles are largely drawn from LexisNexis Butterworths publications. This means that a large number of loose-leaf publications and practitioner texts are potentially available. These include standard practioner texts likely to be found on the bookshelves such as Lester & Pannick, *Human Rights*, and Laddie, Prescott & Vitoria, *The Modern Law of Copyright and Designs*. A number of Tolley's publications, such as *Tolley's Company Law* are also included.

Where libraries have subscriptions to LexisNexis Butterworths databases, only those available for access will be displayed on the initial search menu.

2–4

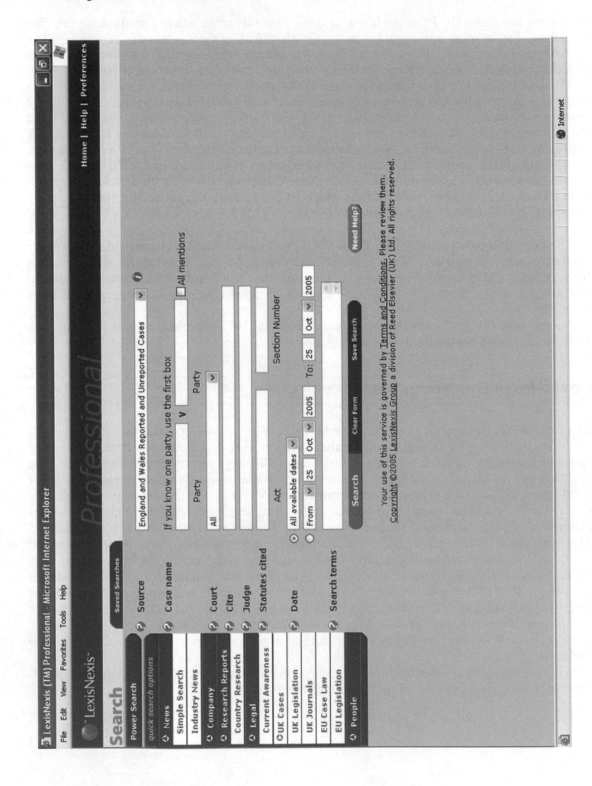

Westlaw UK

Westlaw UK (see figure on p. 12), uses the US-based Westlaw service to provide access to case   **2–5**
law, legislation and journal databases provided by Sweet & Maxwell. As with LexisNexis
Professional, the full text of publicly available legislation and case law is combined with a
range of publications from (in this case) a single UK publisher. The link with the US Westlaw
service also means that the Westlaw UK directory of sources can provide access to North
American content similar to that provided by LexisNexis Professional.

The Sweet & Maxwell content means that Westlaw UK has the most comprehensive case
finding database available for England and Wales case law. Using the indexes and brief case
summaries published in print as *Current Law*, the Westlaw UK *UK Case Locators* database
provides summaries of all reported UK cases, whether published by Sweet & Maxwell or
otherwise, along with citations for each of the law report series that has published a report.
Where relevant, brief case histories are also added, allowing the reader to discover, for
example, which cases have followed the ruling made in a particular judgment and which
cases have considered it. Where the full text of a law report, or a judgment transcript, is
available in the Westlaw UK *UK Cases* database, a link is made from the entry for the case in
the *Case Locators* database to the full text. The 21 law reports available in full text include
the *Law Reports*, the *Weekly Law Reports*, and the *European Human Rights Reports*.

In a similar way, Westlaw UK's *UK Legislation Locators* makes use of indexes and notes
published in *Current Law* to provide information on legislation in force which includes commencement and amendment information along with lists of cases which have cited the legislation where relevant. Links are provided to the relevant sections of statutes and statutory
instruments.

Another unique feature of Westlaw UK is the *Legal Journals Index* database, an online
version of Sweet & Maxwell's *Legal Journals Index*. The database allows articles from a wide
range of UK legal journals to be traced using keywords, author names and other publication details. Sweet & Maxwell published law journals are available in full text in the UK
Journals database and links are made from *Legal Journals Index* entries to the relevant articles. Journals available in full text include the *Criminal Law Review* and the *Statute Law
Review*. Articles from just under 40 journals are available from the mid-1990s onwards.

Lawtel

Although aimed primarily at the legal profession, many university libraries provide access to   **2–6**
Lawtel. Lawtel is essentially a current awareness digest service which provides brief case
reports, usually within a day of a judgment being made. The case reports, which date back to
the mid-1980s, are in turn linked to the full text of judgment transcripts as they become available. A number of additional features include a *Statutory Law* service, which provides update
notes on amendments and repeals made to sections of Acts, and the Articles Index, which provides summaries of articles from over 50 legal and potentially relevant non-legal journals.

The Lawtel service is now a Westlaw UK product, but it has retained its separate role and
identity.

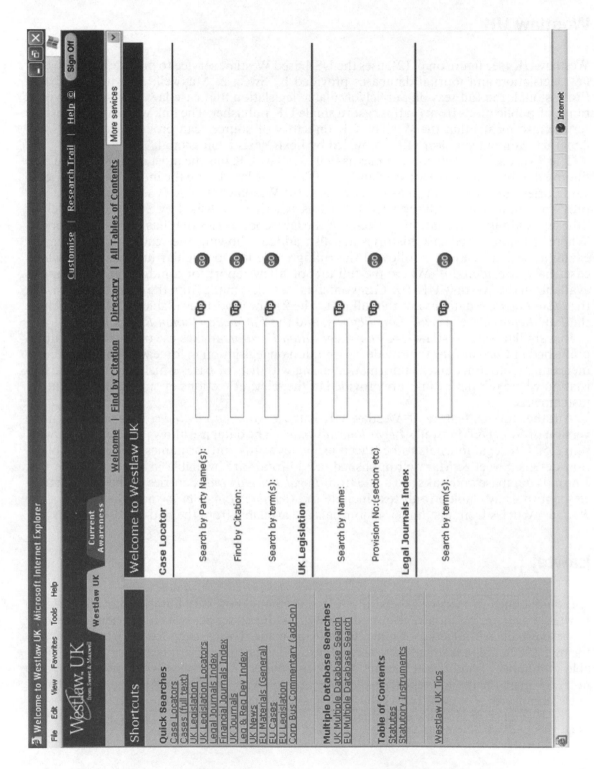

Justis Publishing

Justis Publishing provides access to a number of primary sources not otherwise available   2–7
online. You may find that your library can provide access to one or two of them. Case law from
Justis includes the *Weekly Law Reports* and the *English Reports* (**3–12**), the major source for
law reports published before the *Law Reports* series began in 1864. Justis is also the only online
source for the full text of all Acts of Parliament from 1235 onwards, including all repealed legislation. The other subscription services only include the full text of law in force.

Accessing Subscription Database Services

As already noted, subscription database services are web-based. This means that network   2–8
access requires no more than a PC with an internet connection and a web browser such as
Internet Explorer. There is no specialist software that needs to be loaded or mastered.

However, you will only be able to use these services if your university law library or law
school has paid a subscription. Typically access is licensed to staff and students of a university, either for a limited number of simultaneous users, or more usually, for unlimited
access to any number of users. The licence will have been paid for on an annual basis with
the result that no additional charge is made by the database provider for the connection time
to the database.

Where online services are licensed, the logging on procedure for the service is important,
not just because it provides a way of starting a database query session, but also because it
provides a way of confirming that there is a current valid subscription to access the database. The username and the password you enter confirm that the institution has a current
subscription. Logging in using the correct procedure means that you are recognised as an
authenticated user of the relevant service.

For students in UK universities, the requirement for authentication is provided by a single
intermediary service: the Athens Access Management system. It is not important to understand how the system operates, but its use by UK universities has some important consequences. Firstly, access to a subscription database service such as LexisNexis Professional
or Westlaw UK must be made from a web page link provided by your university library or
law school. If you use your web browser to go directly to the home page of one of these services (e.g. *uk.westlaw.com*), it is not unusual to find login boxes requesting a username and
a password to continue, but you will not be able to access the service in this way. This login
point is for non-academic users. If instead you follow the link to the relevant service provided by your own university, you will be directed to a different login screen, again requesting a username and a password. This will be the username and password valid for the Athens
system (see **2–9** below). Once both username and password have been entered, you will be
directed to the welcome page of the service you wish to use.

Another consequence of the use of the Athens authentication system is that you will only
be asked for your username and password once in any online session. This means that if you
log in first, for example, to a Justis database and then decide to move to Westlaw UK, you
will not be asked for a username and password when you link to Westlaw UK. You are

already recognised as a user with rights to access the service. More importantly, you do not need to be connected to the university network to access any of the subscription services to which you have access. The Athens authentication system operates remotely, allowing you to be recognised as a valid user of a service whether you are logging in from a university hall of residence, from home, or from the other side of the world.

Usernames and passwords

2–9　In most universities a single username and password combination enables a student to log on to both internal computing resources, such as a university email account, and to subscription services such as Westlaw UK or LexisNexis Professional. This is because Athens usernames and passwords are validated locally, using a login page belonging to your own university. As a result your university username and password can be used to access remote subscription services. Both username and password are usually given to you when you first register with the university.

In some cases a different username and password will be needed for accessing remote services and you will be given separate Athens account details. Your university library or computing service should inform you if you need to use an additional Athens account.

Universities are also working towards the provision of a "single sign on" for all networked services. In a single sign on system, once you have logged on to the university network, you will not be asked again for usernames and passwords, whether you are using email accounts, accessing exam results, or using online subscription services.

Library portals

2–10　In many universities access to online resources is now provided by a library portal. The portal consists of special set of library or university web pages that allow you to search many of the online services to which you have access using a single standard search page. The portal then translates the search into the form required for the database selected. A particular advantage of a library portal is that more than one database can be searched in response to a single query.

Unfortunately, the way the major subscription law services structure their databases means that they cannot be searched directly from a library portal search page. Instead, the portal simply provides a link to the "native" interface of the service. You will in effect have to leave the portal pages and use the service in the normal way.

Database Searching

2–11　Although the search pages of services such as Westlaw UK and LexisNexis Professional appear as web pages, and even though the results of a search are presented as a sometimes lengthy list of links to further web pages, when you search a subscription database you are not searching a website. The subscription services provide access to databases constructed from the fully indexed raw text of reports, statutes etc. This has consequences for the way these databases are best searched.

When a database of full text or bibliographic (reference) data is constructed, all uses of a word are automatically indexed and tagged according to their place in the document. Words will be indexed as title words, for example, or as names appearing in the "parties" section of a case report. This will enable searches to be restricted to words in the title or names in the parties section or "field" of the database. If a name, e.g. "Hart" is tagged as the

name of a party to a case, for example, all cases in which someone called Hart is one of the parties will be listed in the computer index used for party names. If you search for Hart as the party to a case, the name you entered is matched against the database indexes and the relevant documents retrieved. The database index works at this level in much the same way as the index to this book, and the database search software is performing an operation that is equivalent to looking up a word in the index and seeing which pages contain relevant information.

This indexing of words makes so-called "Boolean" searching a powerful way of retrieving information from a database. Two examples might help.

Suppose first, that you wish to search the *Legal Journals Index* database (from Westlaw UK) in order to find journal references relevant to the issue of provocation as a defence. You are particularly interested in linking the issue to domestic violence against women. Enter the words

Provocation AND domestic violence

in the subject search area of the search page and click the "go" button. The search software will now retrieve all index entries that are linked both to the term "provocation" and the term "domestic violence". The significance of the "AND" (one of the "Boolean operators") is that it requests this linking of index entries to be made. The result is a list of references which contain both the word "provocation" and the words "domestic violence". (In many databases you need to use quotation marks to indicate that you wish "domestic violence" to be treated as a phrase).

If you wanted to go further with this search, you might also consider that "domestic violence" is not the only phrase of potential interest that could occur in the title or summary of a journal article. Another significant Boolean operator that can help is "OR" which acts as a request to group the index entries for two different words. Using

Battered women OR domestic violence

will widen the scope to the references found to include these using either the phrase "battered women" or the phrase "domestic violence". As there are articles which use the term "battered women" but not "domestic violence", more references will be found. In this case it would be better to make two searches, one for both "Provocation and domestic violence" and the other for "Provocation and battered women".

Suppose now you wish to find cases that have discussed the way the word "charity" has been interpreted in English law. You have decided to look for judgments in which "charity" has been judicially interpreted and are going to search a full text database of case law, such as the Westlaw UK *UK Cases* database, or the LexisNexis Professional *UK Cases* database. Here things can become a little more involved.

An initial consideration might be that because of the complexity of the English language, along with "charity", your keywords might also include, "sense", "usage", or "definition" as well as "interpretation". All these terms should be included in your search (either by repeating searches or using "OR"). Different forms of the same word can also be used. You might want to search for "define", "defines" and "defining" along with "definition" for example. Fortunately most databases allow a truncation symbol which can help, so that "defin*" could cover all of the forms mentioned. Less fortunately, "definite" would also be included in the search, so use truncation with care.

Having thought about your search terms, also make sure that you use the symbol or "search operator" for the database that specifies that your keywords must be found close to each other in the long text of a judgment. Many databases allow "NEAR" to specify a standard proximity, LexisNexis Professional uses "w/" so that "w/6" specifies within 6 words.

Putting these considerations together, a "good" search for judgments on the interpretation of charity, might consist of the following string of words, truncated words and search operators. The brackets ensure that all the alternatives are taken together in one search:

charit* w/6 (defin* OR sense OR usage)

Still other combinations are possible. Though convenient, there is no necessity to make a single complex search in quite this way. Brackets are also not always interpreted in the way you would wish (Westlaw UK databases for example do not allow phrases and brackets to be specified at the same time). Simpler searches could be made and a results list built up by saving the results of each search individually.

The important point to remember is that Boolean searches provide a way of refining the accuracy and scope of your search. No single search is necessarily comprehensive. It is advisable to reconsider your search words and re-edit them as you read your search results and find, perhaps, much more than you had anticipated, or, indeed, much less. Be aware of the coverage of the database you are using, and don't be misled into thinking that any search is final or comprehensive.

Constructing searches in this way differs from the approach you would take if you were searching the internet using a search engine. The way in which results are presented is also different. A database usually lists the results containing your search words in reverse chronological order. A search engine lists a series of web links in which the pages carrying most prominently the word or words you used in your search are listed first. The words "AND" and "OR" also have a particular significance for databases which they do not have for search engines. These differences are worth remembering.

Free Sources of Law on the Internet

2–12   The primary sources of law, the judgments made in the courts, and the statue law made by the UK's various legislative bodies, are not the property of legal publishers or subscription database providers. From the mid-1990s onwards, first the House of Lords and then the Court Service of England and Wales, have put the full text of judgments onto their own web sites;

an example followed in both Scotland and Northern Ireland. During the same period the Office of Public Sector Information (OPSI), in its former guise as HMSO, has placed UK legislation on its own website (**2–13**). Recognising the public nature of this information and the problems caused by the proliferation of websites offering primary sources of law, the BAILII website, launched in 2000, has performed a particularly useful service, by bringing judgment transcripts and legislation together, so they can be searched on a single website (**2–14**).

It should be noted though, that OPSI and BAILII cannot provide some of the "value added" features provided by the commercial database suppliers. Results cannot be emailed and printing can be inconvenient. There are also no hypertext links placed within the text of some documents. More importantly, neither are there the added headnotes and case summaries that are found in the commercially published law reports. It is also only the subscription database services that can offer, for the most part, the amended text of legislation in force.

OPSI

The OPSI website (at *www.opsi.gov.uk*) provides access to the full text of Acts of Parliament   **2–13** from 1988 onwards and Statutory Instruments from 1987. The Northern Ireland, Scotland and Wales legislation pages provide access to the full text of devolved legislation. The text in almost all cases is shown in its original, unamended state, the exception being the Updated Statutes of Northern Ireland 1922 to 2004 pages available on the Northern Ireland Legislation pages.

The website can be searched by type of legislation, by year and by keywords. The keywords search engine uses the "relevance ranking" approach familiar to users of search engines such as Google. As a result it is almost always a good idea to go directly to the "Advanced Search" option which allows the search to be restricted to types of legislation. The problems of using the initial keyword search box

> **SEARCH TIP**
>
> Always look for the "Advanced Search" when searching websites. Limit your search to the kind of document that interests you. Also specify e.g. that "All words" must be found in the pages searched.

rapidly become apparent if a search is made for a Northern Ireland Statutory Rule. Using the words "Northern Ireland" with a general search will ensure that the search results highlight legislation in which the words "Northern Ireland" appear most often. The search results are then dominated by the Northern Ireland Act 1998, not of course a Statutory Rule at all.

BAILII

The BAILII (British and Irish Legal Information Institute) website (at *www. bailii.org*) (see   **2–14** figure on p. 19) provides access to a series of databases derived from public sources of law. The site includes, among other sources, recent House of Lords decisions (from 1996), Court of Appeal and High Court decisions, United Kingdom Employment Appeal Tribunal Decisions, and United Kingdom Social Security and Child Support Commissioner's Opinions. The legislation available on the OPSI site is also included. The great advantage of the site is that all of these disparate sources are brought into a standardised database format, easing searching. The database searching made possible by BAILII is also almost always an improvement on the search facilities available on the home site for the legislation or case law concerned. It is possible to search, for example, using Boolean searching ("AND", "OR" etc) and proximity searches enable the search to specify that keywords should be found close to each other in the full text of case law and legislation. BAILII was launched using systems and approaches developed by AUSTLII (Australasian Legal Information Institute) and this also means that primary sources of law for Commonwealth and former Commonwealth countries can be found from the site.

Internet Gateways

2–15   As you develop your legal research, you may well wish to move beyond the primary sources of law and the discussion and commentary provided by legal journals. Government and Parliamentary publications are covered in chapter 5. However, there are many other internet sites which may be of value. If you are researching environmental law, for example, the websites of environmental organisations may well have material which could be of value to you. Medical and health law websites would have useful content if you are researching medical law, and so on.

One approach is to try putting relevant keywords into a web search engine. Another approach is to use an internet gateway for law resources. A gateway is a single web site that acts effectively as a directory for some part of the internet. For UK law, three valuable sites providing links to legal information are Sarah Carter's *Lawlinks* site on the University of Kent's web pages (at *library.ukc.ac.uk/library/lawlinks*—example on p.20), the Delia Venables site (at *www.venables.co.uk*) and David Swarbrick's site (at *www.swarb.co.uk*). Using the environmental law section of Sarah Carter's website, for example, can provide you with links to environmental law sites such as the *Ecolex* information service on environmental law and the excellent European environmental law pages of the Asser Institute in the Netherlands. Links to relevant organisations such as English Nature and Friends of the Earth can also be found.

The websites of many of the university law schools and law libraries offer additional starting points for UK law. The Faculty of Law at Cambridge (at *www.law.cam.ac.uk*) provides an example of a site with a helpful listing of resources. The *HERO* website provides a full listing of all the UK academic sites (at *www.hero.ac.uk*). Legal material is also accessible via the more general UK academic listings provided by the *BUBL* Information Service (at *bubl.ac.uk*) which links to web sites by subject, and the *SOSIG Social Science Information Gateway* (at *sosig.ac.uk*), which concentrates on evaluating and providing links to a selection of full text resources.

Going beyond UK sources, the US *Findlaw* site (at *www.findlaw.com*) is a valuable starting point for International as well as US law and the law of individual countries. Two sites which bring together legal information with a strong slant towards sources relevant to USA law are *Law.com* (at *www.law.com*) and *Hieros Gamos* (at *www.hg.org*).

British and Irish Legal Information Institute

Access to Freely Available British and Irish Public Legal Information

Find [all of these words ▼]

[   ] [Search]

Tip: To get more control over which BAILII databases you are searching, click on the [Full Search Form] link below.

[Search Help] [**Full Search Form**]   [**Donate to BAILII**]

BAILII Cases & Legislation

- England and Wales
- Ireland
- Northern Ireland
- Scotland
- United Kingdom
- European Union

Other World Collections

- World Collections (WorldLII)
- Australasia (AustLII)
- Canada (CanLII)
- Hong Kong (HKLII)
- Pacific Islands (PacLII)

Other World Law Resources

- England and Wales
- Ireland
- Northern Ireland
- Scotland
- United Kingdom
- Territories & Dependencies

Recent Cases & Other Announcements

Society for Computers & Law

The Society for Computers & Law, as well as offering their innovative Internet-based Webinars, continue to be major sponsors of BAILII.

Recent cases

New cases of interest

English

Recent decisions   Recent accessions

Scottish

Recent decisions   Recent accessions

Northern Irish

Recent decisions   Recent accessions

UK (Privy Council & House of Lords

Recent decisions   Recent accessions

Irish

Recent decisions   Recent accessions

European Union

Recent decisions   Recent accessions

About BAILII
Feedback - Who's Who - Contact Details - Statistics - Copyright Policy - Disclaimers - Privacy Policy - Case law on BAILII

BAILII Support
Sponsors - Other People and Organisations who have helped

Help
Searching Help - Case Law Help - Legislation Help - Citing cases on BAILII

(By permission of BAILII (British and Irish Legal Information Institute) a charity that provides free online access to British and Irish legal information.)

Gateways | UK resources | UK Government | Special legal topics | Other jurisdictions | European Union | International law | Human rights | Private international law | Legal profession & legal education | Legal publishing | Library catalogues general resources

LAWLINKS

UNIVERSITY OF KENT
40 YEARS 1965-2005 ■ ■ ■ ■

INFORMATION SERVICES
TEMPLEMAN LIBRARY ■ ■ ■ ■

KLS
UNIVERSITY OF KENT
AT CANTERBURY ■ ■ ■ ■

LawPaths

Legal information on the internet
An annotated list of web sites
compiled by Sarah Carter

ELECTRONIC LAW LIBRARY	LAW RESOURCES FAQs SEARCH LAWLINKS	Google™

Gateways & portals — Starting points for legal research, providing links to legal resources across the world

UK resources — Primary sources for legislation & case law. Indexes & digests, periodical indexes. Current awareness. Devolved governments

UK government & news — Government departments & agencies. Parliament. Official publications. Sources for news & current affairs

Special legal topics — A selected list of sites by topic, with an emphasis on relevance to UK law. Some international materials.

Other jurisdictions — Sites which lead you to substantive law worldwide. European and other regional jurisdictions

European Union — Official & unofficial resources for European Union law and current affairs

International law — Including treaties & international courts, international organisations.

Human rights — Human rights & international criminal law

Private international law — Including international commercial law, international trade, maritime law and other resources

Legal profession & legal education — Sites for the legal profession, professional organisations, legal directories Legal education and training

Legal publishing — The main UK and European legal publishers. Booksellers. Electronic legal journals

General resources — Library catalogues, general bibliographic sources, email discussion lists for law, search engines

BIALL
BRITISH AND IRISH
ASSOCIATION OF
LAW LIBRARIANS
Winner of the
Wallace Breem
Memorial Award
2000

Winner of the Lex
Website Awards 2000
- Best
Portal/information
resource

[Top of page]

lawZONE.co.uk
Top Site Award

469123
since 29.1.2002

Page last updated August 25, 2005
Editor: Sarah Carter

(Reprinted by kind permission.)

When to use Print Sources

The reasons for using online sources are compelling. Sources of information which you **2–16** may not otherwise be able to use will be available to you and you need never suffer the frustration caused by the discovery that the printed volume you sought on the library shelves is in use, missing or mutilated. More importantly, the availability of full text sources online means that sources of law can be searched in a way that simply wasn't possible when only print indexes were available. It should not be assumed that online sources are always better. For some tasks, such as checking a citation when the name and year of a case is already known to you, a print source can be quicker and easier to use. A fast, accurate result can be achieved, for example, by using the *Current Law Case Citator* (see **3–16**). The full text of an Act of Parliament, or a House of Lords judgment, may also run to many pages. The type-face and layout of the printed versions, combined with the ability to scan and skip easily through the text, can make the printed publication much easier both to read and handle; especially when the alternative is a stack of pages gathered from a computer printer. There is also a significant time investment in getting to grips with an online source of information. The peculiarity of individual online services needs to be mastered, as does the search language associated with database searching. Of course, you cannot even begin, unless you have access to a networked computer.

As a library user, you will also be faced with a limited choice of available sources. Just as the book and journal coverage of a library is limited by the funds available, so too is access to online subscription services. Very few libraries have access to anything approaching the full range of services. Where both print and online services are available, the choice generally depends on the particular resources to hand, the task you have in mind, and, of course, your own personal preferences.

Remember too, that some of the most significant legal resources are still found only in print form. The student textbooks and research monographs which make up much of a library collection are currently available solely in print, and this is still true of many of the authoritative practitioner texts. Some of the journal literature in law is still also available only in print, though this is continuing to change as publishers increasingly provide online access to their journal titles (see **5–2**).

2–17

Combining Print and Electronic Sources

It is important to place electronic resources in the wider context of your legal research. Online resources are an important part of the resources available to you, but you need to learn how to make use of these alongside printed resources. It is not simply the case that "online" means "modern" and "paper" means "old fashioned". Bear in mind that a student textbook usually provides your best starting point when you are new to a subject area. If you wish to find out about the impact of the Human Rights Act 1998 on statutory interpretation, for example, you need to clarify the basic issues. This is often best achieved with the help of a recent textbook and some quality time to think about the core issues. You will find no shortage of textbooks in this area. Books published as "cases and materials" will offer a valuable quick reference as they contain extracts from leading cases and statute law. Only after you have looked at the textbook material will it probably make sense to go online using an index such as the *Legal Journals Index*. You can then search for references to journal articles that have discussed and developed the issues you have identified in your basic preparation. Online access to case law might have its place as you search for judgments that have cited what you now know to be the key cases. Having traced journal articles and cases online, you may finally need to return to print sources and use the library catalogue to locate particular journals or law reports on the library shelves.

To make the best use of law library resources you must learn how to move comfortably between electronic and print sources. The ability to do so will result in better time management and better coverage of the material. The remaining chapters of this book, placing as they do, online resources beside those in print, are designed to enable you to switch research techniques as and when appropriate.

2–18

CD-ROMs

Many of the full-text products of the commercial legal publishers, including the *All England Law Reports*, the *Law Reports* series and *UK Statutory Instruments*, were first made available in CD-ROM form. The Westlaw UK databases first appeared on CD-ROM as Current Legal Information. In general, university libraries no longer carry major databases in this form, though they can still be useful for small organisations. However, CD-ROMs may be used in the library to provide improved search access to some of the key practitioner texts and loose-leaf updating services (where they save on filing).

If you wish to use a CD-ROM held by your library you have to borrow the disc from an issue or information desk. As the CD-ROM requires particular search software to be loaded onto a computer before it can be used, you will be directed to a particular PC or workstation on which the search software is loaded. Alternatively the CD-ROM may be pre-loaded on a particular computer and you will need to locate the one that holds the CD-ROM database. This may or may not be located within the law library. Where CD-ROMs have been networked by your university, it may be possible for any machine on a university's local network to use the CD-ROM database, though again the particular machine may need to have CD-ROM search software pre-loaded. When in doubt ask for advice from the library staff about what is located where in the library.

3   Law reports

Introduction

Law reports are one of the basic (or "primary") sources of English law. Traditionally, the   **3–1**
common law develops through the practical reasoning of the judges. This is based on the particular facts of the case in question, social forces and previous judicial reasoning when it has a bearing on the case being heard. Legal principles stated in earlier decisions are given effect in later cases by the operation of the doctrine of precedent, which is described in detail in most introductory texts to the English legal system. The successful development of the common law depends largely upon the production of reliable law reports which carry not only the facts, issues and decision, but also, most importantly, the legal principles upon which the judgment is made. Currently, the senior judiciary spend most of their court time considering the scope and application of particular Acts of Parliament.

A law report re-prints the full text of a judgment, i.e. the statement of facts and judicial reasoning made by judges in a case and adds additional material. This consists of a summary of the legal issues, lists of other cases cited, legislation referred to, and other key features of the case (see **3–6**).

Only a very small proportion of cases decided by the courts is reported in the law reports. Just because a case is widely reported in the media, it does not follow that it will appear in a law report. A case is selected for reporting if it raises a point of legal significance. Judgments made in cases which are not reported, though publicly available, are referred to as "unreported judgments". Unreported judgments can nonetheless be cited in court cases where it is felt that relevant legal issues are raised. Typescript transcripts of judgments and judgments held on online databases have been referred to in court cases for some time. However, in recent years the availability of judgments has increased greatly as judgments from the High Court, the Court of Appeal and the House of Lords, have been made available on the internet on a variety of non-subscription websites (**3–19**). The judgments made available in this way do not just include those destined to remain "unreported". Judgments made in reported cases are also available.

Despite this, the element of selection provided by the law reports, and the additional explanatory material included, has meant that law reports continue to be the major primary source of case law in the English legal system. Throughout your legal study you will make constant use of law reports, occasionally supplemented by unreported judgments, usually for significant recent cases which have not yet been reported. It is worth remembering, though, that if you do not have access to a particular recent law report, the judgment made in the case reported is almost certainly available online. For 19th and almost all 20th century cases, you will have to rely on law reports.

The History of Law Reports

3–2   Law reports have existed, in one form or another, since the reign of Edward I. These very early law reports are known as the *Year Books*. If you wish to see a copy, reprints of a number of these *Year Books* are available in the series of publications published by the Selden Society, in the Rolls Series and in facsimile reprints issued by Professional Books.

After the *Year Books* had ceased, collections of law reports published privately by individuals began to appear. These reports, the first of which were published in 1571, were normally referred to by the name of the reporter or compiler. For this reason, they are collectively referred to as the *Nominate Reports* and they vary considerably in accuracy and reliability. Few libraries will have a complete collection of these old reports and if you do obtain a copy, you may find that the antiquated print makes it difficult to read. Fortunately, the great majority of these *Nominate Reports* can be found in at least one of the three reprint series, called the *English Reports*, the *Revised Reports* and the *All England Law Reports Reprint* series. The most comprehensive of the three series is the *English Reports*, which is examined in detail later in the chapter (**3–12**).

In 1865, a body called the Incorporated Council of Law Reporting commenced publication of the *Law Reports*, a single series of reports covering all the major courts. These reports were rapidly accepted by the legal profession as the most authoritative version of law reports and, as a result, most of the earlier series published by individuals ceased publication in 1865 or soon after. Judgments in the *Law Reports* have been checked by the relevant judges before publication and are cited in court in preference to any other series. The *Law Reports* series is described in more detail in **3–10**.

Today, there are over 50 different series of law reports for England and Wales. The *Weekly Law Reports* and the *All England Law Reports*, like the *Law Reports*, cover a wide range of topics and are aimed at the lawyer in general practice. There are also a large number of law reports which cover a specialised area of the law, such as the *Criminal Appeal Reports* and the *Road Traffic Reports*.

A case may be reported in more than one series of law reports. For example, a short report may appear in *The Times* newspaper (under the heading "Law Report") a day or so after the judgment is given. A summary or a full report may be published in some of the weekly legal journals, such as the *New Law Journal* and the *Solicitors Journal*, or a case note may discuss the significance of the new judgment. Several months later, the case may be published in one or both of the two general series of law reports which appear weekly, the *All England Law Reports* and the *Weekly Law Reports*, and in specialist law reports and journals (e.g. *Tax Cases*, the *Criminal Law Review*). Some time later, a final, authoritative version checked by the judges concerned may be published in the *Law Reports*. Thus, if your library does not hold the series of law reports given in the reference you have, it is worth checking whether the case is reported elsewhere (see **3–14**).

Citation of Law Reports

Lawyers often use abbreviations when referring to the sources where a report of a case can **3–3** be found. These can appear confusing at first, but constant use will rapidly make you familiar with the meaning of most of the abbreviations used. References to cases (called *citations*) are structured as shown in the following example:

Giles v Thompson[1] [1993][2] 2[3] W.L.R.[4] 908[5].

[1] the names of the parties involved in the case;
[2] the year in which the case is reported. Square brackets indicate that the date is an essential part of the citation. Some series of law reports number the volumes serially from year to year, so the reference is sufficient even if the year is omitted. Round brackets are used if the date is not essential but merely an aid;
[3] the volume number, i.e. the second volume published in 1993. Where only one volume is published in a year, the volume number is omitted unless it is essential for finding the correct volume;
[4] the abbreviation for the name of the law report or journal;
[5] the page number on which the case begins.

Thus, in this example, the case of *Giles* v *Thompson* will be found in the 1993 volumes of the *Weekly Law Reports* (abbreviated to W.L.R.). There are three volumes of the *Weekly Law Reports* containing the cases reported in 1993. The case referred to will be found in the second volume, at page 908.

If you wish to draw attention to a particular phrase or section in the judgment, you should write out the citation for the case, followed by "at" and the page number where the section or phrase is printed, hence:

Giles v *Thompson* [1993] 2 W.L.R. 908 at 910.

Since 2001 reports published by Sweet & Maxwell have been cited using a case number rather than a page number. For example: *Nestle Mars* [2005] 3 C.M.L.R. 12

This refers to case number 12 of volume 3 of the *Common Market Law Reports*. The report begins on page 259 of volume 3.

Neutral citations

In 2001 the High Court and Court of Appeal adopted a neutral, or common, form of cita- **3–4** tion for all cases. These "neutral" citations do not distinguish between print and online media and are independent of any of the published law reports. This form of citation has been adopted in order to make it easier to cite and to trace unreported judgments. The neutral form of citation can be seen in the following example:

R. (Ebrahim) v Feltham Magistrates Court [2001] EWHC Admin 130.

EWHC Admin is the standard abbreviation for the High Court (Administrative Division) for England and Wales. The number 130, placed without brackets after EWHC Admin, tells you that the judgment is judgment number 130 for 2001.

Other abbreviations are EWCA Civ for the Court of Appeal (Civil Division) and EWCA Crim for the Court of Appeal (Criminal Division).

Rather than give page references, these citations use numbers in square brackets which indicate the paragraph of a judgment, e.g.

> *R. (Ebrahim) v Feltham Magistrates Court* [2001] EWHC Admin 130 at [40]–[42].

When judgments are given in the High Court or Court of Appeal the neutral form of citation is always given at least once, ahead of any other citations. *R. (Ebrahim) v Feltham Magistrates Court* has been reported in the *All England Law Reports*, so the case would be cited as follows:

> *R. (Ebrahim) v Feltham Magistrates Court* [2001] EWHC Admin 130 at [40]–[43];
> [2001] All ER 831 at 841.

The House of Lords adopted a similar form of neutral citation in 2001. The 2001 case *Johnson (AP) v Unisys Limited*, for example, is cited using the neutral system as:

> *Johnson (AP) v Unisys Limited* [2001] UKHL 13.

UKHL is the abbreviation for the House of Lords and the number 13, placed without brackets after UKHL, tells you that the judgment is judgment number 13 for 2001. Any numbers in square brackets at the end of the citation represent paragraph numbers, as they do for Court of Appeal and High Court cases.

How to Find the Meaning of Abbreviations

3–5   A variety of different reference sources enable you to check the meaning of abbreviations. The most extensive is the Cardiff Index to Legal Abbreviations (at *www.legalabbrevs. cardiff.ac.uk*). If you are faced with an abbreviation for a law report or journal which you do not recognise, the website's abbreviations search finds matching law publications using a database compiled from a wide range of legal abbreviations. Either exact or close matches can be sought, making it possible to search for the meaning of an abbreviation even if you are not sure of the initial letter. A particular advantage of an online index is the ability it provides to search for the preferred abbreviation of a journal or law report. This can be useful if you have noted the full title of a law report or journal, but are unsure how to abbreviate it for citation purposes.

The *Current Law Monthly Digest* provides a convenient print source for current UK abbreviations. A list of abbreviations of reports and journals cited in *Current Law* (**3–16**) can be found near the front of each issue. The *Digest* (**3–17**) prints a list of abbreviations near the front of Vol. 1(1) which can help with older abbreviations. Most Law Library reference shelves also have Raistrick's *Index to Legal Citations and Abbreviations*. Some of the most commonly used abbreviations are listed in Appendix 2 of this book.

Format of Law Reports

3–6   Page 28 gives a typical example of the first page of a law report. The citation is *Cleveland Petroleum Co. Ltd v Dartstone Ltd and Another* [1969] 1 All E.R. 201. Several key points in the illustration are numbered.

1. The names of the parties. In a civil case, the name of the plaintiff (the person bringing the action) comes first, followed by the name of the defendant. The small letter "v" between the names is an abbreviation of the Latin "versus" but when speaking of a civil case, you say *"and"* not *"versus"*. A criminal case, on the other hand, might appear as *R. v Smith*. R. is the abbreviated form for the Latin words *Rex* (king) or *Regina* (queen). The charge against Smith, the accused, is brought on behalf of the Crown and this case would be said as *"the Crown against Smith"*.

2. The name of the court in which the case was heard, the names of the judges (M.R.: Master of the Rolls; L.JJ.: Lords Justices) and the date on which the case was heard.

3. A summary of the main legal issues of the case. You are advised not to rely on this, as it is not necessarily complete or accurate.

4. The headnote, which is a brief statement of the case and the nature of the claim (in a civil case) or the charge (in a criminal case). Again, do not rely on the publisher's précis but instead read the case.

5. The court's ruling is stated, with a summary of reasons.

6. In certain reports, e.g. the *All England Law Reports*, the major legal points are cross-referenced to *Halsbury's Laws* and *The Digest*.

7. A list of cases which were referred to during the hearing.

8. A summary of the history of the previous proceedings of the case. The final sentence explains where in the report you can find the details of the facts of the case.

9. The names of the counsel (the barristers) who appeared for the parties. Q.C.s (Queen's Counsel) are senior counsel.

10. The start of the judgment given by Lord Denning M.R.

Recent Law Reports

The law is constantly changing, with new cases being reported daily. Therefore be prepared to consult recent reports. This is essential if you are to remain aware of new developments in the law. The most up-to-date reports are found in the some of the national newspapers. *The Times*, the *Financial Times*, the *Daily Telegraph*, *The Independent* and *The Guardian* all regularly publish law reports. These newspaper reports appear ahead of the major law report series, but, unlike them, do not reproduce the full text of judgments. This need not be a problem. If you wish to see the full text of judgments, these are available from a number of websites (**3–19**).   **3–7**

   It is not necessary, however, to scan the print issues of the newspapers themselves to see recent newspaper reports. Your library may provide access to the latest *Times Law Reports*, provided in association with LexisNexis (and linked from the *The Times* website at *www.timesonline.co.uk*). The current week's reports for the *Daily Telegraph* are available from its website (at *telegraph.co.uk*).

First page of a Law Report from the All England Reports. The illustration is taken from the online version available from LexisNexis Butterworths.

[1969] 1 All ER 201

Cleveland Petroleum Co Ltd v Dartstone Ltd and Another①

COURT OF APPEAL, CIVIL DIVISION

LORD DENNING MR, RUSSELL AND SALMON LJJ ②
26 NOVEMBER 1968

Trade—Restraint of trade—Agreement—Petrol filling station—Solus agreement—Lease by garage owner to petrol supplier—Underlease to company to operate service station—Covenant in underlease for exclusive sale of supplier's products—Assignment of underlease by licence granted by supplier—Interim injunction to restrain breach of covenant.

③
S the owner in fee simple of a garage, leased the premises to the plaintiffs for 25 years from 1 July 1960. The plaintiffs granted an underlease to COSS by which COSS covenanted, inter alia, to carry on the business of a petrol filling station at all times and not to sell or distribute motor fuels other than those supplied by the plaintiffs. After several assignments the underlease was assigned to the defendants who undertook to observe and perform the covenants. The defendants thereupon challenged the validity of the ties. The plaintiffs issued a writ claiming an injunction restraining the defendants from breaking this covenant. The plaintiffs obtained an interim injunction against which the defendants appealed.

④
Held—The appeal would be dismissed, the tie was valid and not an unreasonable restraint of trade because the defendants, not having been in possession previously, took possession of the premises under a lease and entered into a restrictive covenant knowing about such covenant, and thereby bound themselves to it (see p 203, letters *c*, *f* and *g*, post).
Dicta in *Esso Petroleum Co Ltd v Harper's Garage* (Stourport) ([1967] 1 All ER at pp 707, 714, and 724, 725) applied.
Appeal dismissed.⑤

Notes
As to agreements in restraint of trade, see 38 *Halsbury's Laws* (3rd Edn) 20, para 13; and for cases on the subject, see 45 *Digest* (Repl) 443–449, *271–297.*⑥

Case referred to in judgment
Esso Petroleum Co Ltd v Harper's Garage (Stourport) [1967] 1 All ER 699, [1968] AC 269, [1967] 2 WLR 871, *Digest* (Repl) Supp.⑦

Interlocutory Appeal
This was an appeal by the defendants, Dartstone and James Arthur Gregory, from an order of Eveleigh J, dated 1 November 1968, granting an interim injunction restraining the defendants from acting in breach of a covenant contained in an underlease made on 1 July 1960 between the plaintiffs, Cleveland Petroleum Co and County Oak Service Station and assigned to the defendants on 30 August 1968. The facts are set out in the judgment of Lord Denning MR.⑧

*Raymond Walton QC and M C B Buckley for the defendants.*⑨
A P Leggatt for the plaintiffs.

26 November 1968. The following judgments were delivered.

LORD DENNING MR.⑩

This case concerns a garage and petrol station called County Oak service station, at Crawley in Sussex. Mr Sainsbury was the owner in fee simple. On 1 July 1960, there were three separate transactions: First, Mr Sainsbury granted a lease.

Finding recent law reports online

Recent law reports, such as those found in the *All England Law Reports* and the *Weekly Law Reports* are straightforward to find if you have a citation. These are the reports which carry the full text of judgments along with other explanatory material as noted in **3–6**. Unlike newspaper reports, these reports usually appear some weeks or months after the judgment date. To find a report, locate the citation search box in the welcome page or the main search page of the appropriate database. Enter the citation exactly as you have been given it, e.g. "[2005] 4 All ER 97". Sources for the major reports are noted below. Take care to ensure that you enter the exact form of the citation before searching.

3–8

The *All England Law Reports* remain the most generally available law reports throughout the legal profession and aim at a general coverage of England and Wales. As a result they are the most widely cited report series for recent cases. The full text of the *All England Law Reports* is available from both LexisNexis Professional (**2–3**) and from LexisNexis Butterworths (**2–4**). On LexisNexis Butterworths, the *All England Law Reports* constitute a single database. Where cases have also been reported in the *Weekly Law Reports* (published by the Incorporated Council of Law Reporting), the *Weekly Law Reports* citation is preferred. The *Weekly Law Reports* are available from Westlaw UK (**2–5**) and from Justis (**2–7**). Most of the cases reported in the *Weekly Law Reports* are destined to be reported some weeks later in the *Law Reports* with a summary of counsel's arguments, having been checked by the judges involved. Although law libraries do not necessarily subscribe to all of the relevant databases, the vast majority will have ensured access to the major general reports through one database service or another.

If you do not have a specific citation, but wish to browse through recent issues of the *All England Law Reports* online, this is most easily achieved using the LexisNexis Butterworths service which allows recent reports to be viewed in the order in which they were printed. Justis provides a similar facility if you wish to browse through recent issues of the *Weekly Law Reports*.

Specialist reports will be available from either Westlaw UK, Justis, or LexisNexis Professional and LexisNexis Butterworths. No one database contains all of the specialist reports, so be prepared to check all available sources for a specialised report. As might be expected, many of the cases reported in the various specialist reports are not reported elsewhere. A property case may only be reported in *Property, Planning and Compensation Reports*; a family case may only be reported in the *Family Law Reports*.

Finding recent law reports in print

If you wish to find a report of a case in the printed *All England Law Reports* or *the Weekly Law Reports* (or indeed most other series of law reports), which has been published in the last few months, you will not find a bound volume on the shelves but a series of paper covered parts, or issues. However, your reference (citation) will make it appear that you are looking for a bound volume. So how do you locate the report? You will find, at the top of the front cover of each unbound issue, the date of this issue, the part (or issue) number, and the year, volume and page numbers covered by this issue, e.g.:

3–9

[2005] 4 All ER 97–208 Part 2, 5 October 2005

This indicates that this issue (Part 2) will eventually form pages 97–208 of the fourth bound volume of the *All England Law Reports* for 2005. Also on the front cover appears a list of all the cases reported in that part, showing the page number on which each report begins.

Many other law reports are published in a number of parts during the current year. At the end of the year, these are replaced by a bound volume or volumes. Every part will indicate on its cover the volume and pages in the bound volume where it will finally appear.

The *Weekly Law Reports* is a series (which commenced in 1953) that you will consult frequently. The arrangement of its weekly print issues is rather confusing. Three bound volumes are produced each year, and each weekly issue contains some cases which will eventually appear in Volume 1 of the bound volumes for that year, and some cases which will subsequently appear in either Volume 2 or Volume 3. The front cover of each issue shows the contents and the volume in which these pages will eventually appear. For example on the front cover shown below is printed:

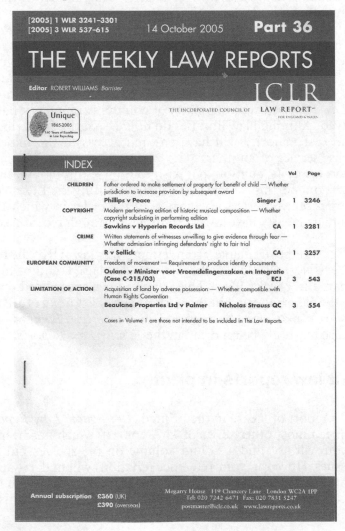

(Reproduced by permission of the Incorporated Council of Law Reporting for England and Wales.)

Part 36
14 October 2005
[2005] 1 W.L.R. 3241–3301
[2005] 3 W.L.R. 537–615

Part 36 therefore contains pages 3241–3301 of what will eventually form Volume 1 of the *Weekly Law Reports* for 2005 and pages 537–615 of Volume 3. A sheet of green paper is inserted in the issue to mark the division between the pages destined for Volume 1 and those forming part of Volume 3. A list of all the cases included in the part is printed on the front cover, and the volume and page number for each case is shown. You may wonder why the publishers (the Incorporated Council of Law Reporting, who also publish the *Law Reports*) have chosen this method of publishing the issues. The reason is that the cases in Volumes 2 and 3 will be republished, after being checked by the judges and with a summary of counsel's arguments, in the *Law Reports*. Those cases appearing in Volume 1, however, will not reappear in the *Law Reports*.

The latest issue of each journal and law reports series is usually displayed in a separate area of the library. The remainder of the issues for the current year may also be filed in this area, or they may be in a box on the shelves alongside the bound volumes.

The Law Reports Series

The publication known as the *Law Reports*, which commenced publication in 1865, was **3–10** originally published in 11 series, each covering a different court. The rationalisation of the court structure since that time has reduced this to four series. These are:

Appeal Cases (abbreviated to A.C.);
Chancery Division (Ch.);
Queen's Bench Division (Q.B.);
Family Division (Fam.).

This is the order in which the bound volumes are usually arranged on the library shelves. Paper-covered parts are issued monthly and are replaced by bound volumes at the end of the year. The monthly issues of the Chancery Division and Family Division, however, are published within the same paper-covered part, although they are bound as separate series.

The location on the shelves of the various earlier series often reflects their relationship to the present four series, for example, the historical predecessors of the present Queen's Bench Division (called the King's Bench Division when a King is on the throne) were the Court for Crown Cases Reserved, the Court of Common Pleas and the Court of Exchequer. These are therefore usually shelved before the Queen's Bench Division reports (because they are its predecessors) but after the Appeal Cases and Chancery Division reports. The same arrangement is applied with the other three current series (i.e. reports of the predecessors of the present courts are filed at the beginning of each series).

Law Reports

TABLE OF THE LAW REPORTS

The mode of citation is given in brackets. In the first, second and third columns, dots (. . .) are put where the number of the volume would appear in the citation. In the fourth column square brackets([ ]) are put where the year would appear in the citation.

1866–1875	1875–1880	1881–1890	1891–present
House of Lords, English and Irish Appeals (L.R. ... H.L.)	Appeal Cases (...App.Cas.)	Appeal Cases (...App.Cas.)	Appeal Cases ([ ]) A.C.)
House of Lords, Scotch and Divorce Appeals (L.R. ... H.L.Sc. or L.R. ... H.L.Sc. and Div.)			
Privy Council Appeals (L.R. ... P.C.)			
Chancery Appeal Cases (L.R. ... Ch. or Ch. App.)	Chancery Division (...Ch.D.)	Chancery Division (...Ch.D.)	Chancery Division ([ ]) Ch.)
Equity Cases (L.R. ... Eq.)			
Crown Cases Reserved (L.R. ... C.C., or, ... C.C.R.)	Queen's Bench Division (...Q.B.D.)		
Queen's Bench Cases* (L.R. ... Q.B.)		Queen's Bench Division (...Q.B.D.)	Queen's (or King's) Bench Division ([ ] Q.B. or K.B.)†
Common Pleas Cases (L.R. ... C.P.)	Common Pleas Division (...C.P.D.)		
Exchequer Cases‡ (L.R. ... Ex.)	Exchequer Division (...Ex.D.)		
Admiralty and Ecclesiastical Cases (L.R. ... A. & E.)	Probate Division (...P.D.)	Probate Division (...P.D.)	Probate Division ([ ]P.) Since 1972 Family Division ([ ]Fam.)
Probate and Divorce Cases (L.R. ... P. & D.)			

* Note that there is also a series called Queen's Bench Reports in the old reports (113–118 E.R.).
† After 1907 this includes cases in the Court of Criminal Appeal, later the Court of Appeal, in place of the previous Court for Crown Cases Reserved.
‡ Note that there is also a series called Exchequer Reports in the old reports (154–156 E.R.).

(Reproduced from G. Williams, *Learning the Law* (12th ed.), p. 40.)

The figure on page 32 shows the way in which the complete series of *Law Reports* are arranged on the shelves in most libraries. The abbreviations used to denote each series are shown, and also the dates during which each series appeared.

Citations for the *Law Reports* have varied over the years as the system of numbering the reports changed. Until 1891, for example, each volume in the various series had its own individual number, running sequentially through the years. The date in the citation is therefore in round brackets, to show it is not essential to the reference. For the *Law Reports* after 1891, however, the date is in square brackets, since the year must be quoted in order to locate the correct volume. The other slight complication in the citation of the *Law Reports* is the use of the abbreviation L.R. (for *Law Reports*) which is placed before the volume number in citation of *Law Reports* before 1875, e.g. *Rylands v Fletcher* (1868) L.R. 3 H.L. 330.

The figure on page 32 also clarifies the use of abbreviations and brackets for the *Law Reports*. It is worth noting, however, that the abbreviation H.L. stands for *Law Reports: English and Irish Appeal Cases* and not, as you might guess, Law Reports: House of Lords.

The *Law Reports* are available online from Westlaw UK (**2–5**), LexisNexis Professional (**2–3**) and Justis (**2–7**).

Older Law Reports

We have concentrated upon the modern series of law reports because these are the reports which you will be using most frequently. However, from time to time you will need to look at older cases, that is, those reported in the first half of the nineteenth century or even several centuries earlier. Reports of older cases can be found in several series: the *English Reports*, *Revised Reports*, the *Law Journal Reports*, the *Law Times Reports* and the *All England Law Report Reprint* series. We shall now look at some of these series in more detail.   **3–11**

The reports published privately by individuals (and known as the *Nominate Reports*) ceased publication around 1865, when the *Law Reports* were first published. If the date of the case you want is before 1865, you are most likely to find it in a series known as the *English Reports*. Many libraries have the *English Reports* in print form. A small number of libraries may also have the full text of the *English Reports* available from Justis (**2–7**).

How to use the English Reports

If you know the name of the case, look it up in the alphabetical index of the names of cases, printed in Volumes 177–178 of the *English Reports*. Beside the name of the case is printed the abbreviation for the name of the original nominate reporter, and the volume and page in his reports where the case appeared. The number printed in **bold** type next to this is the volume number in the *English Reports* where the case will be found, and this is followed by the page number in that volume: **3–12**

Daniel v North[a]   11 East, 372[b]   **103**[c] 1047

[a] name of the case;
[b] volume, name of the original reporter, page number in the original report, i.e. the original report of this case appeared in Volume 11 of *East's Reports* p. 372;
[c] the reprint of the report appears in Volume 103 of the *English Reports* at page 1047.

Table of Cases in the English Reports

424 DAN		Index of Cases	
Ⓐ	Ⓑ		Ⓒ

You will see that Volume 103 of the *English Reports* has the volumes and names of the *Nominate Reports* which are to be found in that volume printed on the spine. Page 1047 appears in its normal position at the top outer corner of the page whilst the volume and page number of the original report are printed at the inner margin.

Sometimes you may only have a citation (reference) to the original nominate report, e.g. 3 Car. & P. (Carrington and Payne); 2 Barn. & Ald. (Barnewall and Alderson). This reference is often printed in an abbreviated form. You do not know the name of the case, so you are unable to look it up in the index to the *English Reports*. Let us suppose, for example, that you have come across a reference to (1809) 11 East 372. Because the date is before 1865, you know that it is likely to be found in the *English Reports*; but you do not know the name of the case. How do you find it? If the name of the report has been abbreviated, e.g. 3 Car. & P., you will need to look in Raistrick's *Index to Legal Citations and Abbreviations* or one of the similar reference works (see **3–5**) to find the meaning of the abbreviation. You then turn to the *Chart to the English Reports*. This may be displayed near the *English Reports*, or it may be a slim volume shelved with the *English Reports* themselves. The Chart contains an alphabetical list of the names of all the reporters whose work has been reprinted in the *English Reports*, showing which volume their work appears in. The Chart indicates that Volumes 7 to 11 of *East's Reports* are reprinted in Volume 103 of the *English Reports*. If you open Volume 103 at random, you will see that, at the top of each page (at the *inner* margin) the volume and page numbers of the original report are printed. Find the volume and page reference which most nearly corresponds to your reference. There is no entry at the top of the page for Volume 11 of *East's Reports*, page 372, but there is an entry, at the top inner margin, for page 371. If you look at the figure on page 24, you will see the heading "11 East 371" at the top of the page. There are also numbers printed, in square brackets, in the body of the text. These indicate when the page numbers in the original report changed. For instance, in the original Volume 11 of *East's Reports*, page 371 began with the words "practice, but a specific notice of trial at Monmouth . . .". Page 372 began with the case of *Daniel* v *North*.

Chart to the English Reports

Table of English Reports				
Old Reports.	Volume in English Reports.	Abbreviations.	Period Covered (approximate).	Series.
Dow & Clark, 1 & 2	6	Dow & Cl.	1827–1832	H.L.
Dowling & Ryland	171	Dowl. & Ry. N.P.	1822–1823	N.P.
Drewry, 1–3	61	Drew.	1852–1859	V.C.
Drewry 4	62			
Drewry & Smale, 1 & 2	62	Drew & Sm. or Dr. & Sm.	1860–1865	V.C.
Dyer, 1–3	73	Dy.	1513–1582	K.B.
East, 1–6	102			
East, 7–11	103	East.	1801–1812	K.B.
East, 12–16	104			
Eden, 1 & 2	28	Eden.	1757–1766	Ch.
Edwards	165	Edw.	1808–1812	Ecc. Adm. P. & D.
Ellis & Blackburn, 1–3	118			
Ellis & Blackburn, 4–7	119	El. & Bl.	1851–1858	K.B.
Ellis & Blackburn, 8	120			
Ellis, Blackburn & Ellis	120	El. Bl. & El.	1858	K.B.
Ellis & Ellis, 1	120	El. & El.	1858–1861	K.B.
Ellis & Ellis, 2 & 3	121			
Eq. Cases Abridged, 1	21	Eq. Ca. Abr.	1667–1744	Ch.
Eq. Cases Abridged, 2	22			
Espinasse, 1–6	170	Esp.	1793–1807	N.P.

Other older law reports

If the *English Reports* are not available in your library, you may find the case you need reprinted in the *Revised Reports*. The *Revised Reports* has similar coverage to the *English Reports* but is not as comprehensive. **3–13**

The *All England Law Reports Reprint* series is another useful source for old cases between 1558 and 1935. The cases are reprinted from the reports which originally appeared in the

Algorithm designed to show how to look up a case in the English Reports

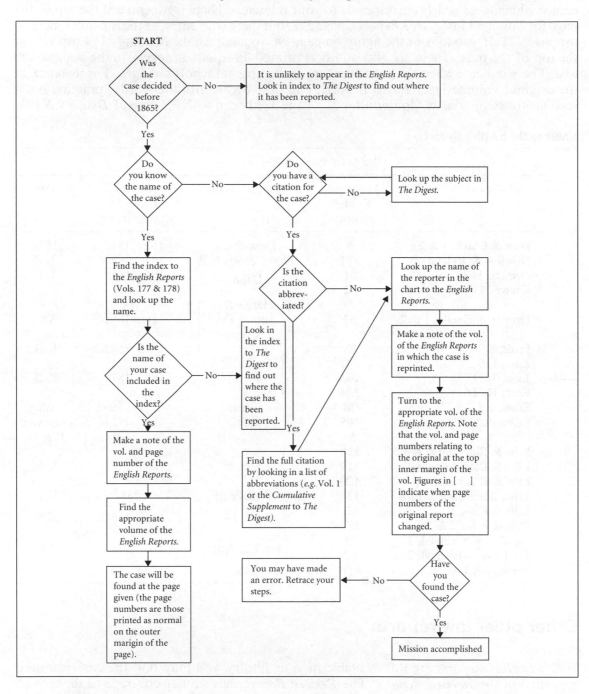

Law Times Reports, which commenced in 1843, and from earlier reports. The *Reprint* series contains some 5,000 cases selected principally upon the criterion that they have been referred to in the *All England Law Reports* and in *Halsbury's Laws of England*. Online access to the full text of the *Reprint* series is available from both LexisNexis Professional (**2–3**) and LexisNexis Butterworths (**2–4**). The *Reprint* cases can be searched alongside more modern cases, or searches restricted to *Reprint* cases only. There is an index volume to the printed series containing an alphabetical list of cases and a subject index of the cases included in the reprint.

Two other series of nineteenth century cases are also referred to regularly: the *Law Journal Reports* and the *Law Times Reports*. The *Law Journal Reports* cover the period 1823–1949. They can be complicated to use because usually two volumes were published each year, both bearing the same volume number. In one volume were printed the cases heard in common law courts, while in the other were printed equity cases. You will need to check both volumes, unless you know whether the case you want is equity or common law. To add to the difficulty, the volume numbering and the method of citation changed during the course of its publication. The first nine volumes (1823–1831) are known as the Old Series (L.J.O.S.). References to the New Series (1833–1949) omit the letters N.S. Citations give the abbreviation for the court in which the case was heard. It is therefore necessary to decide if the court was a court of common law or equity, so that you consult the correct volume. For example, the reference 16 L.J.Q.B. 274 is a reference to Volume 16 of the *Law Journal (New Series)* in the common law volumes (since Queen's Bench was a court of common law), at page 274 of the reports of Queen's Bench. Volume 16 contains law reports from several different courts. Each court's reports have a separate sequence of page numbers. You are looking for page 274 in the sequence of Queen's Bench reports.

The *Law Times Reports* (L.T.) cover the period 1859–1947. Prior to this, the reports were published as part of the journal entitled *Law Times* and these are cited as the *Law Times, Old Series* (L.T.O.S.) which ran from 1843–1860. You may find this Old Series is shelved with the Journals, not with the law reports.

How to Find a Reported case when you only know its name

We will now turn to some of the problems frequently encountered by students and show how these are solved. Often you know the name of a case but you have no idea where the case was reported; or else the reference which you have been given has proved to be inaccurate. How can you find out where a report of the case appears?   **3–14**

The easiest way of tracing a case is to use the Westlaw UK *Case Locator* database (**3–15**), especially if you think your case was probably decided in or after 1947. *The Digest* (**3–15**) can help find older cases. In addition, most series of law reports have indexes to cases reported in their publication.

How to use the Westlaw UK Case Locators database

3–15   The Westlaw UK *Case Locators* database enables you to trace a case when you only have the name of one, or possibly both, of the parties. The database forms part of Westlaw UK (**2–5**) and contains information on all reported England and Wales cases since 1947, taken from the print volumes of *Current Law*, along with keywords and citations for earlier cases where they have been cited by *Current Law*. In addition, the database links directly to cases reported in the *Law Reports* from 1864 onwards.

The *Case Locator* search box boxes are located on the Westlaw UK welcome screen and allow searches using one or both party names. If both party names are known the "v" citation convention can be used to retrieve all cases featuring the two names e.g.

"Douglas v Hello"

A results list for the matching cases is then displayed. A number of separate cases have been reported for "Douglas v Hello" and the results list will include, for example:

Douglas v Hello! Ltd (No.1)

The "No.1" in brackets has been added to distinguish this case from a number of subsequent related cases, e.g. *Douglas v Hello! Ltd (No.9)*. You may need to check to ensure that you are looking at the right case.

> ## SEARCH TIP
>
> The full name of both parties does not need to be entered when searching for a case using party names. Enter the most distinctive elements, e.g. "Factortame", not "Secretary for State for Transport Ex p. Factortame".

Cases which use initials for party names to protect anonymity can cause particular problems. A search for "R v A", for example, finds literally hundreds of potential matches in the *Case Locators* database. A citation becomes essential unless the case name has been extended to include further identification, e.g. *R v A (Complainant's Sexual History)*. The full phrase in brackets can be added to ensure that a match is found for the particular case you are looking for. If you are fairly sure of the keywords likely to be used in a case, an alternative is to use the "Search by term(s)" search.

Selecting a case name from the list of search results provided by the database displays a page of information headed by a list of citations for the case. As already noted, a significant case is likely to be reported in a number of law reports, so that *R v A (Complainant's Sexual History)* has been reported, among other places, in the *Law Reports*, for example, as [2002] 1 A.C. 45, and in the *Human Rights Law Reports* as [2001] H.R.L.R. 48. As the judgment in the case as delivered after 2000, the neutral citation for the case is also included, [2001] UKHL 25. This is not a citation to a law report (see **3–4**).

Example results page from the Westlaw UK Case Locators page

(c) Sweet & Maxwell Limited
R. v A (Complainant's Sexual History)
Also known as:
R. v A (No. 2)
R. v Y (Sexual Offence: Complainant's Sexual History)
(HL) House of Lords
17 May 2001

Where Reported
Summary
Cases Cited
Legislation Cited
History of the Case
Citations to the Case
Case Comments

Where Reported

[2001] UKHL 25
[2002] 1 A.C. 45
[2001] 2 W.L.R. 1546
[2001] 3 All E.R. 1
[2001] 2 Cr. App. R. 21
(2001) 165 J.P. 609
[2001] H.R.L.R. 48
[2001] U.K.H.R.R. 825
11 B.H.R.C. 225
(2001) 165 J.P.N. 750
Times, May 24, 2001
Independent, May 22, 2001
Daily Telegraph, May 29, 2001
2001 WL 513004

Summary

Subject: Criminal evidence

Keywords: Admissibility; Consent; Evidence; Rape; Right to fair trial; Sexual behaviour.

Catchphrases: admissibility; rape; consent; evidence of prior sexual relationship; compatibility with right to fair trial.

Abstract: Following the decision of the Court of Appeal ([2001] EWCA Crim 4) as to the admissibility of evidence, in a rape trial, concerning the alleged previous sexual relationship between a complainant and a defendant in relation to the issue of consent, the House of Lords was asked to determine whether the exclusion of such evidence under the *Youth Justice and Criminal Evidence Act 1999 s. 41* would contravene a defendant's right to a fair trial under the Human Rights Act 1998 Sch. 1 Part I Art. 6.

Summary: Held, dismissing the appeal, that s. 41(3)(c) of the 1999 Act should be construed where necessary by having regard to the interpretative obligation under s. 3 of the 1998 Act and by giving consideration to the need to seek to protect a complainant from indignity and humiliating questions. Evidence of a complainant's previous sexual history was admissible where that evidence, and questioning concerning it, was so relevant to the issue of consent that by not including it the fairness of the trial would be brought into question. The relevance of the previous sexual experience was a matter.

If the full text of the law report is available from the Westlaw UK *Cases (full text)* database, the relevant citation will be shown as a hyperlink. The link opens a new window containing the full text of the report. Within the text asterisked numbers in purple mark the start of the printed pages, enabling precise quotations to be traced. Where cases cited within the report are available from Westlaw UK in full text, citations are again shown as hyperlinks.

For many cases judgment texts are linked from a Westlaw UK case number at the foot of the list of law report citations. This can be helpful if Westlaw UK does not have the full text of a law report online. However, if your library has a subscription to LexisNexis Professional (**2–3**), or to LexisNexis Butterworths (**2–4**) or the Justis databases (**2–5**), it makes sense to search those databases for a full law report, once a citation has been confirmed.

The Westlaw UK *Case Locators* database also provides a significant amount of additional information about a case which can be of value even if the full text or a report or judgment is not available.

Summaries are provided for all of the cases in the database reported after 1947. In addition a "Case History" section of the page shows a list of cases which have followed, for example, the decision made by the case, or been "distinguished" from it. See **7–18** for more on tracing the judicial history of the case. Finally, the *Case Locators* page lists citations for journal articles which have commented on the case.

How to use the Current Law Case Citators

3–16   The print volumes of the *Current Law Case Citator* each have an alphabetical list of the names of cases which have been published or quoted in court between the dates specified on the spine. If you have an idea of the approximate date, and easy access to the *Citator* volumes, they provide a quick and easy way to trace a citation. The *Citator* is published in a number of parts:

1. *The Current Law Case Citator* bound volumes covering cases which were reported or cited in court in the years noted on the Spine, e.g. 1947–1976, 1991–2001, 2002–2004.
2. A paperback issue of the *Current Law Case Citator* including references to cases reported or cited since the last bound volume and before the end of the preceding year.
3. The *Current Law Monthly Digest*. To find cases reported in the current year, look in the Table of Cases in the most recent issue of the *Monthly Digest*. The December issue of the previous year's *Monthly Digest* can be used to find cases in that year, if the cumulative supplement has not yet been published.

The different parts of the *Citator* may at first seem confusing. It is best to look through the *Citators* in chronological order, as above, in order to ensure that you have looked in all the relevant issues.

You may find your library has copies of the *Scottish Current Law Case Citator* for the periods 1948–1976 and 1977–1988. Despite its name, the Scottish version does contain all the English cases but, in addition, it lists Scottish cases in a separate alphabetical sequence at the back of the volume. The two publications have now merged and the *Current Law Case Citator* volumes since 1989 have included Scottish cases. Part 1 of the *Citator* lists all the

English cases, while the Scottish cases are listed in Part 2. Make sure you look for your case in the right section!

In each of the *Citators*, the cases are listed in alphabetical order. Cases which start with a single letter, e.g. *S. v Cox*, are at the beginning of that letter of the alphabet; criminal cases starting with *R.* v are at the beginning of the letter R section. If the title of the case is *Re Smith*, or *Ex p. Smith*, look under *Smith*. When you have traced the case you require, you will find an entry similar to the following:

> Biles *v.* Caesar [1957] 1 W.L.R. 156; 101 S.J. 108; [1957] 1 All E.R. 151; [101 S.J. 141; 21 Conv. 169], C.A. . . .. *Digested, 57/1943: Followed, 59/1834: Applied, 68/2181*; 69/2037

The entry for *Biles* v *Caesar* in the 1947–76 volume shown here gives you a complete "life history" of the case for the years covered by the volume. Like the Westlaw UK *Case Locator* database (**3–15**) it shows you where and when the case was originally reported and where you can find journal articles commenting on the case; there are also citations relevant to its subsequent judicial history (see **7–18**).

The entry for *Biles* v *Caesar* gives the following information:

(1) After the name of the case (*Biles* v *Caesar*) there is a list of three places where you can find a full report of the cases:
   (a) [1957] 1 W.L.R. 156—for the year 1957 in the first of the three volumes of the *Weekly Law Reports* at page 156;
   (b) (1957) 101 S.J. 108—for the year 1957 in volume 101 of the *Solicitors Journal* at page 108 (this, as the name suggests, is a journal, shelved with other journals);
   (c) [1957] 1 All E.R. 151—for the year 1958 in the first volume of the *All England Law Reports* at page 151.
(2) The entries which are enclosed in square brackets in the printed volume—[101 S.J. 141; 21 Conv. 169]—are references to articles or comments in law journals where the case is discussed in some detail. If you select volume 101 of the *Solicitors Journal*, or volume 21 of *The Conveyancer*, you see articles discussing the case of *Biles* v *Caesar*.
(3) The C.A. after the references to the case tells us that it is a Court of Appeal Decision. If the decision of the court of first instance was reported, references to these reports would have been included after the C.A.
(4) The word Digested followed by the figures 57/1943 indicates that you will find a digest (a summary) of the case in the 1957 volume of the *Current Law Year Book* (see **7–13**). Every item in the 1957 volume has its own individual number; you will find that item 1943 is a summary of the facts and decisions in the case of *Biles* v *Caesar*.

You may also wish to know whether the decision given in a particular case has been subsequently approved, i.e. whether the case has been quoted with approval by another judge in a later case. By 1976, when the print *Citator* volume was published, the case of *Biles* v *Caesar* has been quoted in three other cases—in 1959, when the decision was followed, and in 1968 and 1969 when the courts applied the decision in the *Biles* case to two other cases, following the doctrine of precedent. You can find the names of the cases in which *Biles* was referred to by looking in the 1959 *Current Law Year Book*, at item 1834, and in the 1968 and 1969 *Year Books*, at the item numbers given.

If you are using the *Citator* and, as in the above example, you find a reference to your case in the *Citator* for 1947 to 1976, it is still advisable to check through the more recent *Citators* to find the present status of the judgment. You can find out whether since 1976, for example, the case has been taken to a higher court or the decision has been approved or overruled in other judgments.

How to trace a case in The Digest

3–17   Older English and Scottish cases can most easily be traced using *The Digest* (formerly known as the *English and Empire Digest*), as can many cases heard in Irish, European and Commonwealth courts. *The Digest* consists of the main work (around 70 volumes), several *Continuation Volumes*, a *Cumulative Supplement*, a *Consolidated Table of Cases* and a *Consolidated Index*. *The Digest* is in its third edition which is called the *Green Band Reissue* because of the green stripe on the spine. Most of the *Green Band Reissue* volumes have now been updated and reprinted. These volumes say *2nd or 3rd Reissue* on the spine. The date of reissue of any volume is printed on the title page inside the front cover.

   To trace a particular case in *The Digest*, go first to the four-volume *Consolidated Table of Cases*. This contains an alphabetical list of the cases summarised in *The Digest* and gives a reference to the volume in which the case can be found. Page 43 shows the entry in the *Consolidated Table of Cases* for the case of *Bell* v *Twentyman*. This case is included in Volumes 19(9), 35(3) and 36(1) of *The Digest*, since it is relevant to the law of easements, negligence and nuisance. At the front of each of these volumes, there is another Table of Cases which refers you to the *case* number (or *page* number in older volumes—see the heading at the top of the column) where you can find a summary of the case and a list of citations where the full report can be found. If, for example, you wished to find a summary of the negligence aspects of the case of *Bell* v *Twentyman*, you would now look up the name of the case in the Table of Cases at the front of Volume 35(3). Alongside the name of the case is the number 378, which refers you to case number 378 in that volume. The entry is shown on page 44. The case number is given in **bold,** followed by a summary of the case and references to where the full text of the report can be found. The case of *Bell* v *Twentyman* was reported in a number of series. To find the meaning of the abbreviations used, look in the list of abbreviations in the *Cumulative Supplement*. The *Consolidated Table of Cases* is updated and reprinted every two years. To find the latest cases, you will need to look in the annual *Cumulative Supplement*. There is a Table of Cases at the front of the volume, which indicates where in the *Cumulative Supplement* a summary of the case can be found. For more information on *The Digest*, refer to **7–14**.

Tracing a case through the indexes in law reports

3–18   In addition to the *Current Law Case Citators* and *The Digest*, there are a number of indexes to the cases in individual series of law reports. For instance, the *All England Law Reports* has published a volume containing a list of all the cases in the *All England Law Reports Reprint* series (see **3–13**), which covers selected cases between 1558 and 1935. In addition, there are three volumes containing the *Consolidated Tables and Index 1936–1992*. Volume 1 contains

Example Page from The Digest Consolidated Table of Cases A–F

Bell v Twentyman (1841) **19(1) Esmt; 35(3) Negl; 36(1) Nuis**
Bell v Union Bank (1923) (NZ) **3(2) Bank**
Bell v Walker & Debrett (1785) **13 Coprt**
Bell v Wardell (1740) **17(1) Custom; 46(1) Time**
Bell v Welch (1850) **12(1) Contr; 26(1) Guar**
Bell v Wermore (1880) (CAN) **21(2) Exon**
Bell v Wetmore (1880) (CAN) **17(2) Damgs; 27(2) H & W**
Bell v White (1857) (CAN) **7(1) Bounds**
Bell v Whitehead (1839) **13 Coprt**
Bell v Wilson (1865) **17(1) Deeds; 34(1) Mines**
Bell v Wilson (1866) **34(1) Mines**
Bell v Wilson (1900) (CAN) **32(1) Libel**
Bell v Windsor & Annapolis Ry Co (1892) (CAN) **8(1) Carr**
Bell v Wright (1895) (CAN) **44(2) Solrs**
Bell v Wyndham (1865) **25 Fish**
Bell (1827) (IR) **4(2) Bkpcy**
Bell (1867) (IR) **5(2) Bkpcy**
Bell (1870) (AUS) **5(2) Bkpcy**
Bell (1870) (CAN) **5(2) Bkpcy**
Bell (1872) (IR) **4(2) Bkpcy**
Bell (1878) (AUS) **5(1) Bkpcy**
Bell (1922) (CAN) **4(2) Bkpcy; 5(2) Bkpcy**
Bell (or Young or Farrell) v Arnott (1857) (SCOT) **3(1) Arbn**
Bell (Robert) Engine & Thresher Co v Farquharson (1918) (CAN) **39(3) S Goods**
Bell (Robert) Engine Co v Burke (1912) (CAN) **39(2) S Goods**
Bell & Atkins & Durbrow Ltd v Milner (1956) (CAN) **28(5) Injon**
Bell & Barron Ltd, R v (1922) (CAN) **30 Intox**
Bell and Bell v Robutka and Blair & Scott Construction Ltd (1966) (CAN) **40(2) S Land**
Bell & Black, Re (1882) (CAN) **17(1) Deeds**
Bell & Co v Antwerp, London & Brazil Line (1891) **12(2) Contr; 12(3) Contr; 37(2) Prac & Proc**
Bell & Co v Johnstone (1821) (SCOT) **43(2) Ship**
Bell & Davis (1892) (AUS) **4(2) Bkpcy; 5(2) Bkpcy**
Bell and Denver (1886) **21(2) Exon**
Bell & Hill, R v (1956) (CAN) **33 Mags**
Bell and Innes v Martin (1952) **30 Intox**
Bell and Jordan, R v (1877) **14(2) Crim**
Bell & Langley's Case (1587) **13 Cohlds**
Bell and Lucas v King's City County Council (1910) (IR) **14(2) Crim**
Bell and MacLaren v Robinson (1960) (CAN) **35(3) Negl; 35(4) Negl**
Bell & Maedel v Bell & Bell (1957) (CAN) **32(2) Limit of A**
Bell & Moore v Swart (1899) (S AF) **32(2) Limit of A**
Bell and others v Smith and Smith (1968) (CAN) **22(2) Evid**
Bell and Schiesel v Jacobson and Weitzer (1925) (CAN) **18 Distr; 31(3) L&T**
Bell & Sons v Great Crosby UDC (1912) **26(2) Hghys**
Bell, Bell v Agnew, Re (1931) **50 Wills**
Bell, Bell v Bell, Re (1871) (CAN) **24 Exors**
Bell, Bell v Bell, Re (1894) **24 Exors**
Bell Bros, Ex p Hodgson, Re (1891) **9(2) Coys**
Bell Bros v Hudson Bay Insce Co (1911) (CAN) **29(2) Insce**
Bell Bros (HP) Ltd v Reynolds (1945) (SCOT) **34(2) Misrep**
Bell Canada v Office & Professional Employees' International Union, Local 131 (1973) (CAN) **47(3) Trade**
Bell Canada and Palmer, Re (1974) (CAN) **45 Stats**
Bell, Carter v Stadden, Re (1886) **21(2) Exon**
Bell Concord Educational Trust Ltd v Customs and Excise Comrs (1989) **49(1) VAT**

Bell Electric Ltd v Aweco Appliance Systems GmbH & Co KG (2002) **37(3) Prac & Proc**
Bell Engine & Thresher Co Ltd v Gagne (1914) (CAN) **3(2) Barr**
Bell Engine & Threshing Co v Wesenberg (1912) (CAN) **39(3) S Goods; 40(2) Set-off**
Bell Estate, Re (1929) (CAN) **23 Exors**
Bell Estate Montgomery v Marshall, Re (1955) (CAN) **50 Wills**
Bell Etc JJ, R v (1899) **30 Intox**
Bell Group Finance (Pty) Ltd (in liq) v Bell Group (UK) Holdings Ltd (1996) **10(2) Coys**
Bell Helicopter Textron Inc v Brown (1991) (CAN) **28(5) Injon**
Bell Helicopter Textron Inc v Brown, Fretwell et al (1991) (CAN) **11(2) Confl**
Bell Hill Gold-Mining & Sluicing Co Ltd (in liq), Knight (1900) (NZ) **9(1) Coys**
Bell Houses Ltd v City Wall Properties Ltd (1966) **10(1) Coys**
Bell, In the Estate of (1908) **24 Exors**
Bell, In the Goods of (1859) **23 Exors**
Bell, In the Goods of (1878) **23 Exors**
Bell, Jeffery v Sayles, Re (1896) **35(1) Mtge; 48(2) Trusts**
Bell, Lake v Bell, Re (1886) **1(3) Agcy; 35(1) Mtge**
Bell Lines Ltd and An Bord Bainne Co-op Ltd, Ex p (1984) **2 Agric**
Bell London & Provincial Properties Ltd, Ex p (1949) **31(3) L&T**
Bell London & Provincial Properties Ltd v Reuben (1946) **31(3) L&T**
Bell Lumber Co, R v (1932) (CAN) **49(2) Water**
Bell Property Trust Ltd v Hampstead Borough Assessment Committee (1940) **38(2) Rates**
Bell, R v (1730) **13 Corpns**
Bell, R v (1731) **15(1) Crim**
Bell, R v (1737) **15(1) Crim**
Bell, R v (1753) **14(1) Crim; 45 Stats**
Bell, R v (1798) **38(1) Rates**
Bell, R v (1822) **36(1) Nuis; 49(2) Water**
Bell, R v (1829) **15(1) Crim**
Bell, R v (1841) **14(2) Crim**
Bell, R v (1857) (CAN) **28(3) Infts**
Bell, R v (1859) (IR) **13 Crnrs; 15(1) Crim**
Bell, R v (1868) (CAN) **19(1) Elect**
Bell, R v (1871) **5(2) Bkpcy; 15(1) Crim**
Bell, R v (1874) (IR) **14(2) Crim**
Bell, R v (1878) (NZ) **15(1) Crim**
Bell, R v (1919) **15(2) Crim**
Bell, R v (1920) (CAN) **8(2) Comwlth**
Bell, R v (1921) **15(2) Crim**
Bell, R v (1922) **15(2) Crim**
Bell, R v (1924) **28(2) Inc T**
Bell, R v (1925) (CAN) **28(2) Inc T**
Bell, R v (1929) (CAN) **5(2) Bkpcy; 38(1) Pub Hlth**
Bell, R v (1930) (CAN) **15(1) Crim**
Bell, R v (1947) (CAN) **14(2) Crim**
Bell, R v (1959) (CAN) **15(2) Crim**
Bell, R v (1966) (CAN) **14(2) Crim**
Bell, R v (1977) (CAN) **47(1) T & CP**
Bell, R v (1978) **14(1) Crim**
Bell, R v (1984) **15(1) Crim; 39(1) R Traf**
Bell Refining Co v McFadyen (1946) (CAN) **31(1) L&T**
Bell Telephone & Indian Head Town, Re (1909) (CAN) **38(1) Rates**
Bell Telephone Co, Re (1885) (CAN) **1(1) Admin L; 16 Cr Proc**
Bell Telephone Co v Avery (1912) (CAN) **28(5) Injon**

Example Page from The Digest, Vol. 35(3), 3rd Reissue

1 GENERAL PRINCIPLES OF THE LAW OF NEGLIGENCE   Case **384**

goods by order, delivered them at a booking-office, with the customer's address, and booked them, to be forwarded to him, not specifying any particular conveyance, and no particular mode of transmission having been pointed out by the customer.

Quaere: whether the consignor could maintain an action against the office-keeper for a negligent loss of the goods while under his charge.

Gilbart v Dale (1836) 5 Ad & El 543; 2 Har & W 383; 1 Nev & PKB 22; 6 LJKB 3; 111 ER 1270

ANNOTATION **Apld** Mid Ry v Bromley (1856) 17 CB 372

378 No negligence without duty

In case for an injury to plaintiff's reversionary interest by defendant's obstruction of a water-course on his land and thereby sending water upon and under the house and land in the occupation of plaintiff's tenant, defendant pleaded, that the obstruction was caused by the neglect of plaintiff's tenant to repair a wall on the demised land, that in consequence it fell into the watercourse, and caused the damage, and that within a reasonable time after defendant had notice he removed it: *Held* to be a bad plea, it not showing any obligation on the tenant to repair the wall merely as terre-tenant. *Quaere*: whether it would have been good if it had.

Bell v Twentyman (1841) 1 QB 766; 1 Gal & Dav 223; 10 LJQ B 278; 6 Jur 366; 113 ER 1324

ANNOTATION **Distd** Taylor v Stendall (1845) 5 LTOS 214

379 No negligence without duty

A declaration in case stated, by way of inducement, that plaintiff was possessed of a dwelling-house as tenant to defendant, and that defendant, at the request of plaintiff, promised to fit up a cellar for a wine cellar, with brick and stone bins; and then charged that it became the duty of defendant to use due care in fitting up the same, but that he did not, and that the slabs gave way, and broke plaintiff's wine bottles. It was proved that defendant did fit up a wine cellar with brick and stone bins; but that plaintiff afterwards required more bins to be made, and defendant consented to have the partitions carried up to the roof of the cellar. The workmen, however, by plaintiff's directions, erected the new partitions upon the centre of the slabs which covered the bins first made, and the slabs then gave way. It was proved that those slabs would have been strong enough to bear the weight of empty bottles; but some of the witnesses thought not that of full bottles: *Held* under these circumstances no breach of duty was shown, defendant having only undertaken to fit up a wine cellar with brick and stone bins, and not one of any particular character.

Richardson v Berkeley (1847) 10 LTOS 203

380 No negligence without duty

The declaration stated that defendants were possessed of a mooring anchor, which was kept by them fixed in a known part of a navigable river, covered by ordinary tides, that the anchor had become removed into, and remained in, another part of the river covered by ordinary tides, not indicated, whereof defendants had notice, and although they had the means and power of refixing and securing the anchor, and indicating it, they neglected so to do, whereby plaintiffs' vessel, whilst sailing in a part of the river ordinarily used by ships, ran foul of and struck against the anchor, and was thereby damaged, etc: *Held* bad, for not showing that defendants were privy to the removal of the anchor, or that it was their duty to refix it and to indicate it.

Hancock v York, Newcastle & Berwick Ry Co (1850) 10 CB 348; 14 LTOS 467; 138 ER 140

381 No negligence without duty

Negligence creates no cause of action unless it expresses a breach of a duty (*Erle, CJ*).

Dutton v Powles (1862) 2 B & S 191; 31 LJQB 191; 6 LT 224; 8 Jur NS 970; 10 WR 408; 1 Mar LC 209; 121 ER 1043, Ex Ch

382 No negligence without duty

Plaintiff, a carman, being sent by his employer to defendants for some goods, was directed by a servant of defendants to go to the counting house. In proceeding along a dark passage of defendants in the direction pointed out, plaintiff fell down a staircase, and was injured: *Held* defendants were not guilty of any negligence; for if the passage was so dark that plaintiff could not see his way, he ought not to have proceeded; and if, on the other hand, there was sufficient light, he ought to have avoided the danger.

Wilkinson v Fairrie (1862) 1 H & C 633; 32 LJ Ex 73; 7 LT 599; 9 Jur NS 280; 158 ER 1038

ANNOTATIONS **Apld** Lewis v Ronald (1909) 101 LT 534
Consd Campbell v Shelbourne Hotel Ltd [1939] 2 KB 534

383 No negligence without duty

Skelton v London & North Western Ry Co no 828 post

384 No negligence without duty

Plaintiffs, merchants at Valparaiso, received through defendants a telegram purporting to come from London and addressed to them, ordering a large shipment of barley. No such message was ever in fact sent to plaintiffs. The misdelivery of the message was caused by the negligence of defendants, and occasioned heavy loss, to plaintiffs, in consequence of a fall in the market price of barley. In an action to recover the amount of this loss: *Held* there was no duty owing by defendants to plaintiffs in the matter, either by contract or law, and therefore no action would lie.

a list of all the cases included in the *All England Law Reports* between these dates. The reference given is to the year, volume and page number. Cases reported since 1992 appear in the annual cumulative *Tables and Index*, updated quarterly by the *Current Tables and Index*.

If you know that the case you are looking for is old, you can turn to the index in Volumes 177 and 178 of the *English Reports*, and this will tell you if the case is printed in the *English Reports* (see **3–12**). Several other series of law reports also publish indexes and these can be useful if you know that a case is reported in a particular series but you have not got an exact reference.

The indexes to the *Law Reports* are very useful for all but the most recent cases. From 1865 to 1949, a series of *Law Reports: Digests* were published. These contain summaries of the cases reported in the *Law Reports*, in subject order, and a list of cases is usually included. From 1950 this has been published as the *Law Reports Consolidated Index* (lettered on the spine *Law Reports Index*), usually referred to as the *Red Index*. Four bound volumes, each covering cases in a 10-year period, have been published for the period 1951–1990. An annual paper back *Red Index* is published, containing cases indexed to the end of the previous year. This is supplemented by the *Pink Index*, which is issued at intervals during the year and lists all the cases published during the current year. The main arrangement of all the indexes is by subject, but there are two alphabetical lists. The list of Cases Reported, at the front of each volume, covers recently reported cases, whilst the separate list of Cases Judicially Considered, at the back of the volume, gives information on older cases which have been mentioned in court during the period covered by the index. In addition to cases published in the *Law Reports* and the *Weekly Law Reports*, the *Red* and *Pink* indexes also include cases published, in the *All England Law Reports*, the *Criminal Appeal Reports*, the *Lloyd's Law Reports*, the *Local Government Reports*, the *Industrial Cases Reports*, the *Road Traffic Reports* and *Tax Cases*.

Recent Unreported Judgments

Transcripts of judgments made in the Court of Appeal have been added to LexisNexis databases since the 1980s. However, recent judgments have become much more widely available since the late 1990s as courts have added judgment texts to their websites. Transcripts of judgments made in a very wide range of cases are now available on the internet, sometimes within hours of the judgment being handed down. Perhaps the most useful aspect of this development is the opportunity this gives you to find the text of very recent judgments. Where cases have provoked coverage in the newspapers and other media, the availability of judgments on the internet makes it possible to examine the legal issues by going directly to the full text.   **3–19**

The House of Lords led the move towards the publication of judgments on the internet, and has made its own judgments available on the Parliament website (at *www.parliament.uk*) since 1996. As these are the judgments of the court of final appeal, they are the most influential recent judgments available online. The judgments are found in the "Judicial Work" section of the Parliament website. The most recent judgments are listed first as they appear, followed by alphabetical lists of judgments grouped according to the year in which they were made. The "Advanced Search" on the Parliament website allows a search to be restricted so that only the judgments on the website are searched. Keywords, exact phrases or dates can then be added to retrieve particular judgments. The Privy Council has made its judgments available (at *www.privy-council.org.uk*) since 1999. (The Privy Council complements the role of the House of Lords as the court of final appeal for some Commonwealth Countries, the Channel Islands, Isle of Man and UK overseas territories.)

The availability of recent judgments was greatly increased in the late1990s when the Court Service began adding judgments to its website. Now an agency of the Department of Constitutional Affairs, and re-titled Her Majesty's Court Service, the Court Service continues to make recent judgments available from its website (at *www.hmcourts-service.gov.uk*). The judgments can be found in the "Legal/Professional" section of the website, with the most recent judgments listed first on the judgments web page. A search engine on the judgments page also allows searching by keyword or phrase. Judgments are available from the Civil and Criminal Divisions of the Court of Appeal, the Administrative Court and the High Court, though not all cases are included. Instead, cases are made available at the discretion of the presiding judge.

How to find recent judgments

3–20   If you are looking for an extremely recent judgment, perhaps one made the previous day, it makes sense to look for the judgment on the court websites mentioned in **3–19**. However, a number of alternatives are available for locating the full text of recent judgments.

The BAILII web pages (at *www.bailii.org*) provide a convenient way of searching for all recent UK judgments as they bring together judgments from Her Majesty's Court Service, the House of Lords and the Privy Council. Judgments from Scotland and Northern Ireland courts are also available. Judgments can be viewed either alphabetically or by year and month. Select "England and Wales" and then the relevant court to see Court Service judgments, or "United Kingdom" to see House of Lords and Privy Council judgments. A keyword search box on the home page allows the full text of judgments to be searched using keywords and phrases. The "Search Form" link allows judgments to be searched from specific courts or groups of courts.

SEARCH TIP

Use the "neutral citation" (**3–4**) if known when searching for recent judgments, e.g. [2005] UKHL 35. (The citation can be used with paragraph numbers in square brackets when quoting from a judgment.)

Most university libraries can also provide access to the *Casetrack* database (at *www.casetrack.com*). The database provides direct access to Smith Bernal transcripts of judgments made in the Court of Appeal, the Administrative Court and the High Court, along with searchable links to House of Lords and Privy Council judgments. Again, Scotland and Northern Ireland judgments are included. As Smith Bernal is the official reporter to the Court of Appeal and the Administrative Court, judgments from these courts can be made available very quickly, sometimes within hours of being handed down. The database can be searched by case name, date and keyword. Access to the database is restricted to registered users, so you will need to request a username and a password from your law library (*Casetrack* does not use the Athens authentication system—**2–9**).

As the UK's leading current awareness service for law, Lawtel (**2–6**) provides another effective way of searching for recent judgments, though by no means all university law libraries subscribe. The range of judgments available is again wide, and judgments are loaded onto Lawtel databases as soon as they become available. The judgments are linked to brief summaries provided by Lawtel.

It should be emphasised, however, that the greatest benefit of the availability of judgments online, lies in the opportunity it gives the student to find recent judgments which are already known to be of legal significance. The ability to search through large numbers of judgments is not in itself a particular benefit to the law student. Some of the judgments will be reported later, but many will not. About a third of Court of Appeal cases will be reported. As noted in the introduction to this chapter, the aim of law reporting is to make available those cases that raise a point of legal significance. It is unusual for cases which raise a significant legal issue to go unreported.

Summary: How to Find a Case

1. If the date is unknown:
    use the Westlaw UK *Case Locator* database, or the *Current Law Case Citator*; a print alternative is provided by *The Digest*, in the *Consolidated Table of Cases*, and in the *Cumulative Supplement*.
2. If the case is thought to be old look in:
    the *Digest Consolidated Table of Cases*,
    the index to the *English Reports*,
    the index to the *All England Law Reports Reprint*,
    or use the *All England Law Reports Reprint* series online from LexisNexis Professional or LexisNexis Butterworths.
3. If the case is thought to be very recent and unreported, use one of the databases described in **3–19** and **3–20**.
4. If the case is thought to be recent, and reported, look in:
    the Westlaw UK *Case Locator*,
    or the *Current Law Monthly Digest*; the indexes of the *Law Reports*, the *Weekly Law Reports* and the *All England Law Reports* provide further print alternatives.
5. If you know that the case has been reported in one of the leading series, but your reference is incomplete:
    search for the case online (see **7–8**), or look in the printed index to the series if there is one.

How to Trace Journal Articles and Commentaries on a Case

You may want to find journal articles written about a case, or trace comments on a recent **3–21** court decision. Such articles and comments usually explain the significance of the case and relate it to other relevant decisions. Sometimes writers who disagree with a decision made in a case may suggest that the case provides a justification for a substantive change in the law.

If you have used the Westlaw UK *Case Locator* database to find a case (**3–15**), or the *Current Law Case Citator* (**3–16**), you may already have been alerted to the existence of journal articles providing comment and analysis. In the *Case Locator* database, brief journal citations appear at the end of the page of information on a case provided by Westlaw UK. If Westlaw UK can provide access to the full text of the journal article online, the citation appears as a hyperlink. In the *Current Law Case Citator*, journal articles appear in square brackets after citations for law reports. Not all cases attract comment in journals. Significant cases may be referenced many times. *Douglas* v *Hello! Ltd* (No. 1) has been discussed to date in 49 journal articles. Some of the articles will be very brief, others extensive, running to many pages.

Journal titles are given in an abbreviated form in both these sources and the full citation uses a similar format to that used for law reports. Two examples may help:

I.P.Q. 2005, 1, 27–51

refers to an article published in the *Intellectual Property Quarterly* which discussed the case. The article appears on pages 27 to 51 of volume 1 for 2005.

S.J. 2004, 148 (17), 493–495

refers to an article published in volume 148, issue 17 of the *Solicitors Journal* on pages 493 to 495.

Sources explaining the meaning of abbreviations are noted in **3–5**. These can be useful if you need to check a library catalogue to see if a university library holds a particular journal (**1–8**).

However, the Westlaw UK *Case Citator* and the *Current Law Case Citator* provide only the briefest information about a journal article. This can be a problem if you wish to assess the potential value of the article. More information can be found by searching the *Legal Journals Index* database on Westlaw UK, or the Lawtel Articles database. Both services provide brief summaries of articles indexed.

SEARCH TIP

Use both the Westlaw UK Case Locators database and the *Legal Journals Index* when tracing journal articles on a case. Different articles can be indexed.

The *Legal Journals Index* database can be found via a shortcut from the Westlaw UK home page. To use the Index, enter a case citation in the "Case Cited" box of the search menu displayed. A search then displays a results list showing citations of articles discussing the case. This will not be the same list of articles as that provided by the Case Locator database, as indexing for the *Legal Journals Index* is carried out separately. Selecting entries for any of the articles displays the article summary, sometimes no more than a sentence or two, along with additional keywords and citations for any legislation discussed. Articles are indexed from 1986. The Index is also available in print, though not all libraries continue to keep copies. A Case Index can be used to find references to relevant articles, but searching can be cumbersome, especially for cases generating a great deal of comment, perhaps necessitating a trawl through a number of annual volumes.

The Article Index for the Lawtel database (**2–6**) provides an effective online alternative to the *Legal Journals Index* database on Westlaw UK. Although fewer articles are indexed than is the case for Westlaw UK, the summaries provided are somewhat more extensive. Articles are indexed from 1988. To search for case comment on Lawtel, select the "Articles Index" tab on the home page, then "Focused Search". Case names can be entered in the "Case Law Cited" box. A search on "Douglas v Hello" finds slightly fewer articles than the *Legal Journals Index*.

If you are simply looking for any comment on a recent case likely to be of general interest, a more direct approach can be adopted. If you know the date of a case, the relevant issue of weekly journals such as the *New Law Journal* or the *Solicitors Journal* can be checked on the library shelves. These always carry notes and comments on recent cases. Key specialist journals such as *Public Law* and the *Criminal Law Review* can be used in a similar way. Again, these journals always carry notes and comments on recent cases.

How to Find Updates on Recent Cases

A number of online services provide brief summaries of new cases. These enable the legal profession to identify the key features of recent judgments that might be of interest. Cases can be reviewed quickly, without the need to read through the judgments. The brief summaries provided by these services may sometimes be the only text available that notes the content of a judgment.   **3–22**

Updates on recent reported cases can also be found using the *Current Law Digest* (in print) or the Westlaw UK *Case Locators* database.

The *All England Reporter* database is one of the most wide-ranging sources for summaries of new judgments; most appearing soon after the judgment is made. Some of the judgments will later be reported in the *All England Law Reports*, but many will not. The cases that will be reported later are marked with an asterisk against the case name. The *All England Reporter* database can be found in both LexisNexis Butterworths (**2–4**) and LexisNexis Professional (**2–3**).

To access the *Reporter* database in LexisNexis Butterworths, first select "Cases" from the LexisNexis Butterworths home page, then "Browse". Selecting the database displays a list of cases with the most recent cases shown first. Judgment summaries can be selected for each of the cases. Although relatively brief, they are comparable to the summaries provided in the Westlaw UK *Case Locator* and provide information on the key facts of a case. Subject keywords are also added. To use LexisNexis Professional, choose the "Current Awareness" search option on the LexisNexis home page and search for "Cases". Results can again be browsed by date. Judgments can also be viewed by legal practice area in both services ("Banking", "Civil Procedure" etc).

The summaries can be cited using *All England Reporter* reference numbers and the month of the judgment, e.g.

R v D [2005] All E.R. (D) 64 (Sep)

A more selective alternative to the *All England Reporter* database is provided by the Incorporated Council for Law Reporting. Its *WLR Daily* service (at *www.lawreports.co.uk*) provides digests of cases that will later be reported in the *Weekly Law Reports*. This has the distinct advantage of ensuring that the cases summarised on the database raise questions of legal significance. The site is also a non-subscription site, guaranteeing access to the database content. The summaries provided are reasonably extensive and a full list of keywords is provided. Once a case has been reported in the *Weekly Law Reports* the entry is removed from *WLR Daily*. Cases can be viewed by week, or by court and subject matter. If the latter option is selected, case names and keywords can be viewed by major subject heading (e.g. "Arbitration", "Audit", "Children"). The summaries can be cited using a *WLR Daily* reference number as follows:

Mabon v Mabon and Others [2005] W.L.R. (D) 68

Not all libraries provide access to Lawtel (**2–5**), but Lawtel's *Case Law Service* provides another rapidly updated source of summaries of judgments. An advantage of the *Case Law Service* is that the case report summaries provided are always linked to the full text of judgments.

Though these services are highly effective, the availability of online summaries of recent judgments can nonetheless be a mixed blessing, especially when the database providing the summaries is as wide-ranging as Lawtel's *Case Law* service or the *All England Reporter*. Though the specialist practitioner, or legal academic, may be able to sift through case summaries and decide which raise legal issues of significance, this is not easily accomplished by the law student. Finding information and interpreting it are two separate tasks involving different skills and levels of expertise.

Updates on recent reported cases, though less immediate, are more likely to yield new cases that might be important. The *Current Law Monthly Digest* prints summaries of cases under major subject headings (along with notes of journal articles and new legislation). A Cumulative Table of Cases in each monthly issue enables cases to be traced by name for the current year. The relevant month and entry item number is noted against each case. The same information can also be found using Westlaw UK's *Case Locators* database. First select the "Case Locators" shortcut from the Westlaw UK home page. Searches can then be limited so that only recent cases are shown. A search can be limited, for example, to cases added to the database in the last six months. Subject keywords (e.g. "Privacy") can then be entered to find new reported cases of interest.

European Human Rights Case Law

3–23 The Human Rights Act 1998 incorporated into UK law the principles of the European Convention for the Protection of Human Rights and Fundamental Freedoms. Although the Convention had been of potential relevance to the law of the UK before the Human Rights Act, the Act requires that courts take Convention case law into account in all cases where it might be considered relevant, greatly increasing its importance to UK domestic law. As a result, knowing how to find and cite European Convention case law has become an essential skill for students of UK law.

The European Convention is a treaty agreed by the member states of the Council of Europe—not to be confused with the European Union, though many of its 46 member states are also members of the EU. The UK ratified the Treaty in 1951 and it came into force in 1953. The Convention established both the European Court of Human Rights and the European Commission of Human Rights and both bodies have played a role in the creation of Convention case law. The role of the European Commission is now subsumed into that of the European Court.

European Convention case law consists of both judgments and decisions. Judgments are made by the full sessions of the European Court of Human Rights, sitting in Strasbourg.

Decisions are admissibility decisions which determine whether a case should proceed to a full hearing of the European Court. Before 1998 admissibility decisions were made by the European Commission of Human Rights. Decisions are now made by a committee of the European Court of Human Rights itself. Both judgments and decisions are relevant to the interpretation of the European Convention and must be taken into account under the Human Rights Act 1998.

All applications to the European Court of Human Rights are given an application number consisting of five digits plus two digits for the year the application was lodged. Where a case is unreported, this application number can be used to cite both judgments and decisions, e.g.

B.B. v the United Kingdom no. 53760/00, 10 February 2004

specifies the judgment made in the case;

B.B. v the United Kingdom (dec.), no. 53760/00, 27 May 2003

specifies the decision made in the same case.

An abbreviation such as ECHR or ECtHR is often added where it may not be obvious that a European Court case is being cited. The citation format noted for judgments follows the Council of Europe's specification. The practice of UK publishers does not always follow the Council of Europe specification.

Tracing European Convention case law

The full text of European Convention case law can be found on the European Court of Human **3–24** Rights website (at *www.echr.coe.int*). Judgments and decisions are held in the HUDOC database, part of the European Court of Human Rights Portal. The database contains all judgments made by the European Court of Human Rights since 1959 and all admissibility decisions made since 1986. Some decisions are also available for the period 1955 to 1986.

If you have the application number for a case, use the full number in the "Application Number" search box of the HUDOC database, to retrieve a link to the full text (e.g. "44875/98"). Tick boxes allow judgments, decisions or both to be selected for searching. Resolutions of the Committee of Ministers of the Council of Europe are also included, though these are not often cited in legal discussion.

If you do not have the application number for a case, the name of the case can be entered under "Case Title" (e.g. "B.B." or "Hobbs"), along with the respondent state (e.g. "United Kingdom"). The use of abbreviations in case titles and the need to have an exact case name can cause problems. It may be necessary to try likely subject keywords in the "Text" box to find a case.

Printed judgments and decisions

Judgments made before 1996 were published by Carl Heymanns Verlag in *Series A* of the **3–25** Publications of the Court. Each judgment has a number within the series, so that a full citation is as follows:

CONSEIL
DE L'EUROPE

COUNCIL
OF EUROPE

COUR EUROPÉENNE DES DROITS DE L'HOMME
EUROPEAN COURT OF HUMAN RIGHTS

FOURTH SECTION

CASE OF PERKINS AND R. v. THE UNITED KINGDOM
(Applications nos. 43208/98 and 44875/98)

JUDGMENT

STRASBOURG

22 October 2002

FINAL
22/01/2003

This judgment will become final in the circumstances set out in Article 44 § 2 of the Convention. It may be subject to editorial revision.

Soering v the United Kingdom, judgment of 7 July 1989, Series A no. 161 References to pages or paragraph numbers may follow (e.g. pp. 40–41; para. or § 65).

The text of individual judgments was also printed by the Council of Europe and distributed to libraries up until 1997. Some law libraries which do not hold the *Series A* text of a judgment may have retained these individually printed transcripts. Confusingly, they have their own numbering system. This is not used in citation.

From 1996 onwards selected judgments and decisions have been published (again by Heymanns Verlag) as *Reports of Judgments and Decisions*, and cited e.g. as:

Robins v the United Kingdom, judgment of 23 September 1997, Reports 1997-V

Pages and paragraph numbers may again be added to the citation.

Decisions made between 1974 and 1995 were published by the Council of Europe as *Decisions and Reports* (DR). These are cited as follows:

Hewitt and Harman v the United Kingdom (1989) 67 DR 88

Here, 67 specifies the volume number and 88 the first page of the report. Only a few law libraries hold the full *Decisions and Reports* series, which can be a problem as the HUDOC database does not contain all decisions made before 1986. Decisions made between 1960 and 1974 were published by the Council of Europe as *Collection of Decisions of the European Commission on Human Rights* (C.D.). These are rarely cited.

Other sources of European human rights Law

Most of the human rights cases cited in UK courts have been reported in either the *European Human Rights Reports* (E.H.R.R.) or *Butterworths Human Rights Cases* (B.H.R.C.). Digests are also available in the *European Human Rights Law Review* (E.H.R.L.R.). These are commercial publications available both in print and online. The full text of the *European Human Rights Reports* and the *European Human Rights Law Review* are available online from Westlaw UK (**2–5**). *Butterworths Human Rights Cases* is available online from LexisNexis Butterworths (**2–4**) and LexisNexis Professional (**2–3**). Citations from these publications use the standard format for UK law reports and journals. As with other Sweet & Maxwell law reports, the *European Human Rights Reports* from 2001 onwards are referenced using a case number rather than a page number, e.g.

3–26

> **SEARCH TIP**
>
> Use Westlaw UK and LexisNexis Professional to search for ECHR cases reported in UK law reports. These are the cases most often cited in UK legal discussion.

Bubbins v United Kingdom (2005) 41 E.H.R.R. 24

Here the reference is to case 24 of the 2005 reports volume. Summaries and extracts of reports are also included in the *European Human Rights Reports*, and these are referenced as e.g.

Brinks v Netherlands (2005) 41 E.H.R.R. SE5

Some admissibility decisions are reported in a separate section of the E.H.R.R. and are cited as E.H.R.R. C.D.

Although the *European Human Rights Reports* concentrates on European Convention case law, *Butterworths Human Rights Cases* is more wide ranging, including cases from other common law countries which may be of relevance to the human rights law of the UK. Cases might be reported from the Constitutional Court of South Africa for example, or the United States Supreme Court. These appear alongside reports of UK cases.

Textbooks on UK human rights law also refer to cases from the Court of Justice of the European Union (**8–13**) where these concern European Convention principles.

Summaries of European Court of Human Rights cases have also been published in book form. Vincent Berger's *Case Law of the European Court of Human Rights* for example was published in three volumes and covers the period 1960 to 1993. Peter Kempees' *Systematic Guide to the Case Law of the European Court of Human Rights* covers the period 1960 to 1998 in four volumes, arranging summaries according to the relevant article or articles of the European Convention within each volume.

The *Human Rights Information Bulletin*, produced by the Council of Europe, provides extensive summaries of recent judgments along with information on cases currently pending. Current issues are available from the Council of Europe website (at *www.coe.int/Human_rights*), along with back issues from no. 41 1997. The European Court of Human Rights has issued an *Information Note* since 1999 which contains brief summaries of judgments arranged by Convention article.

Tribunals

3–27   The establishment of the welfare state led to the creation of a large number of tribunals. They were set up to resolve disputes over entitlement to welfare benefits. Subsequently, other areas, such as problems between landlords and tenants, and between employer and employees because of unfair dismissal, became subject to resolution through tribunals. Tribunals can be extremely busy, hearing many thousands of cases each year, but only a small number of cases are eventually reported in the law reports. Some law reports, such as the *Industrial Cases Reports* and *Immigration Appeals*, carry reports of appeals from the tribunal to an appeal court, but the vast majority of cases heard by tribunals are not reported. However, relatively recent decisions from a wide range of tribunals can by found on the BAILII website (at *www.bailii.org*). These include, for example, decisions of the Employment Appeal Tribunal (from 1999) and the Financial Services and Markets Tribunal (from 2003). The full listing can be found under "BAILII Cases & Legislation" and "United Kingdom". The full text of judgments can then be found. Where Tribunals also put the text of judgments made on their own websites, these can usually be traced from the relevant page of the BAILII website. For reported and unreported decisions of the Social Security and Child Support Commissioners, see **3–28**. Unreported decisions of tribunals can be cited using unique appeal numbers, e.g. Appeal No UKEAT/0879/04 for an Employment Appeal Tribunal case.

Social welfare law

The most important decisions taken by the Social Security and Child Support **3–28** Commissioners are found on the Commissioners' website (at *www.osscsc.gov.uk*). To find them, select "Search Decisions" from the home page. The decisions available on the website include reported decisions from 1991 to date, all decisions from 2002, and "starred decisions" from 1990 to 2001. Starred decisions were decisions the Commissioners thought should be published in print. The practice was discontinued in 2001 and references to starred decisions are to be removed from the website.

Between 1976 and 1990, bound volumes of decisions were published by HMSO, the last appearing in 1993 as *Reported Decisions of the Social Security Commissioner. Vol 13. 1989–1990*. Reported decisions between 1948 and 1976 were published in the seven volumes of the *Reported Decisions of the Commissioner under the Social Security and National Insurance (Industrial Injuries) Acts*, known as the *Blue Books* because of their colour.

The form of citation for Commissioners' decisions differs from that used in conventional law reports and references to cases do not include the names of parties. All reported cases since 1950 bear the prefix R, followed, in brackets, by an abbreviation for the series. For example, the prefix R(U) indicates a Commissioner's decision on unemployment benefit, and R(P) a decision on entitlement to pensions. Within each series, reports are cited by the report number and the year: R(U) 7/62 indicates a reported unemployment benefit decision, case number 7 of 1962. The following abbreviations are in use:

R(A)	Attendance allowance
R(CS)	Child Support
R(DLA)	Disability Living Allowance
R(DWA)	Disability Working Allowance
R(F)	Family allowances and child benefit
R(FC)	Family Credit
R(FIS)	Family Income Supplement
R(G)	General—miscellaneous (maternity benefit, widow's benefit, death grant, etc.)
R(I)	Industrial injuries
R(IS)	Income Support
R(M)	Mobility allowance
R(P)	Retirement pensions
R(S)	Sickness and invalidity Benefit
R(SB)	Supplementary benefit
R(SSP)	Statutory Sick Pay
R(U)	Unemployment benefit

Unpublished decisions are prefaced by C instead of R. For example, CP3/81 is a reference to an unpublished 1981 Commissioner's decision on pensions and CSB 15/82 is an unreported decision on supplementary benefits. The year in "starred" cases (1987–2001) is given in full, e.g. CDLA 1347/1999.

Reported cases from 1948–50 had a different method of citation. They were prefixed by C, followed by a letter (*not* enclosed in brackets) representing the area of law covered. Thus, CI denotes an early decision on industrial injuries. Scottish or Welsh cases were prefixed with

CS and CW respectively. The cases were numbered in sequence. However, only a minority were printed, which has resulted in gaps in the numerical sequence. For example, CWI 17/49 is followed by CWI 20/49. Cases numbered 18 or 19 of 1949 are unreported. The abbreviation (KL) after the citation is an indication that the case has been reported, whilst the suffix (K) denotes a decision of limited value.

Decisions on a particular subject can be traced using *Neligan: Social Security Case Law: Digest of Commissioner's Decisions*. The *Digest* is available from the Department of Work and Pensions website (at *www.dwp.gov.uk*). To find the publication, use the website's search engine and search for "Neligan". *Neligan* summarises the majority of the reported decisions, under appropriate subject headings. Appendix 3 of the work provides a list of decision numbers which allow you to trace the summary of a particular case should the full report of the Commissioner's decision be unavailable. A general subject index is also provided.

Reported decisions of other tribunals

3–29   The wide range of tribunals makes a complete guide to reported decisions impossible within the available space. What follows is selective.

Immigration appeals are covered by *Immigration Appeals*, published by TSO. Also available from TSO are the *Value Added Tax and Duties Tribunals Reports*.

Many Lands Tribunal cases appear in the *Property, Planning and Compensation Reports* and in the *Estates Gazette* and the *Estates Gazette Law Reports*. The latter series also covers leasehold valuation tribunals. Barry Rose published a series of volumes entitled *Lands Tribunal Cases*.

Most reported cases, in subjects other than welfare law, appear in standard series of law reports and are conventionally cited. *Current Law* contains references to many tribunal decisions, under appropriate subject headings, and provides a summary for each one. Looseleaf encyclopedias frequently refer to both published and unpublished decisions in the appropriate subject.

The *Industrial Tribunal Reports*, published until 1978, now form part of the *Industrial Cases Reports*. These contain many cases heard by the Employment Appeal Tribunal and many E.A.T. decisions also appear in the *Industrial Relations Law Reports*.

4 Legislation

Introduction

When a Bill (**6–6**) has been approved by both Houses of Parliament and has received the Royal Assent, it becomes an Act of Parliament. The Act is made available on the Office of Public Sector Information (OPSI) website (at *www.opsi.gov.uk/legislation*) and the first printed version is published by TSO, usually within a few days of receiving the Royal Assent. **4–1**

There are two types of Acts. Public General Acts deal with public policy and apply to the whole population, or a substantial part of it. Local and Personal Acts, on the other hand, affect only a particular area of the country, or a named organisation or group of individuals. This chapter will concentrate on Public General Acts, which you are more likely to use regularly. Local and Personal Acts will, however, be examined in **4–25**.

The Structure of an Act

A copy of the Ragwort Control Act 2003 is reproduced below. This is an unusually short Act, as most Acts are many pages in length. All Acts are structured in the same way, although some of the parts described below are not included in every Act. **4–2**

The parts of an Act (see the illustration) are:

1. *Short title*;
2. *Official citation* (see **4–3**);
3. *Long title*. This may give some indication of the purpose and content of the Act;
4. *Date of Royal Assent*;
5. *Enacting formula*. This is a standard form of words indicating that the Act has been approved by Parliament;
6. *Main body of the Act*. This is divided into sections, which are further divided into subsections and paragraphs. When referring to a section, it is usual to abbreviate it to "s." Whilst subsections are written in round brackets. You would therefore write section 2, subsection 1 as s.2(1);

Ragwort Control Act 2003①

2003 Chapter 40②

An Act to amend the Weeds Act 1959 in relation to ragwort; and for connected purposes.③

④[20th November 2003]

BE IT ENACTED by the Queen's most Excellent Majesty, by and with the advice and consent of the Lords Spiritual and Temporal, and Commons, in this present Parliament assembled, and by the authority of the same, as follows:-⑤

1 Control of ragwort

After section 1 of the Weeds Act 1959 (c. 54) there is inserted-

"1A
Code of practice: ragwort⑥

(1) The Minister may make a code of practice for the purpose of providing guidance on how to prevent the spread of ragwort (*senecio jacobaea L.*).
(2) Before making the code the Minister must consult such persons as he considers appropriate.
(3) The Minister must lay a copy of the code before Parliament.
(4) The Minister may revise the code; and subsections (2) and (3) apply to the revised code.
(5) The code is to be admissible in evidence.
(6) If the code appears to a court to be relevant to any question arising in proceedings it is to be taken into account in determining that question."

2 Wales

(1) The reference to the Weeds Act 1959 in Schedule 1 to the National Assembly for Wales (Transfer of Functions) Order 1999 (S.I. 1999/672) is to be treated as referring to that Act as amended by this Act.
(2) Subsection (1) does not affect the power to make further Orders varying or omitting that reference.

3 Short title, commencement and extent

(1) This Act may be cited as the Ragwort Control Act 2003.
(2) This Act comes into force at the end of the period of three months beginning with the day on which it is passed.⑦
(3) This Act extends to England and Wales only.⑧

7. *Date of commencement.* A specific date may be set for the Act to come into force. Alternatively, the Act may give a Minister of the Crown the power to bring it into force at a later date. This will be done through a commencement order, which is a form of delegated legislation. If there is no commencement section at the end of an Act, it comes into force on the date of the Royal Assent;

8. *Extent.* Acts of Parliament usually apply to the whole of the United Kingdom, unless specified otherwise in an extent section.

Schedules and tables are sometimes included at the end of an Act. They may contain detailed provisions not included elsewhere in the Act or may summarise and clarify the effect of the Act. They help to prevent the main body of an Act becoming too cluttered with detail and are used in the same way as appendices in a book. Until 2001 the text of an Act also included helpful marginal notes, explaining the contents of a section.

Citation of statutes

Statutes (or Acts) are commonly referred to by a shortened version of their title (the short title) and the year of publication, e.g. the Theft Act 1968. Every Act published in a year is given its own individual number and Acts may also be cited by the year in which they were passed and the Act (or chapter) number. Thus the Theft Act was the 60th Act passed in 1968 and is cited as 1968, c. 60. "Chapter" is abbreviated to "c." when written, but it is spoken in full.   **4–3**

The present system of citing statutes by their year and chapter number began in 1963. Before that date, the system was more complicated. Prior to 1963, statutes were referred to by the year of the monarch's reign (the "regnal year") and the chapter number. For example, a citation 3 Edw. 7, c. 36 is a reference to the Motor Car Act 1903, which was the 36th Act passed in the third year of the reign of Edward VII.

A session of Parliament normally commences in the autumn and continues through into the summer of the following year. A "regnal year" is reckoned from the date of the sovereign's accession to the throne and a session of Parliament may therefore cover more than one regnal year. In the case of Queen Elizabeth II, who came to the throne in February, the first part of a Parliamentary session, from the autumn until February, falls into one regnal year, whilst the latter part of the session of Parliament falls into a different regnal year. Statutes passed before February bear a different regnal year to those passed after the anniversary of her accession to the throne. Two examples make this clearer:

1. The Children and Young Persons Act 1956 received the Royal Assent in March 1956, when the Queen had just entered the fifth year of her reign. It was the 24th Act to receive the Royal Assent during the Parliament which commenced sitting in the autumn of the fourth year of her reign, and which continued in session during the early part of the fifth year of her reign. The Act is therefore cited as 4 & 5 Eliz. 2, c. 24.

2. By contrast, the Air Corporations Act 1956 was passed during the following session of Parliament and it received the Royal Assent in December 1956, when the Queen was still in the fifth year of her reign. Since, at that time, there could be no certainty that the Queen would still be on the throne in two months' time or that Parliament would still

be in session in February, when she would be entering the sixth year of her reign, the statute was cited as 5 Eliz. 2, c. 3 (i.e. the third Act passed in the Parliament held in the fifth year of the reign). When the Queen subsequently survived to enter her sixth year, the statute would henceforth be referred to as 5 & 6 Eliz. 2, c. 3.

Both these Acts are to be found in the 1956 volumes of the statutes, which contain all the Acts passed during that year, regardless of the session of Parliament in which they were passed.

Until 1939, the volumes of the statutes contained all the Acts passed in a particular session of Parliament. After that date, the annual volumes contain all the statutes passed in a calendar year. This can give rise to some confusion. For instance, the volume for 1937 contains the statutes passed in the parliamentary session which extended from November 1936 to October 1937. Thus, some Acts which actually bear the date 1936 are included in the 1937 volume. The volume for 1938 includes some statutes passed in December 1937 (which one might normally expect to find in the 1937 volume). The simple rule with older Acts is: if it is not in the volume you expect to find it in, look in the volumes on either side of it!

Citation of the names of monarchs and their regnal years

4–4   The names of the monarchs are abbreviated as follows:

Anne	Ann.
Charles	Car., Chas. *or* Cha.
Edward	Edw. *or* Ed.
Elizabeth	Eliz.
George	Geo.
Henry	Hen.
James	Ja., Jac. *or* Jas.
Mary	Mar. *or* M.
Philip and Mary	Ph. & M. *or* Phil. & Mar.
Richard	Ric. *or* Rich.
Victoria	Vict.
William	Will., Wm. *or* Gul.
William and Mary	Wm. & M., Will. & Mar. *or* Gul. & Mar.

A list of the regnal year of monarchs showing the equivalent calendar year is found in *Sweet & Maxwell's Guide to Law Reports and Statutes* (4th ed.), pp. 21–33; and at the back of *Osborn's Concise Law Dictionary*.

Modern Statutes

4–5   Acts of Parliament can be found on the OPSI website (at *www.opsi.gov.uk/legislation*) from 1988 and in print as *Public General Acts & Measures*. These are the official sources of statutes (**4–6**). However, a number of alternative sources for statutes are also available.

Which source to use may not be obvious. The following considerations can help ensure that you choose an appropriate source for modern statute law.

First, you should consider whether you need to consult the current amended text of an Act. Is it important that you are consulting law in force? If so, you should consider using one of the sources introduced in **4–12**. These include subscription databases such as the *UK Legislation* databases of Westlaw UK (**4–15**) or LexisNexis Professional (**4–14**), also the print volumes of *Halsbury's Statutes of England* (**4–16**).

If it is important to see the full text of legislation as originally enacted, then turn to the sources noted in the following sections.

Having decided this, it is useful to consider whether you need to consult a particular section of an Act, or the Act as a whole; online sources are usually best if you wish to find a particular section of an Act (especially if you already have the relevant section number). This could be done using one of the subscription sources of law in force noted above, or a free public source of legislation as enacted. This might be the OPSI website (**4–6**) or the BAILII website (**4–8**).

If you wish to gain an understanding of an important piece of legislation taken as a whole, it is worth turning to print editions. Important legislation can be extensive, making it difficult to read and review an entire Act on screen. Your library is likely to have the print volumes of both *Public General Acts & Measures* (**4–6**) and *Current Law Statutes* (**4–11**). These are sources of statutes as originally enacted. *Halsbury's Statutes of England* (**4–16**) is the only print source for statutes in force.

An additional advantage of some print editions is the inclusion of often extensive annotations, which can help direct your understanding of legislation. Both *Current Law Statutes* and *Halsbury's Statutes of England* provide annotations. These are not available in the online databases.

There are also books devoted to particular key Acts of Parliament. These can be particularly helpful as they combine detailed comment with a reprinted version of the Act itself. Relevant secondary legislation is usually included. Extracts of Parliamentary Debates and government white papers might also found. *Blackstone's Guide to the Human Rights Act 1998* (3rd edition 2003) and *The Criminal Justice Act 2003: a practitioner's guide* (Ward and Davies 2004) are examples of such works.

Official sources of statutes

The OPSI website lists Public General Acts on its legislation pages (at *www.opsi.gov. uk/leg-*   **4–6** *islation*). There are also links to Northern Ireland, Scotland and Wales legislation. Acts are listed on the page by year of enactment, both alphabetically and chronologically (i.e. in chapter number order). Selecting the title of an Act displays the full text with hyperlinks from the list of sections near the start of most Acts to the relevant section. In most cases a number of sections of an Act are reproduced on a single web page, making printing cumbersome. All Acts passed by Parliament from 1988 onwards can be found on the site.

Acts are also printed individually as they appear. At the end of each year bound annual volumes are then published as the official *Public General Acts & Measures* of 2006, 2007 etc. This series of red volumes has been published since 1831 (originally under the title *Public General Acts*). There are now a number of volumes for each year. At the front of the annual volumes there is a list of all the Acts passed during the year, in alphabetical order, showing where they are to be found in the bound volumes. There is also a list in chapter number order giving the same information. The General Synod Measures of the Church of England are printed in full at the back of the annual volumes of the *Public General* Acts. A list of Local and Personal Acts published during the year is also printed in the annual volume, although the texts are not included. Most law libraries keep both individually printed Acts for the current year and the bound volumes.

Alternative sources for the official text of statutes

4–7   The BAILII website (**4–8**) reproduces the full text of statutes available on the OPSI website. Although the text available is identical, the layout of the website and the search engine used might be preferred, especially by anyone also using BAILII as a free source of case law. However, complete historical coverage online is only offered by Justis UK Statutes (**4–9**). This is a subscription database and not all law libraries can provide access. There are two current print series which reprint the text of statutes as originally enacted. *Law Reports: Statutes* (**4–10**) reproduces the *Public General Acts & Measures* text in a smaller, more easily handled, format. *Current Law Statutes* (**4–11**) prints the same text with additional annotations. Most law libraries will have one or both of these print series.

BAILII United Kingdom Statutes

4–8   Statutes can be found on the BAILII website (at *www.bailii.org*), under the "United Kingdom" heading. They are available from 1988 onwards. Acts can be found by year of enactment and also alphabetically, using a single A–Z listing for all of the Acts on the site. If you are unsure of the year of an Act, this makes the BAILII site a little easier to use than the OPSI alternative. However, each Act is reproduced on the site as a single continuous web page. You need to be sure that you want the entire text of an Act before you click to print. As is the case in the OPSI website, the section names in the list of sections near the start of most Acts are hyperlinked to the relevant section. Northern Ireland, Scotland and Wales legislation is also available.

Justis UK Statutes

4–9   The Justis *UK Statutes* database is the only complete source of United Kingdom statute law available online, containing the full text of all Acts of Parliament from 1235 onwards. It is one of a number of Justis subscription databases (see **2–7**), so you need to check if your law library can provide access. Though the text of statutes is presented as enacted, a particular feature of the database is the ability it provides to trace the path of amendment and repeal from one statute to another. For each statute, any amending legislation is presented as a family tree, with the relevant links leading you from statute to statute. Justis *UK Statutes* is the best source available for tracing the historical development of statute law. Acts are presented section by section in the database, making printing easier than is the case with the BAILII or OPSI websites.

Law Reports: Statutes

The Incorporated Council of Law Reporting publishes a series called *Law Reports: Statutes*   **4–10**
alongside the *Law Reports* and the *Weekly Law Reports*. The unbound parts issued through
the year share the same A4 page size and publishing format. Each contains the reprinted text
of one or more Acts, though there may be some delay between an Act receiving the Royal
Assent and its appearance in *Law Reports: Statutes*. At the end of the year annual volumes
are printed which replace the loose parts. The page size of the reprint can make the bound
volume appreciably easier to manipulate than the large Royal Octavo volumes of *Public
General Acts & Measures*. As a result some law libraries hold the reprint series as well as
Public General Acts & Measures.

Current Law Statutes

Current Law Statutes reprints the full text of all Public General Acts soon after they receive   **4–11**
the Royal Assent. They are printed in booklet form on grey paper and are filed into a loose-
leaf *Service File* in chapter number order. The grey paper denotes that the Act is a reprint of
the Queen's Printer copy. Some months later, the Act printed on grey paper is replaced by the
annotated version which is printed on white paper. At the front of the *Service File* are alphabetical and chronological lists of all the Acts included. If the Act you want to look at is in
italic type in the contents list, it means that it has not yet been published in this series.

The annotations give a detailed account of the background to the Act, including references to discussions on the Bill in the Houses of Parliament as reported in *Hansard*. The
annotations also include a summary of the contents of the Act, as well as definitions and
explanations of the meaning of individual sections of the Act. The annotations are in
smaller print to avoid confusion with the Act itself. Although the annotations have no
official standing, they are extremely useful. The author is often a leading authority on the
subject matter.

The information in the *Service File* is reissued during the year in bound volumes. *Current
Law Statutes* covers all Public General Acts since 1948, when the series commenced publication. Until 1994 the series was known as *Current Law Statutes Annotated*.

Sources of statutes as currently in force

The LexisNexis Butterworths *UK Parliament Acts* database (**4–13**), the LexisNexis   **4–12**
Professional *UK Legislation* database (**4–14**) and the *UK Legislation* database from Westlaw
UK (**4–15**) all provide online access to statutes as currently in force. Your library should be
able to provide access to at least one of these sources. The volumes of *Halsbury's Statutes
of England* (**4–16**) provide a print alternative. The Department of Constitutional Affairs is
currently working with the publisher TSO to revive plans for a "Statute Law Database"
which would provide alternative free public access to legislation in force. No release date has
yet been set for the database.

It is important to keep in mind the difference between the amended text of legislation provided by these sources and the unamended text of statutes as originally enacted provided by
the sources noted in **4–6** and **4–7**. A simple example might help.

If you look for the text of the Dangerous Dogs Act 1991 using any source of law in force, you will find that some of the text is printed between square brackets. This is text "inserted" under the provisions of another, later, Act; in this case the Dangerous Dogs (Amendment) Act 1997. This is one of the many Acts whose sole purpose is to revise the provisions of an earlier Act. Sometimes complete new sections are added. These have letters attached to their numbers in order to retain the numbering of the original Act. The text of the Dangerous Dogs Act 1991, for example, now contains a section "4A" inserted by the later amending Act (see the illustration below). This new section makes a significant change to the law on the destruction of dangerous dogs. Note that the amended Dangerous Dogs Act 1991 is still the Act to turn to find the relevant legislation on dangerous dogs. It is not superseded by the later Act.

Section 4A of the Dangerous Dogs Act 1991 (reproduced from the Westlaw UK UK Legislation database)

SWEET & MAXWELL UNITED KINGDOM LAW IN FORCE
DANGEROUS DOGS ACT 1991 CHAPTER 65
UK Statutes Crown Copyright. Reproduced by permission of the
Controller of Her Majesty's Stationery Office.
In-force date: June 8, 1997 (see Analysis Tab for Commencement Information)

s 4A Contingent destruction orders.

[

4A.—Contingent destruction orders.

(1) Where—

(a) a person is convicted of an offence under *section 1* above or an aggravated offence under *section 3(1)* or *(3)* above;

(b) the court does not order the destruction of the dog under *section 4(1)(a)* above; and

(c) in the case of an offence under *section 1* above, the dog is subject to the prohibition in *section 1(3)* above.

the court shall order that, unless the dog is exempted from that prohibition within the requisite period, the dog shall be destroyed.

(2) Where an order is made under subsection (1) above in respect of a dog, and the dog is not exempted from the prohibition in *section 1(3)* above within the requisite period, the court may extend that period.

(3) Subject to subsection (2) above, the requisite period for the purposes of such an order is the period of two months beginning with the date of the order.

(4) Where a person is convicted of an offence under *section 3(1)* or *(3)* above, the court may order that, unless the owner of the dog keeps it under proper control, the dog shall be destroyed.

(5) An order under subsection (4) above—

(a) may specify the measures to be taken for keeping the dog under proper control, whether by muzzling, keeping on a lead, excluding it from specified places or otherwise; and

(b) if it appears to the court that the dog is a male and would be less dangerous if neutered, may require it to be neutered.

(6) *Subsections (2) to (4) of section 4* above shall apply in relation to an order under subsection (1) or (4) above as they apply in relation to an order under *subsection (1)(a)* of that section.

] *[FN1]*

[FN1] added by *Dangerous Dogs (Amendment) Act (1997 c.53), s 2*

Sections or subsections of an Act can also be "deleted" by later amending legislation. The brief statement in subsection 5(4) of the Dangerous Dogs Act has been deleted in this way. This is shown by the presence of three dots against the subsection. For some Acts, only a single section or part of a section remains in force. This is true of the oldest Acts still in force. Examples can be found if you search for the various Treason Acts in databases of law in force; the earliest one still partly in force dates from 1351.

When using online sources of statutes in force to find legislation, it is important to check that you have the correct title and year for an Act, including the relevant year. There is only one Human Rights Act for example, but many Education Acts. If you type "Education Act" into the title search of either LexisNexis Professional or Westlaw UK and search the database, the result will be an extremely long results list that displays sections from different Acts (there are just under 7,000 sections in total). Databases of legislation in force treat sections of Acts as discrete database items. If you search using just the title words of an Act, your results list contains all the sections of Acts indexed under those words. As a result, searching on "Education Act" means you find all the sections of all the Education Acts.

Sections of Acts are the basic units of databases of legislation, because in most legal discussion, it is particular sections of Acts that need to be referred to, not the Act as a whole. Making sections the basic database unit also means that links can be created, for example, that take you directly from a reference to legislation in a judgment, to the full text of a section of an Act in a legislation database. The text

> **SEARCH TIP**
>
> Always enter the exact title of legislation (including the year) when searching databases of legislation in force. Check the title using other sources (e.g. print indexes and textbooks) if you are not sure.

of law reports available online from LexisNexis Butterworths and Westlaw UK is linked to legislation in precisely this way. It is sections of Acts, rather than whole Acts, that can be emailed, printed or saved using these databases (though Westlaw UK provides a partial exception to this—see **4–15**). Notes of amending legislation and relevant secondary legislation are also placed at the end of each section of an Act, not at the end of the Act as a whole.

LexisNexis Butterworths UK Parliament Acts

If your law library has a subscription to LexisNexis Butterworths *UK Parliament Acts*, **4–13** the database will be found from the LexisNexis Butterworths home page under the "Legislation" tab. Enter the title of the Act you wish to find in the title search box, ensuring to include the year, if known. The title of the Act is then displayed. Select the title to view the full text of sections of the Act. Hyperlinks within the text link to other sections within the Act and to other legislation where cited. Many law libraries combine a subscription to *UK Parliament Acts* with LexisNexis Butterworths subscriptions to both the *All England Law Reports* and *Halsbury's Laws of England* (**7–3**). This means that hyperlinks to sections of Acts in both databases open screens displaying the text found in *UK Parliament Acts*.

LexisNexis Professional UK Legislation database

UK statutes can be searched in LexisNexis Professional from the "UK Legislation" link on **4–14** the home page. Titles and sections can be entered in the relevant search boxes. However, there is no hyperlinking within the text of the Act. Where references to legislation are found elsewhere in LexisNexis Professional databases, they are not linked to the text of the legislation.

Westlaw UK UK Legislation database

4–15   Statutes can be searched by title directly from the Westlaw UK home page. Include the year of the Act in the title search box. Additional search options are available under the "UK Legislation" shortcut. The most significant of these is the ability to search for a PDF file of an entire Act, a format designed for printing and saving entire documents. These PDF files are unofficial consolidated versions of Acts, providing the current amended text. Square brackets and dots (ellipses) for deletions are not used. It is possible to select individual pages of the document for printing, so there is no necessity to print the entire Act. Full pages are printed, rather than individual sections. There are no hyperlinks between sections in these PDF documents. However, they are present in the text of legislation displayed if you use the standard *UK Legislation* search.

Halsbury's Statutes of England

4–16   *Halsbury's Statutes* differs from the other annotated series of statutes available in print. These reproduce Acts as they were originally printed. The purpose of *Halsbury's Statutes* is to provide the correct and amended text of all legislation in force, whatever the date of Royal Assent. It includes all Public General Acts in force in England and Wales, although the texts of some Acts of limited importance are not printed. The text of each Act is accompanied by notes which provide, for example, details of amendments and relevant case law.

   Halsbury's Statutes is in its fourth edition. The main work consists of 50 volumes, which are arranged alphabetically by subject. Hence, Volume 1 contains the Acts dealing with admiralty, agency and agriculture, whilst Volume 2 contains the law of allotments and small-holdings, animals, arbitration and so on. Legislation post-dating the volumes appears in the *Current Statutes Service* binders. The annual *Cumulative Supplement* summarises and explains the effect of new Acts, statutory instruments and case law on existing legislation and this in turn is kept up to date by a looseleaf *Noter-Up* service.

   If you know the name of an Act, the easiest way to find it in *Halsbury's Statutes* is by looking in the Alphabetical List of Statutes in the front of the annual paper-covered *Consolidated Index* volume. An example page from the Alphabetical List is shown on page 68. The entry tells you the volume number (in bold type) and the page number in *Halsbury's Statutes* where you will find the full text of the Act. If the volume number in the Alphabetical List of Statutes is followed by (S), you will find the Act printed in the loose-leaf *Current Statutes Service* under the volume and page number given. Some Acts are not printed in full in one place, but are divided up, each portion of the Act being printed under the most appropriate subject title. If you want to look at the complete text of an Act which has been split up this way, it may be easier to find the Act in one of the other publications outlined above.

   If you want to find the text of a very recent Act, look in the Alphabetical List of Statutes which appears in the first volume of the *Current Statutes Service* under the heading "Contents". The entries give the volume number and page where the text of the Act will be found in the *Current Statutes Service* binders.

Once you have located your Act, either in the main volumes or in the *Current Statutes Service* binders, you will find the official text of the Act. Following each section there are the notes, in smaller type, giving the meaning of words or phrases used, referring to cases on the interpretation of that section and providing details of any amendments which have been made to the text of the Act since it was first passed. You will also find references to statutory instruments which have been passed under the authority granted by that Act. At the beginning of each Act, you are informed when it became law and provided with a summary of the main provisions of the Act. An example page from Volume 48 of *Halsbury's Statutes* is shown on page 69.

It is important to check that the information on the Act is still up to date (i.e. it has not been amended or repealed). To do this, you will need to consult both the *Cumulative Supplement* and the looseleaf *Noter-up* service.

Let us take an example to see how this works. Suppose you want to know whether there have been changes to the Trade Marks Act 1994 since it was passed. You have looked in the Alphabetical List of Statutes (see p. 68) and found the relevant part of the text of the Act in Volume 48 (see p. 69). To find out if this Act has been amended since Volume 48 was published, turn first to the Cumulative Supplement and look at the entries for Volume 48. The Cumulative Supplement lists, volume by and page by page, changes which have occurred in the law since each of the main volumes was published. There are a number of entries showing changes to the Trade Marks Act 1994. These include amending legislation and new Statutory instruments issued under authority granted by the Act (see p. 69).

The information in the *Cumulative Supplement* is up to date to the end of the preceding year. For more recent changes to the Act, you should consult the looseleaf *Noter-up* service under the appropriate volume and page number. This will tell you of any changes in the law in the last few months.

Summary: Finding Up-To-Date Information on an Act Using Halsbury's Statutes

1. Look for the name of the Act in the Alphabetical List of Statutes in the paper-covered *Consolidated Index* volume. This will refer you to the appropriate volume (in **bold** type) and page number. An (S) following the volume number refers you to the *Current Statutes Service*.
2. If the Act is very recent, consult the Alphabetical List of Statutes at the front of Volume 1 of the *Current Statutes Service*.
3. Look up the Act in the appropriate volume, or the *Current Statutes Service*, and note the volume number and the page which contains the relevant information.
4. Look to see if there is an entry for your volume and page number in the *Cumulative Supplement*. If there is an entry, there has been a change in the law. Whether or not there is a relevant entry in the *Cumulative Supplement*, you should now turn to the *Noter-up* service (see below).

Example Page from the Alphabetical List of Statutes in Halsbury's Consolidated Index

Example Page from Halsbury's Statutes, Volume 48

12 Exhaustion of rights conferred by registered trade mark

(1) A registered trade mark is not infringed by the use of the trade mark in relation to goods which have been put on the market in the European Economic Area under that trade mark by the proprietor or with his consent.

(2) Subsection (1) does not apply where there exist legitimate reasons for the proprietor to oppose further dealings in the goods (in particular, where the condition of the goods has been changed or impaired after they have been put on the market).

NOTES

General Note. The general principle that, once goods have been marketed with consent in the European Community under a particular trade mark, the rights in that mark are exhausted and can no longer be used to oppose further dealings in the goods has been established by the jurisprudence of the European Court of Justice; see in particular *Centrafarm v Winthrop* [1974] ECR 1147. There may be exceptions to this principle where there exist legitimate reasons for opposing further commercialisation of the goods, in particular where the condition of the goods is changed (eg by re-packaging) or impaired after they had been put on the market; see *Hoffman-La Roche v Centrafarm* [1978] ECR 1139.

This jurisprudence is embodied in Art 7 of EEC Council Directive 89/104. As regards the United Kingdom, once a trade mark had been applied by the proprietor or other authorised person, the rights of the proprietor were exhausted (subject to the Trade Marks Act 1938, s 6 (repealed by s 106(2), Sch 5 post)) when the goods were first put on the market. This section implements the said Art 7, and overcomes the shortcomings of s 6 of the 1938 Act. (See Chapter 3, paras 3.33–3.36 of the White Paper "Reform of Trade Marks Law" (Cm 1203) (September 1990).)

Use of the trade mark. For the burden of proving use of a trade mark, see s 100 post.

European Economic Area. Ie the area established under the Agreement signed at Oporto on 2 May 1992 (Cm 2073) as adjusted by the Protocol signed at Brussels on 17 March 1993. For the countries which are included in the area, see the notes to the European Economic Area Act 1993, s 1, Vol 17, title European Communities.

By the proprietor or with his consent. As to the construction of references to the proprietor of a registered trade mark in the provisions of this Act relating to infringement, see s 31(1), (2) post. As to the construction of references to consent, see s 28(3) post, and see also s 82 post (acts done by authorised agents).

Transitional provisions. See s 105, Sch 3, para 4 post.

Definitions.

"consent": s 28(3)
"proprietor": s 31(2)
"registered trade mark": s 63(1)

"trade mark": s 1
"use": s 103(2).

13 Registration subject to disclaimer or limitation

(1) An applicant for registration of a trade mark, or the proprietor of a registered trade mark, may—

    (a) disclaim any right to the exclusive use of any specified element of the trade mark, or

    (b) agree that the rights conferred by the registration shall be subject to a specified territorial or other limitation;

and where the registration of a trade mark is subject to a disclaimer or limitation, the rights conferred by section 9 (rights conferred by registered trade mark) are restricted accordingly.

(2) Provision shall be made by rules as to the publication and entry in the register of a disclaimer or limitation.

NOTES

General Note. This section replaces the requirement under the Trade Marks Act 1938, s 14 (repealed by s 106(2), Sch 5 post), in the case of a trade mark containing non-distinctive matter, for a disclaimer to be made before it can be registered with a system of disclaimers made on a voluntary basis (see Chapter 4, para 4.16 of the White Paper "Reform of Trade Marks Law" (Cm 1203) (September 1990)).

5. Finally, look for any entries for your volume and page number in the *Noter-up* service. Read this information (if there is any) in conjunction with the information in the main volume and the *Cumulative Supplement*.

Remember the stages:

main volume;
Cumulative Supplement;
Noter-up service;

and consult them in that order.

Checking Whether Legislation is in Force or has been Amended

4–17   The full provisions of an Act do not necessarily all come into force on the same day. The dates of commencement for some sections may differ from those of others. As a result, it is sometimes important to check the commencement date of an individual section of an Act in order to discover the day on which that section came into force, or is due to come into force.

The Westlaw UK *UK Legislation Locators* database (**4–18**) and the statute law pages of the *Current Law Legislation Citator* (**4–19**) provide the most useful means of tracking both commencement dates and amendments and repeals. Both sources have the advantage that relevant case law is cited. However, *Is it in Force?* provides a useful alternative if you only wish to check commencement dates for legislation.

Is it in Force? is available online from LexisNexis Butterworths as *Halsbury's Is it in Force?* and in print as a single annual volume associated with *Halsbury's Statutes of England* (**4–16**). Both sources list commencement dates for statutes passed since 1980 by year and then alphabetically by title. Commencement dates are noted by section if there is no single date of commencement for the Act. *Halsbury's Is it in Force?* can be found under the "Commentary" tab on LexisNexis Butterworths and has the advantage that commencement dates are added as Acts receive the Royal Assent. The print volume only lists Acts previous to the year of publication. Updates are available in the *Noter Up* service binder of *Halsbury's Statutes*. The *Cumulative Supplement* and *Noter Up* services of *Halsbury's Statutes* also enable you to find out if a statute has been repealed or amended. The *Chronological Table of the Statutes* provides a means of checking amendments to older statutes (**4–20**).

Lawtel (**2–6**), if available, provides an additional online means of checking commencement dates of law in force, along with details of repeals and amendments. Lawtel's *Statutory Law* database provides a "Statutory Status Table" for an Act which lays out amendments and commencements section by section.

It might also be important to legal research to gain an understanding of the way an Act has been amended. This necessitates an understanding of the particular impact of one Act on another. This is complicated by the fact that not all amendments are made using amendment

Acts such as the Dangerous Dogs (Amendment) Act 1997. Changes can be much harder to track. How has the Education Act 2005, for example, affected the provisions of the Special Educational Needs and Disability Act 2001? Online sources of the full text of law in force (**4–12**) could be used to discover this information, but displaying the text of a series of sections of Acts and checking the notes at the end could prove tedious. Fortunately, the *UK Legislation Locator* on Westlaw UK provides an ideal way of tackling the problem.

How to use the UK Legislation Locators on Westlaw UK

To check commencement dates and amendments using the *UK Legislation Locators*, select the "UK Legislation Locators" shortcut from the Westlaw UK home page. If you search by the title of legislation (including date), the numbers and titles of the individual sections of an Act are displayed on the results screen (see page 72), just as they are for full text legislation on Westlaw UK. Select the entry for a particular section of an Act to find a summary of commencement dates and amendments for that section. A link is provided to the full text in the *UK Legislation* database.   **4–18**

If you search for information on the Dangerous Dogs Act 1991 (the example used in **4–12**) and select the entry for section 4 (s.4), commencement dates are shown for the subsections that came into force in 1991 and remain in force, along with those of the subsections added in 1997 by the Dangerous Dogs (Amendment) Act 1997. The dates are recorded as "In Force" dates. An in force date of April 1 2005 is also noted for a small change in wording introduced by the Courts Act 2003. All amending legislation is listed in the "Historic Law" section of the results page.

> **SEARCH TIP**
>
> Use the "Search in Results" feature of the *UK Legislation Locators* database to trace how an Act has amended earlier legislation.

If you wish to discover the precise nature of changes made to an Act by another amending Act, search first for the earlier Act in the *UK Legislation Locators*, e.g. the Special Educational Needs and Disability Act 2001. Then, when the results for the Act are displayed, use the "Locate in Result" feature to search the results list for the name of the amending legislation which interests you, e.g. the Education Act 2005. In this case, four sections of the Educational Needs and Disability Act 2001 are highlighted as having been amended by the Education Act 2005.

Cases which have interpreted the words of a particular section of an Act are referenced under "Cases Citing" at the end of the results page. A number of cases have cited s.4, the most recent being *R. v Haynes (Rodney)*, [2003] EWCA Crim 3247; [2004] 2 Cr. App. R. (S.) 9. Case citations are linked to the case summaries in the Westlaw UK *Case Locator* (**3–15**). The full text can then be found if available in the *Cases* database. Amendments and commencement dates are available for all statutes amended or repealed since 1947.

How to use the Current Law Legislation Citator

The *Current Law Legislation Citator* enables you to track changes to legislation in print, using a series of bound volumes listing references to amending legislation. Commencement orders can also be traced. The first volume details changes to Acts (of whatever age) that   **4–19**

Example results page from the Westlaw UK UK Legislation Locators

SWEET & MAXWELL UNITED KINGDOM LAW IN FORCE
DANGEROUS DOGS ACT 1991 CHAPTER 65
(c) Sweet & Maxwell Limited

Current Law in Force
Commencement Information
Read With
Cases Citing
General Legislative Materials

Current Law in Force:

Dangerous Dogs Act 1991 c 65, s 4A
In Force Date : June 8, 1997

Commencement Information:

1. s 4A (1)
In Force Date : August 12, 1991
2. s 4A (1)(a)–(6)
In Force Date : June 8, 1997

Read With

s 4A to be read with
1. *Dangerous Dogs (Amendment) Act 1997 c 53, s 4 (1) (a)* - Applying
s 4A (1) to be read with
2. *Dangerous Dogs (Amendment) Act 1997 c 53, s 4 (1)* - Applying

Cases Citing
Cases Citing s 4A
1. *R. v Haynes (Rodney), [2003] EWCA Crim 3247; [2004] 2 Cr. App. R. (S.) 9 (CA (Crim Div))*
UK ST 1991 c 65 s 4A

took place between 1947 and 1971. A number of other volumes cover the changes made in following years (again irrespective of the date of the statute changed), concluding with the most recent full year. More current developments can be checked in the Statute Citator section of the *Current Law Monthly Digest*. The *Current Law Legislation Citator* volumes feature both a "Statute Citator" section and a "Statutory Instrument Citator" section. The exception is the first volume in the series, which was published as the *Current Law Statute Citator*.

Acts are listed by year and in chronological (i.e. chapter number) order in each of the volumes. A helpful alphabetical list of statutes at the start of each bound volume can be used to check the chapter number if this is not already known. If changes have occurred to an Act, these are listed section by section in the volume covering the years in which the changes were made. The year and chapter numbers are given of amending Acts, and commencement orders are referred to by statutory instrument number. As a result, the information contained in each volume can take time to decode, as the relevant Act or statutory instrument needs to be found in order to check the details of an amendment, or the date legislation came into force. Citations are also given for Cases which have interpreted a particular section of an Act.

It is important to remember that it may be necessary to use more than one volume of the *Citator* to gain a complete picture of legislative change or relevant case law. Details of the changes made to the Dangerous Dogs Act 1991, for example, need to be traced in the *Current Law Legislation Citator* volumes covering 1989 to 1995 and 1996 to the present. The changes made by the Dangerous Dogs (Amendment) Act 1997 can only be found in the volume covering 1996 to 1999. For the most recent case law interpreting the Act, and details of the change made by the Courts Act 2003, you need to use the volume covering 2002 to 2004.

Chronological Table of the Statutes

The *Chronological Table of the Statutes* is an official publication which lists every statute   **4–20** which has been passed since 1235, and shows, for each one, whether it is still law. This is done by the use of different type faces—an entry in *italic* type indicates that the statute in question is no longer law, whilst entries in **bold** type represent Acts which are still wholly or partly in force.

Entries for Acts are arranged in date order in two print volumes. Part 1 currently covers 1235–1969; Part 2 covers 1970–2001. If a complete section of an Act, or an entire Act, has been repealed, the abbreviation "r" is used, followed by a note of the repealing legislation. Other abbreviations used are explained at the front of Part 1.

Unfortunately, the *Chronological Table* is usually two or three years out of date. It is updated by the annual publication entitled *The Public General Acts and General Synod Measures: 20 . . .: Tables and Index*, under the heading "Effect of legislation". This shows whether the Acts passed during that year have amended or repealed any previous legislation. As in the *Chronological Table*, the entries in this index are arranged by the date of the original Act, so that it is possible to tell at a glance if there has been any change to a particular statute. The *Public General Acts: Table and Index* is published separately by TSO and it is also printed at the end of the annual volumes of the *Public General Acts and Measures*.

Older Statutes

4–21   Acts, or sections or Acts, which are in force, whatever their date, can be found in the online and print sources introduced in **4–12**. However, it will sometimes be necessary to look at an Act of Parliament which is no longer in force and dates back beyond 1831 when the *Public General Acts* series (**4–6**) was first published. These can be found in the collections described below and in the Justis *UK Statutes* database (**4–9**).

   The earliest statute which is still part of the law of the land was passed in 1267. The first parliamentary statute dates from 1235 (the Statute of Merton), although some collections of the statutes commence in 1225. Collections of the legislation prior to 1225 do exist (e.g. A. J. Robertson, *The Laws of the Kings of England from Edmund to Henry I*) but they are not regarded as forming part of the statutes of the realm.

Statutes of the Realm

4–22   Produced by the Record Commission, *Statutes of the Realm* is generally regarded as the most authoritative collection of the early statutes. It covers statutes from 1235 to 1713, including those no longer in force, and prints the text of all Private Acts before 1539. There are alphabetical and chronological indexes to all the Acts and there is a subject index to each volume, as well as an index to the complete work.

Statutes at Large

4–23   The title of *Statutes at Large* was given to various editions of the statutes, most of which were published during the eighteenth century. They normally cover statutes published between the thirteenth and the eighteenth or nineteenth centuries. The text used in the Justis *UK Statutes* database (**4–9**) is taken from Ruffhead's editions of *Statutes at Large* for the period pre-dating the *Public General Acts* series.

Acts and Ordinances of the Interregnum

4–24   Acts passed during the Commonwealth are excluded from the collections of the statutes mentioned above. They can be found in C. H. Firth and R. S. Rait, *Acts and Ordinances of the Interregnum 1642–1660*.

Local and Personal Acts

4–25   In addition to Public General Acts, which apply to the whole population or a substantial part of it, there are also passed each year a few Local and Personal Acts. These Acts affect only a particular area of the country or a particular individual or body, e.g. Railtrack (Waverley Station) Order Confirmation Act 2000; Colchester Borough Council Act 2001.

The chapter number of a Local Act is printed in roman numerals, to distinguish it from the Public General Act of the same number. Thus the Railtrack (Waverley Station) Order Confirmation Act 2000 may be cited as 2000, c. vi (i.e. the sixth Local Act passed in 2000), whilst 2000, c. 6 is the citation for a Public General Act, the Powers of Criminal Courts (Sentencing) Act 2000.

Personal Acts are cited in the same way as Public General Acts, but with the chapter number printed in italics, e.g. *c. 3*. The citation of Local and Personal Acts was amended in 1963. Prior to that date, they are cited by regnal years, in the same way as Public General Acts, e.g. 12 & 13 Geo. 5, c. xiv relates to a Local Act, whilst 12 & 13 Geo. 5, c. 14 is a Public General Act (**4–3**).

Local and Personal Acts are listed in alphabetical order in the annual *Local and Personal Acts 19 . . .: Tables and Index*, which can also be found in the bound volumes of the *Public General Acts and Measures*. From 1991 onwards, they are available on the OPSI legislation web pages (at *www.opsi.gov.uk/legislation*). In addition, HMSO published two cumulative indexes: the *Index to Local and Personal acts 1801–1947* and the *Supplementary Index to the Local and Personal Acts 1948–1966*.

Although most libraries will possess copies of the Public General Acts in some form, printed copies of the Local and Personal Acts are not so widely available. Those which are published are listed in the *TSO Daily Lists*, which are cumulated in the *TSO Catalogues*. Local Acts since 1992 are printed in the final volume of *Current Law Statutes Annotated* each year. To obtain a copy of the text of an older Local Act or a Personal Act, you may need to contact the local library or the organisation affected by the legislation.

Statutory Instruments

In order to reduce the length and complexity of statutes and increase flexibility in the light of changing circumstances Parliament may include in an Act an "enabling" section, which grants to some other authority (usually a Minister of the Crown) power to make detailed rules and regulations on a principle laid down in general terms by the Act. The various Road Traffic Acts, for example, give the Secretary of State for Transport power, amongst other things, to impose speed limits on particular stretches of road, to vary these limits at any time, to create experimental traffic schemes, to introduce new road signs, to control the construction and use of vehicles and to impose regulations concerning parking, pedestrian crossings, vehicle licences, insurance and numerous other aspects of the law relating to motor vehicles. An advantage of this power is that the rules can be readily changed, without the necessity for Parliamentary debate and approval of every amendment.

4–26

Statutory instruments, together with statutory codes of practice and byelaws, form what is called *secondary* or *subordinate* legislation, often also called *delegated* legislation, since Parliament has delegated the power to make this legislation to another authority.

The term *statutory instruments* is a generic one, and includes rules, regulations and orders. Commencement orders are a particularly important type of statutory instrument, since they set the date for the commencement of an Act or bring certain provisions of an Act into force (see point 7 of **4–2**). Like statutes, statutory instruments may be of general or of purely local interest. Local instruments are not always printed and published in the normal way. An Order of Council, made by the Queen and her Privy Council, is also a form of statutory instrument. These are printed as an appendix to the annual volumes of statutory instruments, together with Royal Proclamations and Letters Patent.

Citation of statutory instruments

4–27 Each statutory instrument published during the year is given its own number. The official citation is: SI year/number. For example, the Genetically Modified Organisms (Contained Use) Regulations 1993 was the 15th statutory instrument to be passed in 1993 and its citation is therefore SI 1993/15.

Statutory instruments typically have a title which includes the word "Rules", "Regulations" or "Order", e.g. Rules of the Supreme Court, the Safety of Sports Grounds (Designation) Order, the Registration of Births and Deaths Regulations. If you are undecided whether the document you are seeking is a statutory instrument, check in the Alphabetical List of Statutory Instruments in *Halsbury's Statutory Instruments*.

Tracing statutory instruments

4–28 Statutory instruments are listed by year and number on the legislation page of the OPSI website (at *www.opsi.gov.uk/legislation*). The full text is available and coverage begins in 1987. Paper copies of single statutory instruments can also be purchased from TSO and your library may hold these for the current year. Details of new statutory instruments are published in the TSO *Daily Lists* (**6–15**). Bound volumes are available for previous years. The instruments have been printed in numerical order since 1962; before that date, they were arranged by subject. The last volume of each yearly set contains a subject index to all the instruments published during the year.

All the statutory instruments that were still in force at the end of 1948 were reprinted in a series of volumes entitled *Statutory Rules and Orders and Statutory Instruments Revised*. This was arranged in subject order, showing all the instruments which were then in force.

The full, unrevised, text of statutory instruments from 1987 onwards is also available online from the BAILII website (**2–14**) and the Justis *UK Statutory Instruments* database (**2–7**). The Justis UK *Statutory Instruments Archive* provides online access to the full, unrevised, text of all statutory instruments published between 1671 and 1986. Both Justis databases are subscription databases, so you will need to check if your library can provide access.

The databases of law in force noted in **4–12** contain both statutes and statutory instruments in their legislation searches. Use the full title (including year and statutory instrument number if known) when searching these databases. Database results are presented as described in **4–12**. The print volumes of *Halsbury's Statutory Instruments* (**4–29**) provide an alternative approach to tracing statutory instruments in force.

Halsbury's Statutory Instruments

Halsbury's Statutory Instruments provides up-to-date information on every statutory instrument of general application in force in England and Wales. It does not reproduce the text of all statutory instruments in force. Instead it reproduces the text of a selected number and provides summaries of others. The work consists of 22 volumes, in which the statutory instruments are arranged in broad subject categories. The service is kept up to date by a *Service* binder containing notes of changes in the law and the text of selected new instruments.

4–29

If you know the year and number of a statutory instrument, the easiest way to locate it in *Halsbury's Statutory Instruments* is through the Chronological List of Instruments in the *Service* binder. Alternatively, if you know the name of the statutory instrument, look in the Alphabetical List in the back of the annual paper back volume of the *Consolidated Index*. You may, for example, be looking for information on the Part-Time Workers (Prevention of less Favourable Treatment) Regulations 2000. The relevant page from the Alphabetical List is shown on page 78. The list tells us that the number of the statutory instrument is 1551 and that it has been allocated the subject title "Employment" in *Halsbury's Statutory Instruments*. (Entries in the Chronological List in the *Service* binder are displayed in the same way.)

On the inside front cover of each of the main volumes, there is a list of subject titles, indicating in which volume they are printed. "Employment" is located in Volume 7. Turn to the Chronological List of Instruments at the beginning of the section headed "Employment" in Volume 7. A page reference is given for the entry in the volume for the statutory instrument itself. The text of the Part-Time Workers (Prevention of Less Favourable Treatment) Regulations 2000 is printed in full in the 2003 issue of Volume 7 with a note stating that the Regulations are printed as amended by SI 2002/2035.

Subsequent changes are recorded in the Monthly Survey Section of the *Service* binder. The Monthly Survey is arranged by subject titles as in the main volumes. Look for the number of the instrument in the "Amendments and Revocations" section.

Checking whether a statutory instrument is in force or has been amended

If you have searched for and found a statutory instrument using one of the online sources of legislation in force (**4–12**), you do not need any further confirmation that it remains in force. The same applies if you are using the print volumes of *Halsbury's Statutory Instruments* (**4–29**). However, for some important statutory instruments, you may wish to track whether the statutory instrument has been amended, and if so, the dates at which different provisions came into force. This might be the case, for example, if you were tracking the way EU directives have been implemented in the UK, since implementation generally makes use of statutory instruments rather than statutes. The Westlaw UK *Legislation Locators* database provides the best way of tracking such changes. Suppose you wish to track changes to the Working Time Regulations which implement EU legislation on working time. You might begin by searching for the Working Time Regulations 1998/1833 using the *Legislation Locators* title search. Commencement information and amending legislation can then be checked for the separate parts of the Regulations, just as it can for the sections of an

4–30

78 Legislation

Example Page from The Consolidated Index

Act (**4–18**). You will also find links to the full text of the Regulations as currently in force along with the text of various amending statutory instruments. These might include Regulations that you were not initially aware of. The Working Time Regulations 1998/1833 have been amended, for example, by the Working Time (Amendment) Regulations 2003/1684 and the Working Time Regulations 1998 (Amendment) Order 2005/2241. Case law citing the different parts of the 1998 Regulations can also be found.

The Statutory Instrument Citator section of the *Current Law Legislation Citator* provides a print alternative to the *Legislation Locators* database. Search for statutory instruments by year and number.

Tracing statutory instruments made under a particular Act

The Westlaw UK *Legislation Locators* database (**4–18**) provides an effective way of search-   **4–31**
ing for statutory instruments made under a particular Act. Search for an Act by title and check the entries for individual sections to find a list of statutory instruments made under powers granted in that section. Links are available to the full text of the relevant statutory instrument. In the entry for section 1 of the Dangerous Dogs Act 1991, for example, an entry can be found for the Dangerous Dogs (Designated Types) Order 1991/1743.

Lawtel (**2–6**) provides an alternative online approach to tracing statutory instruments made under an Act. For statutes passed since 1984, Lawtel provides links to all statutory instruments which are enabled by the Act. Again, search by the title of the Act. The "Statutory Status Table" provides a links to the relevant statutory instruments. *Halsbury's Statutes* (**4–16**) provides a print alternative for tracing statutory instruments made under an Act.

Wales legislation

Under the Government of Wales Act 1998, the National Assembly for Wales has taken over   **4–32**
powers formerly exercised by the Secretary of State for Wales. This means in practice that the Assembly is able to debate and approve secondary or delegated legislation for Wales. Its legislation takes the form of statutory instruments which are cited in the same way as other statutory instruments, e.g. Children's Homes Amendment (Wales) Regulations 2001. This particular statutory instrument is numbered as No. 140 (W. 6), the "W. 6" denoting the sixth regulation made by the Assembly for 2001.

The Government of Wales Act 1998 does not lay out broad areas of legislative competence; instead the powers of the Assembly are defined in relation to some 300 Acts of Parliament. The Acts themselves are listed in the National Assembly for Wales (Transfer of Functions) Orders made in 1999 and 2000. Broadly speaking, the Assembly can make regulations in the areas of industrial and economic development, education and training, health, agriculture, local government, housing, social services, transport and the environment and arts and cultural heritage.

Statutory instruments made by the National Assembly can be found on the Wales Legislation page of the OPSI website (at *www.opsi.gov.uk/legislation/wales*). Draft statutory orders can be found on the National Assembly of Wales website (at *www.wales.gov.uk*), along with links to Assembly business and other information about the Assembly. Proceedings of the Assembly are not available in print form. The Wales Legislation Online website (at *www.wales-legislation.org.uk*), managed by Cardiff Law School, contains a Digest of National Assembly Functions & Subordinate Legislation which lists the powers of the National Assembly for Wales and its subordinate legislation by subject area. Using the site it is possible to take a given Act, e.g. the Environment Act 1995, and find out which sections list functions that are exercised solely by the Assembly, which list functions that are shared between the Assembly and a Minister of the Crown, and which list functions which have not been devolved to the Assembly. Legislation made by the Assembly is to be added to the entries for each Act where relevant.

5 Journals

Types of Journals

Journals (or periodicals) are important to lawyers: they keep you up to date with the latest **5–1** developments in the law, and provide comments and criticisms of the law. In your preparations for seminars, essays and moots, it is essential to show that you are aware of what has been written in journals. You cannot rely exclusively on textbooks which are always, to some degree, out of date, and which may provide inadequate information on some topics. Journals help to keep you up to date with recent cases, statutes, official publications, comments and scholarly articles.

For convenience, we can divide journals into four different types, although there is some overlap between them. However, they are treated similarly in libraries. There are a number of weekly publications, such as the *New Law Journal, Justice of the Peace*, the *Solicitors Journal* and the *Law Society Gazette*, which aim to keep practitioners and students up to date. They provide reports and comments on recent cases, statutes, statutory instruments and the latest trends and developments in the law, together with some longer articles, usually on topical or practical subjects. In contrast are the academic journals, which are published less frequently. They contain lengthy articles on a variety of topics, comments on recent cases, statutes and government publications, and book reviews. Some examples are the *Law Quarterly Review*, the *Modern Law Review* (six issues a year) and the *Journal of Law and Society* (four issues a year). The third category is the specialist journal dealing with particular aspects of the law. Some specialist journals combine notes of recent developments with longer articles on aspects of that area of the law. Examples of these journals include the *Criminal Law Review* (monthly), *Legal Action* (monthly) and *Family Law* (ten issues a year). Other specialist journals are more like newsletters and are designed as current awareness bulletins for practitioners. These journals (e.g. the *Property Law Bulletin, Simon's Tax Intelligence*) are only a few pages in length and summarise and briefly comment on the latest developments. The final category is foreign journals. English-language publications, particularly from common law jurisdictions, are of assistance in providing a comparative view of similar UK issues. Examples of this group are the *Yale Law Journal* (eight issues a year), the *Harvard Law Review* (eight issues a year), the *Canadian Bar Review* (four issues a year) and the *Australian Law Journal* (monthly).

Online Access to Journals

5–2   Since the late 1990s, most legal journal publishers have allowed access to online versions of journal articles, either from their own website, or from an intermediary site. Some journals can be accessed using web-based services such as *SwetsWise* or *ScienceDirect*, which act as agents for publishers, many more can be found in the full text journal databases available from LexisNexis Professional (**2–3**) or Westlaw UK (**2–5**). This means there is no single route to online versions of journal articles, making access unnecessarily complicated.

Your library website is the best place to start if you wish to access a journal online. It is here that you can discover the appropriate online source for a particular journal. A–Z lists of journals by title are often linked to the appropriate website for accessing the full text of articles online. Entries made for a journal in the Library catalogue may also feature links to websites providing full-text access. In many cases you will have to find the library link to the online source of a journal in order to gain access to the full text. As noted in **2–8**, you need to use the library (or other institutional) link to a journal website in order to confirm that you have access rights. A subscription must be paid for online access to journals; often the same subscription covers both online access and the print copies of journals on the law library shelves. The appropriate access route is one which confirms that your university has subscribed to a journal or database service. The relatively small number of law journal articles that can be found on public internet sites (perhaps placed there in "pre-print" versions by the author) can be found using Google Scholar (at *scholar.google.com*). This is worth trying if subscription routes have failed.

As many of the law journals available online can be found on either LexisNexis Professional or Westlaw UK, it is worth familiarising yourself with the journal titles available from the two database services if both are available. The can be done by checking the information links for the journal databases they contain. LexisNexis Professional holds the full text of LexisNexis Butterworths titles, along with journals from some other publishers (over 50 titles in all). Westlaw UK provides access to approximately 40 Sweet & Maxwell journal titles. There is no overlap in the journal coverage provided by the two services. Some of the journals available from LexisNexis Professional and Westlaw UK are also available from the publisher's website. This is true of the *Oxford Journal of Legal Studies*, for example, which can be found on LexisNexis Professional and also accessed from the publisher's website, using the appropriate subscription access route.

Online access to journals published before the mid 1990s is more limited. Most universities have a subscription to the JSTOR journals archive, which contains a significant number of politics and social science journals of potential value for legal research. Some university libraries may also subscribe to HeinOnline, an American archive of online journal articles which has been adding increasing numbers of UK journals. UK titles include the *Modern Law Review* and the *European Journal of International Law*. Check library database and journal lists for access. Online journal archives always provide access from the first published issue of a journal onwards, but the most recent issues will not be available. For these you will need to turn to the law database services and links to journal publishers.

Example page from an article in The Criminal Law Review [2005] Crim. L.R. 937–950

The Criminal Cases Review Commission and the Court of Appeal: The Commission's Perspective

By Graham Zellick[*]

PhD, LLD, AcSS, Chairman of the Criminal Cases Review Commission

Summary: *This article discusses the relationship between the Court of Appeal and the Criminal Cases Review Commission. It highlights the Commission's perspective on the exercise of its statutory jurisdiction to refer cases to the Court of Appeal and comments on a recent analysis of the relationship.*

The Criminal Cases Review Commission ("CCRC") is a unique part of the justice system. It alone has the power to re-open a criminal conviction and secure a fresh appeal once the appeal process has been exhausted. Most of the cases examined by the Commission are convictions in the Crown Court in England. They will therefore find their way back to the Court of Appeal, Criminal Division only if the Commission finds that there is a real possibility that the conviction will be quashed (or sentence altered). Likewise, the remaining cases—the 96 per cent which are rejected by the Commission—are decided on the basis of applying the same test, which involves an assessment of how the Court of Appeal would treat that case if it were referred. The relationship between the Commission and the court is therefore of considerable interest and critical importance. This article seeks to describe that relationship from the Commission's perspective and, in so doing, to shed some light on the role played by the Commission in the criminal justice system. It also provides an opportunity to comment on the recent article by Richard Nobles and David Schiff on the same theme.[1]

There is, I have no doubt, deep mutual respect between the court and the Commission. My colleagues hold the court's judges in high regard and admire greatly the overall quality of the court's output. Likewise, I know from my own contacts with the judges, as from relevant judgments, that our work is valued and respected, and for that I pay tribute to the judges. In particular, both of the previous

---

[*] Honorary Professor, School of Law, University of Birmingham; Emeritus Professor of Law in the University of London; Bencher of the Middle Temple; and Honorary Fellow of Gonville and Caius College, Cambridge. This article is based on my Keynote Address at the Sweet & Maxwell Criminal Appeals Conference 2005. I am most grateful to the Commission's Legal Adviser, John Wagstaff, and Laurie Elks, a Commissioner, for their assistance. The views expressed are personal.

[1] "The Criminal Cases Review Commission: Establishing a Workable Relationship with the Court of Appeal" [2005] Crim.L.R. 173.

Finding a Journal Article Online If You Already Have a Reference

5–3   Journal references, or citations, in the bibliographies of books, or on course reading lists, need to be deciphered before you can find the article online. A journal citation, like those for law reports, uses standard abbreviations for the journal name, whereas library catalogues and databases use the full spelled-out version. The *Cardiff Index to Legal Abbreviations* (at *www.legalabbrevs.cardiff.ac.uk*) provides the best online source for interpreting abbreviations and additional print sources are noted in **3–5**.

    Once you have the full title of the journal, check library A–Z journal lists or the library catalogue for access. If access is provided from the publishers website or an intermediary database (such as *SwetsWise*), library links may simply provide access to the source website. You then have to search the publisher's site or the intermediary database in order to find the relevant year and issue of a journal, before selecting the full text of an article. Most sites provide access using web versions of the contents page of individual journal issues. You will almost certainly be asked to provide your university authentication (id and password) if you are accessing the journal off-campus. Many universities have now simplified this process through the use of software which provides an additional search menu when you select a link to a journal. The menu prompts for the year, volume, issue number and first page of the journal article and then provides a direct link to the full text of the article on the appropriate website. The search menu page often also links to additional services—the ability to search other catalogues for a reference for example, or perhaps request an inter-library loan if your library does not have a subscription to a journal.

    If the journal article you wish to find is available on either LexisNexis Professional (**2–3**) or Westlaw UK (**2–5**), you need to use an entirely difference approach. If the journal is available on LexisNexis Professional, select the "UK Journals" link from the LexisNexis Professional home page. The title of the journal can be selected from a drop-down menu on the *UK Journals* search page. Add the title of the journal article in the "Title" search and search the database to retrieve the full text. The process is much the same for the *UK Journals* database on Westlaw UK. Select the shortcut for the database from the home page, then enter the title of the journal article in the "Article Title" search. To restrict the search to a single journal, you need to type in the full name of the journal in the "Journal Title" search box. It is not possible to browse the contents pages of journals on either Westlaw UK or LexisNexis Professional.

Finding a Journal Article in the Library

5–4   If you have a reference to a journal article, the relevant abbreviations will need to be deciphered as noted in **5–3** before you can find the article in print. The Library catalogue can then be searched using the full title of the journal in order to confirm that the library holds the journal. You may find this is not the case. Even the largest law libraries lack print copies of some journals. If a journal is not listed in the catalogue, check online access, as print and online access are not always identical. Then consider requesting an inter-library loan (**5–23**).

If a journal is held by your library, there should be some indication of its location. Often the last copy received is noted if there is a current subscription to the journal. Law journals are usually arranged alphabetically by title in a single sequence. Remember though, that the most recent issues may well be shelved in a separate current journals or periodicals area.

Tracing Articles in Legal Journals

You could rely on footnotes in recent books or journal articles to provide references to   **5–5** articles on a particular topic. If an article is well researched, it may give numerous citations to journal articles worth reading. You are likely, however, only to get coverage of those articles which support the view of the author. Using footnotes from textbooks and citations from key articles is a good way to widen your search for documents on a subject, but for the most comprehensive and recent coverage, you must also make use of indexes to journal articles.

There are several indexes you can use to find journal articles on a subject or on a particular case, statute or other document. All of them are available online. The most relevant indexes are described below. Although you would not need or wish to consult every index every time you require articles on a topic, you should remember that the information given, and the journals covered, varies. If you use only one index, you may miss helpful material.

Legal Journals Index

The *Legal Journals Index* began publication in 1986 and is the most useful source for tracing   **5–6** law articles in journals published in the UK. It is currently available online as part of Westlaw UK (**2–5**). All *Legal Journals Index* coverage is included in Westlaw UK from 1986 onwards, along with entries from the print *European Legal Index*, which has carried references to articles on EC law since 1993. The index covers articles from approximately 260 legal journals and provides the most comprehensive coverage of articles on UK law. Some libraries may continue to keep the print volumes of both the *Legal Journals Index* and the *European Legal Index*, though online access has made them largely redundant.

Each entry in the Legal Journals Index database includes details of the title and the author (or authors) of the journal article, along with details of the journal in which the article is published. The volume, issue and page numbers of the article are also included. An abstract, or summary, of the content of each journal article is also provided, though some of the earlier summaries contained in the database may only consist of a single sentence. Ahead of the summary, subject keywords are added, to aid searching. The "Subject Keyword" entries correspond to the subject headings used in the subject index of the printed volumes and use a standard vocabulary. Other potentially useful search words are added under "Terms".

*Example results page from the **Legal Journals Index** on Westlaw UK*

File Edit View Favorites Tools Help

Back | ✕ | Search | Favorites

Address http://uk.westlaw.com/search/default.wl?rs=WLUK5.10&tempinfo=%7dMethodTNC%7cdbLJI%7ctidljuk_u%7cTermsFNprivacy+and+human+rights+and+media%7cT(▼ Go

Links »

Westlaw. UK
from Sweet & Maxwell

Westlaw UK | Current Awareness

Result List
127 Docs
<< Full Screen List
Edit Search | Locate in Result

Related Info

Supp (Information Access and Privacy Practice Update), 8

5. Human rights; Intellectual property; Media and entertainment Review of the law of privacy. Ent. L.R. 2005, 16(7), 174-181

6. Human rights; Intellectual property; Media and entertainment (Case Comment) Confidence, privacy and unlawful interference with business. Ent. L.R. 2005, 16(7), 184-187

7. Intellectual property; Human rights; Media and entertainment Confidence, privacy and human rights: English law in the twenty-first century. E.I.P.R. 2005, 27(11), 405-411

8. Human rights; Intellectual property; Media and entertainment (Case Comment) Image rights and privacy: after Douglas v Hello. E.I.P.R. 2005, 27(10), 384-387

9. Intellectual property; Human rights; Media and entertainment (Case Comment) Confidential information: privacy. E.I.P.R. 2005, 27(10), N207-208

10. Intellectual property; Damages; Human rights; Media and entertainment (Case Comment) Confidentia information - damages. E.I.P.R. 2005, 27(9), N190-19;

Welcome | Find by Citation | Directory | All Tables of Contents

Customise | Research Trail | Help ⓒ | Sign Off

More services

QUICK PRINT | PRINT | EMAIL | OTHER

THOMSON
SWEET & MAXWELL

Legal Journals Index

Abstract

(c) Sweet & Maxwell Limited

Article - Journal
(Case Comment)

Confidential information.
Katharine Stephens.
C.I.P.A.J. 2005, 34(6), 407-409
[Chartered Institute of Patent Agents Journal]
Publication Date: 2005

Subject: INTELLECTUAL PROPERTY. Other related subjects: **Human rights. Media and entertainment**
Keywords: **Breach of confidence;** Celebrities; Damages; Exclusive publishing agreements; Photographs; **Privacy**

Abstract: Examines the Court of Appeal ruling in Douglas v Hello! Ltd on whether OK! was entitled to damages following the publication of photographs in Hello! of the Douglases' wedding on the grounds of the exclusive publishing contract. Discusses the consideration of the law of **privacy**.

Case referred: Douglas v Hello! Ltd (No.6) [2005] EWCA Civ 595; [2005] 4 All E.R. 128 (CA (Civ Div))
END OF DOCUMENT

◄ Term ► ◄ Doc 1 of 127 ►

Tools

Internet

It is important to bear in mind when you use keywords to search the database, that references to articles are only found if the words you have used match words used either in an article title or the brief abstracts and lists of subject keywords provided by the *Index*. The *Legal Journals Index* does not contain the text of journal articles. Getting the best from the index requires that you first think of likely keywords for your subject and then combine keywords using "and" to focus and refine your search (see **2–11**).

Suppose that you are interested in finding articles which discuss privacy issues in the context of the Human Rights Act. To see the full range of search options for the *Legal Journals Index*, first select the *Index* from the shortcuts on the Westlaw UK home page. You might start by searching for index entries that contain both "privacy" and "human rights". To do this, enter "privacy and human rights" in the *Index* "Terms" search. Your search then retrieves all index entries for articles that contain both words somewhere in the text (keywords, title, summary etc.) Your first discovery will be that there are very many articles which have been indexed using both words. As a result, it makes sense to add further search words to reduce the number of matching index entries. Think of ways in which you can narrow your search. Perhaps media intrusion is the focus of your interest, in which case simply add "media" and search for "privacy and human rights and media".

Once you have begun to narrow the range of articles referred to in your results page, take a look at the index entries made for some of the most relevant articles found and pay particular attention to the subject keywords which have been used in the index entries. You will often be able to find more relevant articles by searching again using the keywords which seem to offer the closest match to your interests. You

> **SEARCH TIP**
>
> When you have made an initial search for articles using the *Legal Journals Index*, look at the keywords added to the entries for the articles found. They can give you ideas for new searches.

might note that "celebrities" has been used as a keyword, or that articles discussing the various *Douglas v Hello!* cases have been found, and that these are indexed under "breach of confidence". If your interest in privacy issues had been sparked by the *Douglas v Hello!* cases, you could narrow your search using "breach of confidence and privacy and human rights". As noted in **2–11**, there are no right answers, and it is advisable to try out different searches, saving references of particular interest as you examine the results of each search. Individual entries can be marked (ticked) on the results screen and details of those articles later emailed or saved to a file. There is no need to write down the references you find to useful articles.

The full text of journal articles found in your search can be retrieved if the articles are available in Westlaw UK's *UK Journals* database. If full text is available, the article citation is shown as a hyperlink. Bear in mind though, that Westlaw UK contains only some of the journal articles available online. Once references to articles have been found using the *Legal Journals Index*, all of the potential online and print sources of the articles need to be pursued as described in **5–3** and **5–4**. It would be unduly restrictive to narrow your interest to articles available in full text on Westlaw UK (effectively articles published by Sweet and Maxwell).

Index to Legal Periodicals & Books

The *Index to Legal Periodicals & Books*, which commenced in 1908, is published in the US.   **5–7**
Most of its coverage is of American journals, but it includes some journals from the UK,

Canada, Ireland, Australia and New Zealand. The index is available online from a number of sources. If your library has a subscription to the *Index* as a database provided by the OCLC FirstSearch service you must select the database from a database list. The link to the *Index* is abbreviated as Legal Periodical.

Each entry in the database and the printed version of the *Index* contains the title of the article, along with the author name(s) and details of the source of publication: journal title, issue and/or volume number and page numbers. There is also a "subject descriptor", or subject heading added to the article. If your keyword search used the terms "inherent jurisdiction AND Great Britain", you are shown a database entry as follows:

Author(s): Dockray, M. S.
Title: The inherent jurisdiction to regulate civil proceedings.
Source: The Law Quarterly Review v. 113 (Jan. '97) pp. 120–132
Descriptor: Jurisdiction—Great Britain.

The descriptor entry "Jurisdiction—Great Britain" is also a hyperlink which enables you to list references to all the articles that are indexed using the terms "Jurisdiction—Great Britain". As with any index it makes sense to take full note of these descriptor terms or subject headings, as they provide a means of improving the accuracy and relevance of your search results. The headings use American terminology and spelling which may occasionally cause difficulties.

If you wish to search for articles indexed before 1981, you must use the print volumes of the *Index*. Check if these are available in your library.

Lawtel

5–8   The Lawtel service includes an articles index which contains references to the contents of 57 UK publications. The emphasis is on publications that are likely to be of interest to legal practitioners. *Corporate Briefing, Counsel* and *Pensions World* are included, for example, along with academic law journals such as the *New Law Journal* and *Modern Law Review*. References to the legal sections of *The Times, The Guardian* and *The Independent* are included. Most of the publications are indexed from 1998 onwards, a few from 1995.

Each entry for the article index has a paragraph summarising the contents of the article along with references to any case law or legislation cited in the article. As with other indexes it is possible to search for articles using a case name or the name and section of a statute. You can also search using subject headings.

Index to Foreign Legal Periodicals

5–9   The *Index to Foreign Legal Periodicals* commenced in 1960. It indexes articles on international and comparative law and the municipal law of countries other than the US, the UK and the common law of Commonwealth countries. Close to 500 legal journals are indexed. The *Index* is available online from 1985 onwards.

Legal Resource Index (LegalTrac)

The *Legal Resource Index* indexes over 800 legal publications, most of which are American,   **5–10**
although a few UK journals are included. The index is made available online as the
LegalTrac database.

Halsbury's Laws

Halsbury's Laws of England is available from LexisNexis Butterworths and references to   **5–11**
journal articles are included. Only a small range of journals is covered. The print version of
Halsbury's Laws includes a Table of Articles in Binder 2. References to articles are arranged
alphabetically by title within broad subject areas. As a result, this is not the easiest way to
locate specific articles.

The Table of Articles in Binder 2 is updated by the latest copy of the *Monthly Review* in
Binder 1. The *Monthly Review* summarises changes in the law by broad subject area and new
articles are listed at the beginning of each section.

The *Annual Abridgement* to *Halsbury's Laws* includes a Table of Articles. This gives a
selection of the journal articles written on a subject during that year. The *Annual
Abridgement* replaces the information in the Table of Articles in Binder 2. *Halsbury's Laws*
is described in more detail in **7–3**.

Tracing Law-Related Journal Articles

The effective study of law will of necessity take you into other disciplines. Articles on law   **5–12**
related aspects of housing, delinquency, sentencing, families and education are found in a
wide range of journals, many of which are not solely concerned with law and which as a
consequence are not usually found in a law collection. You may wish to consult journals
which carry articles by sociologists, economists, criminologists, social administrators or
historians. To trace social science and humanities material, you need to use a different
selection of databases. The coverage of some of these databases is noted in the following
paragraphs.

If your library has a "search portal" for database searching on its website, the contents
of these indexes can be searched using a single search page which forms part of the library
website. This means that you do not have to learn how to use a new set of search pages
when you turn to an unfamiliar index. It is usually also possible to search more than one
index at a time. To do this, select the indexes you wish to use from subject lists on the portal
web pages. Search results are amalgamated into a single web page with links provided to
the full-text source of journal articles if available. Unfortunately, search portals cannot
currently be used to search law indexes (with the exception of the *Index to Legal
Periodicals*).

Index to Periodical Articles Related to Law

5–13   This index commenced in 1958. It contains a selective coverage of English-language articles not included in the *Legal Journals Index*, or the *Index to Legal Periodicals & Books*. It is not available in electronic form. There is an index to articles by subject, a list of journals indexed and an author index. All the entries from 1958 to 1988 have been published in one cumulative volume. Thereafter, the index appears quarterly, with the last issue of the year being an annual cumulation.

Applied Social Sciences Index and Abstracts (ASSIA)

5–14   ASSIA is aimed at those in practice in social services, prison services, employment, race relations, etc., and includes articles on many aspects of the law. Articles from approximately 650 journals are indexed. Although produced in Britain, the index covers English-language journals from 16 countries.

British Humanities Index

5–15   This covers a broad range of subjects and includes articles from British newspapers and popular weekly journals, as well as more scholarly periodicals. Online coverage is from 1985 onwards.

Social Sciences Index

5–16   This index, which took over from the *Social Sciences and Humanities Index*, includes articles on law, criminology, sociology, political science, sociological aspects of medicine and other socio-legal topics. Online coverage is from 1983 onwards.

Psychological Abstracts (PsycINFO)

5–17   The scope of this is far wider than the title suggests, covering abortion, drug use, alcoholism, etc. Over 1,300 journals are indexed and dissertations, books and book chapters are included. Online coverage begins as early as 1887.

Current Contents

5–18   *Current Contents* provides access to tables of contents from over 7,000 journals, including many social science titles. This is essentially a current awareness service.

The Philosopher's Index

This index contains references (with abstracts) to articles found in almost 500 philosophy **5–19** journals from a wide range of countries. Records of books and contributions to anthologies are included. Online coverage is from 1940 onwards.

Sociological Abstracts

Sociological Abstracts includes coverage of law, penology and the police and is available **5–20** from a variety on online sources. Online coverage is from 1963 and abstracts are added to records from 1974 onwards.

Social Sciences Citation Index

The *Citation Index* is so called because, in addition to the usual bibliographic details, every **5–21** entry in the index database carries a list of the articles referred to (or "cited") by the article in question. It is possible, using the index, to begin with a particular article, found perhaps after a subject search, and then trace details of the articles which have in turn discussed or used the article you started with. This is particularly useful if you already know of a key article and wish to find the latest articles in a long-running debate in the literature. In addition to the *Social Sciences Citation Index*, there is also an *Arts and Humanities Citation Index* and a *Sciences Citation Index*, all of which are available online as part of the Web of Science service (itself part of "Web of Knowledge").

These are by no means the only subject indexes to the contents of journals. Indexes exist covering many different subjects. The library staff will help you find out which indexing or abstracting services are available to cover the subjects that interest you.

Newspaper Articles

In addition to factual reporting, newspapers often contain commentary, analysis and back- **5–22** ground information on recent legal developments and controversial topics. If your law library has a subscription to LexisNexis Professional (**2–3**), the full text of most UK national (and regional) newspapers is available from the mid 1980s onwards. Some libraries with no LexisNexis Professional access may have made the same data available as an additional subscription on Westlaw UK (**2–5**).

All UK national newspapers can be searched under the LexisNexis Professional "News" search heading, or individual newspaper titles selected. The news coverage of even a single newspaper over a number of years is, however, considerable, so it is advisable to make full use of the options which restrict the way in which your search is carried out. To continue with the example used in **2–5**, you might wish to find newspaper articles which discuss

> **SEARCH TIP**
>
> Use the options available in newspaper data-bases to limit your search words e.g. to "major mentions". If using multiple search words ensure that they must be found close to each other in the text of newspaper articles.

privacy as a human rights issue, so the keywords "privacy" and "human rights" would need to be included in the search. It would not be especially helpful, though, to find all articles which happen to include these words. Once you have entered your search terms, drop-down menus can be used to specify, for example, that only a "major mention" of a term retrieves an article, or that the search term must occur in the headline or the first paragraph. As a search for articles including "privacy" and "human rights" combines two search terms, the proximity of the two terms can also be specified using an additional drop-down menu. Instead of both terms simply appearing somewhere in the article, it can be specified that the terms must occur within 5 words of each other, or in the same sentence. Finally individual newspapers with specialist legal coverage, such as *The Times* or *The Independent*, could be specified. Limiting searches in this way can mean that a search for "privacy" and "human rights" can be restricted to produce a long but manageable results list of perhaps a hundred or so articles over a number of years, some of which will provide useful leads to important legal issues. These might be pursued using the academic coverage provided by legal journals. The *UK News* database contained in Westlaw UK provides the same UK news coverage as LexisNexis Professional and can be searched in much the same way. Similar options are provided to specify the way search terms are used. Again, individual newspapers can be selected.

The current awareness features of both LexisNexis Professional and Westlaw UK can also be used to find newspaper articles on recent legal developments. In LexisNexis Professional the "Current Awareness" shortcut is found under the legal search options and includes a "Latest Legal News" section. Links are provided in the section to the full text of legal coverage in the major national newspapers. News, comment and law reports are included, with the most recent items displayed first (usually news items from the current issue of the newspaper). The "My Practice Areas" section of the current awareness page enables the latest news items to be viewed for particular subject areas, such as corporate law or civil procedure.

Westlaw UK's current awareness features can be selected from a "Current Awareness" tab on the home page. Notes of recent newspaper articles are combined with details of recently indexed journal articles in the "Newspapers & Journal Articles" link. Unlike LexisNexis Professional, the full text is not provided. However, the brief summaries make it possible to review items quickly. Newspaper articles are also included in the "Browse by Legal Subject" section of the current awareness page. The newspaper current awareness summaries are available even if your law library does not subscribe to the full text *UK News* database on Westlaw UK. If your library does not subscribe to *UK News*, the news databases of LexisNexis Professional are the most likely alternative source for the full text of newspaper articles.

Locating Journals from other Libraries

5–23   If the journal is not available in your library, you may wish to obtain it from elsewhere. One approach would be to use the online catalogues of other libraries, which contain details of the journal titles held by the library (see **7–29**). Most online catalogues allow you to limit your title search to a "journals only" section of the catalogue. If you are searching for older journal titles, the *Union List of Legal Periodicals*, published by the Institute of Advanced Legal Studies, may be of use. It lists the locations of journals throughout the UK, though it is now extremely dated. The second edition was published in 1978 (although take comfort from the knowledge that libraries are unlikely to discard journal collections).

If you wish to consult a large number of journals or reports, it may be more convenient to go to another library and use the material there. If only a few articles are required, it may be easier to obtain them through the inter-library loan service. Details of this service are available from your librarian. If you wish to use this service, plan ahead and allow time for your request to be processed and for the material to arrive. The process can take several weeks, but usually around one to two weeks.

Copies of journal articles can be obtained directly from a wide range of organisations offering a document supply service. Even if you have to pay for copies from your own library, copies supplied by these services are likely to be more expensive, as a copyright fee is usually charged by publishers. This fee is added to the cost of supply. A university or other educational or public library does not charge this copyright fee. The British Library (at *www.bl.uk*) has an Articles Direct service for one-off orders using a web page order form which exists alongside its "inside" service, designed to provide document delivery to subscribing organisations.

6 UK official publications

Introduction

6–1 A great deal of official publishing now takes place on the internet. This includes parliamentary publications and the publications of government departments and other official bodies. As a result, official publications have become much more accessible than they once were. However, tracing official publications is not always straightforward. This is a field in which you should not hesitate to seek the advice of library staff whenever you have a difficulty. Most libraries which have a collection of official publications have at least one person who is responsible for helping readers find this material, whether online or in print.

The Stationery Office (TSO) publishes a high proportion of UK official publications. As a result, TSO web pages, and the TSO bookshop catalogue, are significant sources for tracing official publications (**6–15**). TSO is not, however, the only source of UK official publications. Some of the publications you may wish to consult will have been published elsewhere, often on the websites of government departments and other official bodies. Databases are available to help trace these publications (**6–16**).

Before privatisation in 1996, UK official publishing was undertaken by Her Majesty's Stationery Office (HMSO), which acted as the government printer. HMSO still exists as a residual body, responsible for Crown copyright. Since 2005, it has been part of the Office of Public Sector Information (OPSI). For this reason, legislation is found on OPSI web pages.

Parliamentary publications are the most important category of UK official publications for the law student. These include papers brought before Parliament (Command Papers), Bills, House of Commons Papers and *Hansard* reports of parliamentary debates. Most of this chapter is concerned with these sources. Acts of Parliament, which are also official publications, are covered in Chapter 4. Parliamentary Papers are published by TSO.

Documents other than parliamentary publications published by, or on behalf of, government departments or other official bodies, are often referred to as non-parliamentary publications. These items vary considerably and include, for example, public information pamphlets such as the *Highway Code* and directories such as the *Civil Service Yearbook*, which lists Civil Service departments, provides contact details, and gives the names of senior civil servants. TSO publishes only some of these non-parliamentary publications.

Parliamentary Publications

Most recent Parliamentary Papers are now available online. All Command Papers   **6–2**
and House of Commons Papers from the 2005/2006 parliamentary session onwards are
available from TSO (at *www.official-documents.co.uk*). Selected papers are available for the
period 1994–2005. Online access to the text of Bills before Parliament (**6–9**) and *Hansord*
debates (**6–11**) is explained in the relevant sections. If your library has a complete collection
of printed parliamentary publications, they may be bound together in volumes containing
all the material produced during a particular session of Parliament. These volumes are
known as *sessional papers* or *sessional sets*. A Sessional Index provides a subject approach
to the material. The sessional papers are also available on microfiche. These are arranged by
type of material (Bills, Command Papers, etc.) and then in numerical order within each
session.

Libraries with large collections of government publications do not usually enter parliamentary publications in the library catalogues, relying instead on the indexes produced by
TSO and others (**6–14**) to trace relevant material. If, however, your library has only a small
collection of parliamentary publications, they may be catalogued individually.

In many libraries, recent parliamentary publications are gathered together in boxes. Every
parliamentary paper has its own individual number and the papers will usually be arranged
by these numbers in boxes comprising:

> House of Commons Papers;
> House of Commons Bills;
> House of Lords Papers and Bills;
> Command Papers.

These recent publications can also be traced through various indexes (**6–14**). You will
probably find that all the parliamentary publications have been housed in an official publications collection, in a separate area of the library (which may not form part of the law
library). Therefore, you should ask the librarians whether there is a collection of official
publications available and get them to show you where they are located and how they are
arranged.

Older parliamentary papers may only be available in your library on microfiche or
microfilm or in the form of reprints published by bodies such as the Irish University Press.
(These reprints are arranged in subject order.) If your library does not have a complete
collection of older material, it may be possible to trace a summary of a report in the
BOPCRIS database (**6–16**). Material which is still in print may be purchased from any
branch of TSO (addresses appear on the *Daily Lists* and in the monthly and annual *TSO
Catalogues*) or through any bookseller. Photocopies of out-of-print publications can be
purchased from TSO. Publications may also be available on loan through the inter-library
loan service.

We shall now look in more detail at some of the most important types of parliamentary
publications.

Command Papers

6–3   This is a very important category of parliamentary papers and one to which you may frequently be referred. It includes many major government reports, e.g. *A Fairer Deal for Legal Aid* (2005), some, but not all, of the reports of the Law Commission and the reports of all Royal Commissions. A Command Paper is, as it states on the front cover, presented to Parliament "By Command of Her Majesty." In practice, this means that it is presented to Parliament by a Minister of the Crown on his or her own initiative; its preparation has not been requested by Parliament. Command Papers are often statements of government policy, which are likely to be the subject of future legislation, or they are presented for the information of the Members of Parliament. Command Papers include:

statements of government policy (often referred to as *White Papers*);
some annual statistics and annual reports (many more are issued as non-parliamentary publications);
reports of Royal Commissions;
reports of some committees (other committee reports may be issued as non-parliamentary publications);
reports of tribunals of inquiry;
state papers (including the Treaty Series).

Citation and location of Command Papers

6–4   Command Papers are each given an individual number, prefaced by an abbreviation for the word "command". This abbreviation and the number are printed at the bottom left-hand corner of the cover of the report. The numbers run on continuously from one session of Parliament to another. The present abbreviation "Cm." has been used for publications issued since1986. Prior to 1986, different abbreviations of the word "command" were used. They are:

1st series 1833–1869	[1]–[4222] (the abbreviation for "Command" was omitted in the first series)
2nd series 1870–1899	[C. 1]–[C. 9550]
3rd series 1900–1918	[Cd. 1]–[Cd. 9239]
4th series 1919–1956	[Cmd. 1]–Cmd. 9889
5th series 1956–1986	Cmnd. 1–Cmnd. 9927
6th series 1986–	Cm. 1–

(The use of square brackets was abandoned in 1922.) It is important to note exactly the form of the abbreviation so that you have some idea of the date of the report. For instance, Cmd. 6404, which relates to social insurance and allied services (the Beveridge Report), is a different item from Cmnd. 6404, which is an international agreement relating to pensions. One was published in 1942 and the other in 1976.

If your library keeps all the Command Papers together in boxes arranged by command numbers, you will have no difficulty in tracing the report you want. However, if the publications are arranged by sessions or are bound into sessional sets (see **6–2**), it will be necessary to have some idea of the date of the Command Paper. You may find the *Concordance of Command Papers 1833–1972*, which is in J. E. Pemberton, *British Official Publications* (2nd ed.), pp. 66–66, useful for older papers. Occassionally, a report is published later than the Command Papers with adjoining numbers, with the result that it appears in a different session of Parliament (and is therefore in a different sessional set (**6–2**)). If you know the Command Paper number of a publication issued before 1979–80 and wish to locate it in the bound sessional sets, first ascertain the correct session by consulting Pemberton's list or the *HMSO Annual Catalogues* (see **6–14**). Until the 1979–80 session, Command Papers were not arranged in number order in the sessional sets. They were arranged alphabetically by subject in a sequence with all reports, accounts and papers. To find a Command Paper in the sessional sets before 1979–80 therefore, you need to consult the Sessional Index at the back of the last volume of the session. There you will find a list of Command Paper numbers indicating, for each one, the volume and page within the sessional set where it can be found. Command Papers bound in the sessional sets since 1979–80 can be readily traced under the Command Paper number.

Some Command Papers also form part of another series. For instance, some of the reports of the Law Commission (but not all) are Command Papers: but each Law Commission report also bears its own running number. For convenience, law libraries may keep all law Commission reports together, regardless of whether they are issued as Command Papers, House of Commons Papers, or non-parliamentary papers (and some of the series have been issued in all these categories). Another major series within the Command Papers are the state papers known as the Treaty Series. These are Command Papers and each has a number, but, in addition, each has its own Treaty Series number. If they are not bound into the sessional sets, the library may keep all the Treaty Series together. There are separate annual and three- or four-yearly consolidated indexes to the series; in addition, they also appear in the monthly and annual *TSO Catalogues*. Both the Treaty Series number and the Command Paper numbers are given. In 1970, HMSO published an *Index of British Treaties 1101–1968* (compiled by Clive Parry and Charity Hopkins). There are entries under subjects (Volume 1) and by the date of the treaties (Volumes 2 and 3).

Papers of the House of Lords and House of Commons

Until 1988, the House of Lords Papers and Bills were issued in a common numerical sequence, so the Papers and Bills were integrated. Since then, they have been issued in separate numerical sequences in the same way as the House of Commons Papers.   **6–5**

The number of each House of Lords Paper is printed in round brackets at the foot of the front cover. The citation is: H.L. session (paper number), e.g. H.L. 1993–94 (7) 1st Report [Session 1993–94]: Enforcement of Community Competition Rules: Report with Evidence—Select Committee on the European Communities.

The Papers of the House of Commons include reports of some committees, together with accounts, statistics and some annual reports which are required by Parliament for its work. The citation of a House of Commons Paper contains the initials H.C., the session and the paper number. e.g. H.C. 2005–06 167 is the *Annual Report* 2004/05 of the Legal Services Commission.

Bills

6–6   Bills are the draft versions of Acts, laid before Parliament for its consideration and approval. If your library has a complete collection of parliamentary papers, the Bills will be shelved with this collection; if not, they may be available in the law library. If the library's parliamentary papers are bound up into sessional sets, the Bills will form the first volumes of each set. The most recent Bills are likely to be shelved separately in boxes.

A Bill may be introduced into Parliament by a Member of Parliament (or by a peer) as an independent action (called a Private Member's Bill), or it may be introduced by a Minister as a Government Bill. Ultimately, however, if it is passed, it becomes a Public General Act whoever introduces it. Private Members' Bills are not always published by TSO: if not otherwise available, they can usually be obtained by writing directly to the Member of Parliament concerned.

Stages in the passage of a Bill

6–7   Before a Bill can become law, it passes through a number of stages. The exact stage which any Bill has reached on its passage through Parliament can be discovered by consulting the *House of Commons Weekly Information Bulletin* (**6–8**). A Bill may be introduced into the House of Lords or the Commons. If they commence in the House of Commons, Bills progress through the following stages. Bills fail if they do not pass through all these stages before the end of the parliamentary session.

(i)   *First Reading*—a purely formal reading of the Bill's title by the Clerk of the House; after this, the Bill is printed, a day is fixed for its Second Reading and it becomes available to the public.

(ii)   *Second Reading*—the principles of the Bill are debated. If the Bill fails to gain the approval of the House at this stage, it cannot proceed. The debate is reported in *Hansard* (see **6–11**).

(iii)   *Committee stage*—the whole House may sit in committee to examine the clauses of a Bill. More usually, the Bill is discussed in a Standing Committee consisting of approximately 20 Members of Parliament. The Standing Committee debates are found on the Parliament website (at *www.parliament.uk*), on the "*Hansard*" pages. The link to the debates is under the main *Hansard* heading, where they are arranged by session (chronologically), and then alphabetically by the name of the Bill under discussion. TSO also prints the text of the debate on the particular Bill as an individual item. Bound volumes are issued as *Parliamentary Debates. House of Commons Official Report. Standing Committees.* A number of volumes are published for each session and their publication lags two to three years behind the debates themselves.

If you are using the print copies of the debates you will need to find out which committee discussed the Bill you are interested in. This can be done by looking in the *House of Commons Information Bulletin* (**6–8**). Standing Committees can also be traced using the TSO website (**6–15**) or the UKOP catalogue (**6–16**). If you are searching using UKOP you will find that the name of the committee appears in the title area of the records used. Particular debates can be found by combining the Bill's title with "standing committee" or "grand committee".

(iv) *Report stage*—if the Bill has been amended by the Standing Committee, this stage gives the House an opportunity to consider the changes. If necessary, the Bill may be referred back to the committee. (If the Bill was debated and approved without amendment in a Committee of the whole House, then this stage is a formality.)

(v) *Third Reading*—a general discussion of the Bill as amended, after which it is passed to the House of Lords for its approval.

(vi) *Lords' stages*—The Bill is reprinted when it is passed to the Lords for their consideration and approval. If the Lords make any amendments, these are referred back to the Commons for their approval. Normally, both Houses must be in agreement on the text before the Bill can receive the Royal Assent. The Parliament Acts 1911 and 1949 provide for certain exceptions to this rule. Finance Bills are the standard exception.

Changes to the text of a Bill

Bills before Parliament are found on the Parliament website (at *www.parliament.uk*). Public **6–8** Bills are arranged in an alphabetical sequence on the "Bills before Parliament" page. Bills which originated in the House of Lords have [H.L.] after the title. The Bills are available in the form in which they are currently being considered by Parliament and carry a note explaining their status, as, e.g., a Bill passed by the House of Commons and introduced in the House of Lords, or "under consideration by Standing Committee F". If you are looking at the text of a Bill which has already passed through the House of Commons, this means you will see the Bill on the Parliament website as a House of Lords Bill. Because of the amendments made in the Commons, the text of the Bill will not be that of the original House of Commons Bill. If you want to go back to the text of the Bill as introduced to the Commons, you need to find the printed copy of the Bill published at first reading in the House of Commons. Consequently, the exact citation of a Bill becomes crucial.

The paper versions of a Bill can be printed more than once within each House as its content is changed. Thus, it is important to distinguish one printing of a Bill from another. There can be multiple printed versions of a Bill as a House of Commons Bill for example, as well as multiple versions of a Bill as it proceeds through the House of Lords. Most Bills are printed and placed on sale to the public by TSO as soon as they are given their first reading and the first number a Bill will carry is allocated at this point. This will be its number as a Bill introduced in either the Commons or the Lords. The Child Benefit Bill, for example, was allocated the number 13 for its first printing as a House of Commons Bill. As it received its first reading in the 2004–05 session, the full citation of the Bill at this point is therefore Child Benefit Bill [H.C.] [2004–05] 13.

When Parliament discusses the Bill, some amendments may be incorporated. If a major alteration is made, the complete text is reprinted, and this reprinted version is given a completely new number. The Child Benefit Bill was for example reprinted and renumbered 43 for the House of Commons, and the full citation for this version of the Bill is the Child Benefit Bill [H.C.] [2004–05] 43. If a significant number of amendments have been made to a Bill then a marshalled list of amendments may be published which bears the same number as the original Bill, but with the addition of a roman number, e.g. 123 II.

As most Bills require the approval of both Houses of Parliament, a House of Commons Bill will be renumbered when it passes to the House of Lords and becomes a House of Lords Bill. When it became a House of Lords Bill, the Child Benefit Bill for example became the Child Benefit Bill [H.L.] [2004–05] 23.

If you wish to trace the various printed copies of a Bill, the *House of Commons Weekly Information Bulletin* can act as your guide. The entry on page 101 from the *Bulletin* for 9th April 2005 relates to the Prevention of Terrorism Bill which was introduced into the House of Commons by Mr Charles Clarke. The Bill was printed six times during its passage through the Commons as H.C. Bills 61, 80 and 84–86, all printed in the 2004–2005 Parliamentary Session. The first version of the Bill to be considered by the House of Lords was H.L. Bill 34, there were later printings as H.L. Bills 37, 38 and 41 incorporating subsequent amendments. The Bill received its first reading in the House of Commons (1R) on February 22, 2005. The following stages of the Bill are then noted with the appropriate abbreviation. The Bill received the Royal Assent on March 11, 2005 and became law as the Prevention of Terrorism Act 2005 (c.2). A full list of abbreviations can be found in the *Weekly Information Bulletin* under "Legislation—General Notes". The debates on the Bill are found in *Hansard* (**6–11**) on the appropriate dates.

In summary, the Parliament website shows you the current state of a Bill, but if you want a series of snapshots of the passage of a Bill through Parliament, this can only be obtained by tracing the various versions of a Bill. This can be complex and you require the exact citations of the Bill as it progresses and changes through its Parliamentary life.

Tracing recent Bills

6–9   The full text of a Bill as currently before Parliament can be easily traced using the "Bills before Parliament" page of the Parliament website (at *www.parliament.uk*). If you wish to trace the development of legislation, however, you will need to trace the various versions of a Bill which were printed as it was amended in both houses of Parliament. The House of Commons *Weekly Information Bulletin* can be used to discover the numbers of the relevant Bills as noted in **6–7**, but you will need to know the date of Royal Assent in order to pick a *Bulletin* which will give a full picture of the Bill's passage through Parliament. An alternative is to search for the name of the Bill in either the TSO catalogue (**6–15**), or the UKOP catalogue (**6–16**). Both catalogues list individual printings of Bills.

If your library holds a set of the printed copies of Bills, these should be shelved in session and number order. If not, printed Bills can be requested through your libraries inter-library loan service or purchased from the TSO website. The House of Lords text of recent Bills can be found under the House of Lords section of the *Hansard* web pages.

Tracing older Bills

6–10   It is not often that you will need to refer to Bills from earlier sessions, for either they will have become law (in which case you should consult the resultant Act) or they will have lapsed. However, when you do need to consult older Bills, if your library has the bound sessional sets available, the text of all the versions of the Bill, together with all amendments, will be found in alphabetical order in the volumes entitled *Bills* at the beginning of the sessional set. If the bound sets are not available, details of all the published versions of the Bill will be found at the beginning of the *TSO or HMSO Annual Catalogue* and in the *House of Commons Weekly Information Bulletins* during that session. Publication details for Bills from the 1970s onwards can also be found using TSO's website (**6–15**) or the UKOP catalogue (**6–16**).

Example page from the Weekly Information Bulletin

→ **PREVENTION OF**   Mr Charles
TERRORISM (G)   Clarke/Baroness
    Scotland of
    Asthal

Commons: (61, 80, 83, 84, 85, 86)	1R:22.2.2005	2R: 23.2.2005	Prog: 23.2.2005	MR: 23.2.2005
Prog: 28.2.2005	RS: 28.2.2005	Prog: 8.3.2005	LA: 8.3.2005	LA: 10.3.2005
Lords: (34, 37, 38, 41)	1R: 1.3.2005	2R: 1.3.2005	Comm**: 3 & 7.3.2005	RS: 8.3.2005
CA: 9.3.2005	CA: 10.3.2005			

Royal Assent: **PREVENTION**
11.3.2005 (Ch.2)   **OF TERRORISM**
    ACT 2005

PREVENTION OF   Mr William Cash
TERRORISM
(No.2) (P)

Commons: (78)	1R: 8.3.2005	Bill dropped

PRIVATE PARKING   Annette Brooke
ENFORCEMENT
(REGULATION) (T)

Commons: (95)	1R: 22.3.2005	Bill dropped

PROCEEDS OF   Brian White
CRIME
(COMPENSATION
OF PROSECUTION
COSTS) (T)

Commons: (88)	1R: 15.3.2005	Bill dropped

PROCUREMENT   Mrs Anne Campbell
OF INNOVATIVE
TECHNOLOGIES
AND RESEARCH (P)

Commons: (93)	1R: 22.3.2005	Bill dropped

PUBLIC SERVICE   Claire Ward
(BANK
HOLIDAY) (T)

Commons: (53)	1R: 2.2.2005	Bill dropped

PUBLIC SERVICES   Lord Evans of
OMBUDSMAN   Temple Guiting /
(WALES) [HL] (G)   Peter Hain

Lords: (3, 20, 29)	1R: 24.11.2004	2R: 16.12.2004	Comm**: 25.1.2005	Rep: 10.2.2005

3R: 2.3.2005

Parliamentary debates (Hansard)

6–11   The first semi-official reports of Parliament's debates were published in 1803 by William Cobbett. The man whose name is so closely linked with the publication, Hansard, was a subsequent printer of the reports. There have been six series of *Parliamentary Debates*. The first series covered 1803–20, with subsequent series for 1820–30, 1830–91, 1892–1908 and 1909–1981. The sixth series covers 1981 to the present. Since 1909, the *Official Reports of Parliamentary Debates* have been published by the House of Commons itself. The House of Lords Debates have been published separately since 1909; previously, Lords and Commons Debates were published together.

To follow debates in the current session of Parliament, you need to consult a series of daily editions of *The Official Report of Debates (Hansard)*. These are available both online from the Parliament website and in print. Debates from earlier sessions are arranged first by session and then by date, either on the Parliament website, or in bound volumes of debates. House of Commons debates are available online from the 1988/89 sessions onwards on the Parliament website (at *www.parliament.uk*). House of Lords debates can be found in full text on the same site from 1994/95. Indexes are available, both online and in print, for both Houses, which can help trace a debate if you do not have an exact date, though these appear some months after debates have taken place. Both debates and indexes can be found on the Parliament website under "Hansard".

> **SEARCH TIP**
>
> Use the "Advanced Search" on the Parliament website to search *Hansard* using keywords. Searches can be limited to *Hansard* indexes (rather than debates) increasing the potential relevance of your results.

For the House of Commons the *Indexes to the Daily Parts of the House of Commons Parliamentary Debates* provide an alphabetical index listing of the subjects of debates and the names of speakers, along with the subject of written questions and the names of those asking them. References are to the column number of the printed *Hansard*, rather than page numbers. These are linked to the full text of *Hansard* in the online version. Index references ending in 'w' indicate written questions. The *Weekly Indexes to the House of Lords Parliamentary Debates* are set out in the same way. There are also indexes to the bound volumes of *Hansard* (online from 1999/2000) which enable debates to be traced by session.

The search engine for the Parliament website provides an alternative approach to tracing debates. To make the best use of its abilities, select the "Advanced Search" link from any the Parliament web pages. The advanced search menu allows your search to be restricted, so that only *Hansard* debates (or indexes) are searched, and searches can specify that an exact phrase must be matched, to ensure, for example, that the phrase "Prevention of Terrorism Bill" must be matched in the results page. If this is not specified, any document in which "prevention" and "terrorism" are prominent will be returned in the results screen. The search engine still returns all mentions of a Bill though, not just debates on a Bill, when an exact match is specified, making results sometimes difficult to interpret. Searches matching exact phrases within a Bill are more likely to be successful. The Parlianet database (**6–12**) provides a more effective way of tracing successive debates on a Bill. Alternative full text search options are available if your library holds the CD-ROM of House of Common Debates from 1988/89 onwards produced by Proquest.

Example Page from the Volume Indexes to the House of Commons Parliamentary Debates (Hansard)

Association of Chief Police Officers

294w

Astute class submarines

1540–1w, 1849w

Asylum

730–1w, 1401–10w, 1412–4w, 1573–4w, 1605–6w, 2046–51w, 2068w, 2093w
Administrative delays *1014–6*
Appeals *47–8w, 467w, 1411–2w*
Applications *1572–3w*
Children *757w, 1573w, 2051w*
Detainees *47w*
Domestic violence *1423w, 1583–5w*
EC countries *1094–5w*
Expenditure *1411w, 1582–3w*
Falun Gong *1428w*
Greater London *47–8w, 1092–4w, 1575–6w*
Housing *48w, 1428w*
Legal aid (16.11.04) *366–73wh*
Location *79–80ws*
Motor vehicles *1575w*
North Korea *1549–50w*
Reading Berkshire *1575w*
Scotland *1274w*
Sudan *1284–5w*
Wales *1276w, 1574–5w*
Zimbabwe *78–9ws*

Asylum and Immigration (Treatment of Claimants etc) Act 2004

Questions

Prosecutions *1091–2w*

Atherton, Ms Candy

Westminster Hall Debates

Health services, Cornwall (09.11.04) *237wh*

Questions

British Library, Music *510w*
Community support officers, Cornwall *608w*

Example Page from the House of Commons Parliamentary Debates (Hansard)

Illegal Immigration

2. **Mr. Gwyn Prosser (Dover)** (Lab): What plans he has to visit Dover to discuss the impact of his measures to control illegal immigration. [197730]

The Minister for Citizenship and Immigration (Mr. Desmond Browne): Unfortunately, I have no immediate plans to visit Dover in the near future, but I welcome the opportunity to highlight the impact that the asylum and immigration measures that we have taken have had there. We have significantly strengthened our borders by the closure of Sangatte, by deploying new detection technology in France and by developing our juxtaposed controls in northern France, culminating in full United Kingdom immigration controls in Calais, Boulogne and Dunkirk since 3 October 2004. As a result, clandestine entry in Kent fell by 65 per cent. during 2003, compared with 2002. That fall has continued in 2004, with a 23 per cent. decrease in clandestines in Kent in the first six months of 2004, compared with the last six months of 2003.

15 Nov 2004: Column 1012

Mr. Prosser: I thank my hon. Friend for that answer. I assure him that it reflects the situation in Dover, where illegal immigration and working have been reduced hugely. Does he accept that there is still far more to do? Although the number of asylum seekers coming through the port has reduced to just one or two a day, which compares well with figures we had in previous years, we can still take further action. Does he agree that the introduction of a secure identity card will go further towards cracking down on illegal immigrants and on traffickers and illegal working?

Mr. Browne: I thank my hon. Friend for his question, and I agree that the introduction of a secure biometrically based identity card will go a significant way further to secure our borders.

Mr. Eric Forth (Bromley and Chislehurst) (Con): How?

Mr. Browne: A sedentary voice asks "How", and the answer is comparatively simple: it will be done by ensuring that those who are in this country legally have to have a biometrically based identity card. We are confident in the knowledge that the absence of such an identity card—which has, of course, been part of the culture of this country—has been a pull factor to illegal immigrants for many years.

To my hon. Friend the Member for Dover (Mr. Prosser), I may say that there is further evidence on the impact of our measures. The number of detections in Calais increased by 36 per cent. in the first six months of 2004, compared with the first six months of 2003. In addition, my right hon. Friend the Home Secretary met the French Interior Minister Mr. de Villepin in Calais only this morning, and he was shown evidence that when Sangatte was open there were routinely about 2,000 asylum seekers in the Calais area. The police in France now know that there are only about 100 at any given time.

Using online sources to trace debates on a Bill

The "Bill Index" on the Parliament website (at *www.parliament.uk*) can be used to trace **6–12** *Hansard* debates on Bills currently before Parliament. The index can be found on the "Bills before Parliament" page. Brief notes are provided of the various stages a Bill has passed through, along with links to the relevant section of *Hansard*. Links are also provided to supporting documentation, e.g. Command Papers and House of Commons Papers.

Justis *Parlianet* can be used to trace debates on Bills from previous sessions of Parliament. The database is derived from the *POLIS* database prepared by the House of Commons Library. It indexes proceedings of both Houses of Parliament and as a result provides a useful means of tracing the passage of legislation through Parliament. It is a subscription database, so you need to check if your library can provide access. In the current version of the database a "search wizard" takes you through the key steps to be taken if you wish to trace debates and questions relating to a particular Bill. First, "United Kingdom" must be selected as "Legislature"; then the "Tracking Legislation" option must be selected. Particular Parliamentary sessions can be selected, or all sessions. The database indexes proceedings from 1979 onwards. An important final step is to enter the title of a Bill (not an Act) in the "Legislation" search box, i.e. "Prevention of Terrorism Bill", not "Prevention of Terrorism Act". A particular strength of the database lies in the option to sort results in legislation, then date order. This means that you ignore all incidental mentions of a Bill and concentrate only on index entries that relate to its passage through Parliament. Notes of debates are provided along with references to oral and written questions. It is then easy to find, for example, the oral statement that introduced a Bill to one of the Houses of Parliament, before following debates and amendments in sequence. A link to the *Hansard* full text on the Parliament website is usually available from the relevant index entry.

Non-Parliamentary Publications

These are publications which are not presented to Parliament. The term covers a vast range **6–13** of government publications, including statutory instruments (**4–26**). In most libraries, these publications (other than statutory instruments) are entered in the library catalogue, so you should start your search for them in the catalogue. Checking the catalogue is particularly important in those libraries where non-parliamentary publications are scattered among the book collections according to the subject matter of their content, rather than being kept in a single central location. If a central collection exists, additional copies may also be kept in subject collections.

Non-parliamentary publications are increasingly available on the internet, usually on the website of the body responsible for their publication. As there are many official bodies, a useful starting point is the UK online website (at *www.direct.gov.uk*), as this features an alphabetical list of government, or government funded or controlled bodies under the "Directories" link. This allows you to trace relevant or potentially relevant home pages. Home pages of public bodies as diverse as the Child Support Agency, the Commission for Racial Equality and the Employment Appeal Tribunal can be found using the site. Your next step is to explore the site, looking for a publications link, a site map, or a search engine.

Previously, much of the non-parliamentary publishing was undertaken by HMSO, but this is no longer the case, so the current TSO catalogues (**6–15**) are only of limited use. If you wish to trace non-parliamentary papers, the UKOP catalogue is of more use as it includes official publications not published by TSO (see **6–16**). The UKOP database also includes links to non-parliamentary publications found on departmental sites, along with archived copies of some publications from 2000 onwards.

Tracing Official Publications

6–14   A number of sources are available for tracing both parliamentary and non-parliamentary papers. These include *TSO Daily Lists* and catalogues (**6–15**), along with the *UKOP* catalogue and the *BOPCAS* and *BOPCRIS* databases (all covered in **6–16**). It often may not be clear whether a document—an annual report perhaps—is a parliamentary, or a non-parliamentary paper, so the ability to search for all kinds of official publications is helpful.

Stationery Office catalogues and indexes

6–15   The *TSO Daily Lists* are useful for tracing very recent Acts and other recent government publications. The lists appear both in print and on the TSO websites. The current list is on the TSO website (at *www.tsoshop.co.uk/parliament*). The site also features links to previous lists by month and year. Using the *Daily List*, you can find publication details of House of Lords and Commons Papers and Bills, Command Papers, Acts, and Debates at the beginning of the list in the parliamentary section. Non-parliamentary publications appear in the official publications section. Other sections are devoted to Scottish Parliament publications, Northern Ireland Assembly publications and Northern Ireland official publications. The final section is devoted to agency publications. Agency publications, by bodies such as the Council of Europe, the UN and the WHO, are those that are sold, but not published, by TSO.

If your required publication is more than a few days old, it is easier to search using TSO's online bookshop (at *www.tsoshop.co.uk*)—other sources for keyword searching are covered in **6–16**. The TSO bookshop site includes details of all publications sold by TSO and it is possible to keyword search for any TSO publication, along with HMSO publications, including some "print on demand" titles from as early as 1930. Click the link for the "Advanced Search" to limit your search to Bills, Acts, House of Commons Papers, etc. The author search allows searches by the names of chairmen of committees and date limits can also be set. The TSO bookshop site is designed to act for the Stationery Office as an internet bookshop, so along with pricing information, the site provides the ability to order online. If the item you are interested in is out of print, a price is given for TSO's print on demand facility.

Should you want to trace relatively recent publications using print sources, you will find that many libraries hold the printed *TSO Weekly List*. This contains the contents of the week's *Daily Lists* and these are in turn replaced (some months later), by the *Stationery Office Monthly Catalogue*. This has lists of House of Lords and House of Commons Papers arranged in numerical order, a list of Command Papers in numerical order and a list of Acts

(Reproduced with permission of The Stationery Office Limited)

produced during that month. The list of Command Papers can be used to trace the title of publications, if you have only the Command Paper number. Scottish Parliament and Northern Ireland Assembly publications are also included using a numerical sequence. Non-parliamentary and agency publications are listed as indeed they are in the *Daily* and *Weekly Lists*. Finally, a cumulative alphabetical index is included for the year which has entries for subject terms, authors, chairmen and editors. Statutory instruments are not included, as they are included in a separate monthly index. The current *Stationery Office Annual Catalogue* is structured in the same way as the monthly lists.

If you are looking for earlier material, which may not appear on the TSO website, you should use the annual catalogues which appeared as either the *HMSO Annual Catalogue 19 . . .*, or before that, *Government Publications 19 . . ..* As you go back through the catalogues you see that where the name of the Ministry began with the word "Ministry" or "Department", the entry was inverted, as, for example, Environment, Department of. Otherwise the structure and layout of the catalogues remains essentially unaltered.

Every five years a Consolidated Index was produced for the older catalogues, e.g. for 1961–65, 1966–70, 1971–75, 1976–80 and in many libraries, the catalogues for these years are bound together. To allow for this, the pagination of the catalogues was continuous over the five year period.

Other sources for tracing official publications

6–16   The *UKOP* (UK Official Publications) database combines details of official publications published by TSO with details of official publications published by other sources. This means that almost all publications by government departments are included—whether published by TSO or not—along with the full range of TSO published parliamentary papers. Coverage begins in 1970 and since 2000 links have been added to the full text source of many publications. Some of these are archived digital copies only available from *UKOP*. *UKOP* is a subscription database, so you need to check if your library can provide access.

UKOP can be searched for publications by title, in much the same way as the TSO book-shop catalogue, in order to trace Command Paper or other parliamentary reference numbers, or information on which branch of government was responsible for the publication. But be warned, the use of automatic keyword searching, and the relevance ranking of results, means that some documents can be almost impossible to find. A search for the government white paper *Justice for All* (Cm. 5563), retrieves a list of 1,000 possible matches featuring "Justice". Further details, preferably including a date, are needed to find the document with its Command Paper number.

UKOP is better designed for subject searching, allowing a trawl through often long results lists for potentially useful or relevant documents on a subject. Its "Advanced Search" facilitates subject searching using either a "Flexible Search" or a "Boolean Search" (see **2–11** for more on Boolean searching). The "Flexible Search" option automatically adds additional search words to the ones you have entered using the *UKOP* thesaurus of subject terms, so that if you search for publications relating to "asylum seekers", publications with titles featuring the words "immigration"

SEARCH TIP

Use the "Boolean Search" (under "Advanced Search") when searching the *UKOP* database. Combine search keywords using "AND".

and "refugees" are also found. However, this kind of searching can be all too inclusive. A "Flexible Search" for "asylum seekers" finds over 1,000 references, so additional, more specific, search terms need to be added to create a meaningful search. A "Boolean Search" for "asylum AND seekers" finds well under 200 references.

Your library may subscribe to the *BOPCAS* database service as an alternative to *UKOP*. The service is provided by the University of Southampton, which has catalogued parliamentary papers, along with non-parliamentary papers taken by the university's Ford collection since 1996. The service includes emailed current awareness updates on new official publications in an area.

The Justis *Parlianet* database (**6–12**) provides another subscription route for tracing recent official publications. Like the previous databases, it includes both parliamentary and non-parliamentary papers. A "search wizard" can be used to specify "Publications", excluding the details of parliamentary debates and other material held on the database. Subject keywords can then be used to search for official publications. Title and author searches are also possible.

If you wish to trace older official publications, the *BOPCRIS* database (at *www.bopcris. ac.uk*) provides selective coverage of the entire period from 1688 to 1995. The database provides abstracts for 23,000 key documents, most of which are parliamentary papers, though some non-parliamentary papers are included. Selection is based on the Ford lists and breviates, a series of print publications which have provided the standard selection of important official publications for most of the period covered by the database. Many of the abstracts are extensive, making keyword subject searching particularly effective. The database was funded by UK universities enabling database access to be free of charge.

Another source for tracing older parliamentary papers is the *Index to the House of Commons Parliamentary Papers* on CD-ROM, which contains references to Bills, Command Papers and House of Commons Papers. Coverage begins in 1801. Nineteenth Century references are taken from the *Subject Catalogue of the House of Commons Parliamentary Papers, 1901–1900*, by Peter Cockton, and later references are taken from HMSO indexes and the *POLIS* database. Broad subject headings are provided, though for most searches you should rely on keyword searching words appearing in the titles of the papers.

A comprehensive approach to finding older material requires the use of printed indexes. Along with the indexes published by HMSO (**6–15**), the general indexes printed for the House of Commons covering the nineteenth Century should be examined. These provide a detailed alphabetical approach to finding parliamentary papers and were published as the *General Index to the Accounts and papers . . . Printed by Order of the House of Commons or Presented by Command* for 1801–1852, 1852/53 to 1868/69 and 1879–1878/79. The Ford lists and breviates, already mentioned, were published as *Select list of British parliamentary papers for 1833–99*; *A Breviate of Parliamentary Papers*, with volumes covering the period from 1900 to 1954; *Select List of British Parliamentary Papers, 1955–1964*; and *Ford List of British Parliamentary Papers*, with volumes covering 1965–83.

Tracing Law Commission reports and working papers

Some of the Law Commission reports are published as Command Papers and others are House of Commons Papers, whilst many more are non-parliamentary papers. As a result you may find that in your library they are not all shelved as one collection. Every report and   **6–17** working paper has its own individual number. A complete list of all the reports and working papers which have been published is given in the latest copy of the *Law Commission's Annual Report* (issued as a House of Commons Paper). The list gives the Command Paper number or Paper numbers, where relevant, and indicates, for each report, whether the Commission's proposals for reform have been implemented. Law Commission papers can also be traced using TSO's website for recent publications and the HMSO catalogues for older reports and publications.

Tracing press releases

6–18   The press releases of government departments are relatively easy to trace thanks to the UK online website (at *www.direct.gov.uk*). This provides a means of tracing the departmental websites and the press releases they carry. Updates on press releases with brief summaries can be found in the "Current Awareness" section of Westlaw UK. The "Press Releases" link provides coverage of press releases of legal interest from UK government departments, the Commission of the European Communities and the European Court of Human Rights.

Tracing statistics

6–19   The National Statistics website (at *www.statistics.gov.uk*) provides a particularly useful starting point for official statistics. The site includes a link to the StatBase database, which provides a detailed description of the UK Government Statistical Service's data sources, products and services. It provides an authoritative route into the available statistical sources. In some cases statistical data are provided directly, and in others you are given details of a print source or a relevant government department. It is possible to search StatBase by theme (e.g. crime and justice), subject (e.g. court and judicial procedings) and then topic (e.g. children's procedings). A good departmental site for lawyers is the Home Office site, and in particular the Home Office Research Development statistics (at *www.homeoffice.gov.uk/rds*).

TSO publishes the printed *Guide to Official Statistics*, revised annually, which again provides a valuable starting point. It is produced by the Office for National Statistics, now incorporated into National Statistics.

7 How to find information on a subject

Introduction

It is probable that you will frequently be asked to discover the law relating to a particular topic. Your essays, tutorial and seminar preparation will often require you to know not simply the present state of the law but also its development and such criticisms and suggestions for reform as have been made.

    To find information on a subject you will need to consult some or all of the following sources:

Acts of Parliament;
Delegated legislation;
European Communities legislation, and International Treaties and Conventions;
Cases;
Textbooks;
Journal articles;
Relevant government publications, including Law Commission Reports (especially those which have made suggestions for reform of the law);
Reports and comments in newspapers;
Bills and Parliamentary Debates.

In order to tackle a legal problem, you may need to ask yourself the following questions:

QUESTION: Where can I find a general statement of the law on this subject?
ANSWER: In encyclopedias, such as *Halsbury's Laws* (**7–3**) and in textbooks (**7–29**).

QUESTION: What books are there on this subject?
ANSWER: Consult library catalogues (**7–29**) and bibliographies (**7–30**).

QUESTION: What journal articles have been written on this subject?
ANSWER: Consult indexes to journals (**5–5**).

7–1

QUESTION: What cases have there been on this topic?
ANSWER: Use either electronic databases or print indexes (**7–8**).

QUESTION: What judicial interpretation has been placed on particular words?
ANSWER: Look in *Words and Phrases Legally Defined* and similar works (**7–19**).

QUESTION: Which Acts of Parliament deal with this subject and are in force?
ANSWER: Use online databases (**7–21**) and (**7–22**) or *Halsbury's Statutes* (**7–24**).

QUESTION: Are there any relevant statutory instruments?
ANSWER: Use online databases (**7–26**) or *Halsbury's Statutory Instruments* (**7–27**).

QUESTION: Have there been any government reports or Law Commission reports on this topic?
ANSWER: Use the TSO or UKOP databases (**6–15** and **6–16**) and the *Annual Reports* of the Law Commission (**6–17**).

QUESTION: Are there any Bills before Parliament which would change the law on this subject? Has the issue been discussed in Parliament?
ANSWER: Consult the *House of Commons Weekly Information Bulletin* (**6–8**) and *Parliamentary Debates* (**6–11** and **6–12**).

Having mapped out the ground, you can now proceed to tackle these questions. If you encounter any difficulties in carrying out a search on a legal subject, never be afraid to ask the library staff or your lecturer for help. Remember that other students may also be working on the same subject—start work well within the time limits set, otherwise you may discover that the material is unavailable because of high demand.

Legal Encyclopedias

7–2   These contain a detailed up-to-date statement of the law on a particular subject. The major general legal encyclopedia is *Halsbury's Laws of England*, which is now in its fourth edition. It is a most useful source of information on a wide variety of topics. In addition, there are a number of more specialised encyclopedias, many of them available online, or issued in looseleaf form so that the information can be kept up to date.

Halsbury's Laws of England

7–3   *Halsbury's Laws* covers all areas of English law and is a useful starting point for research on any legal topic. Because it is kept up to date, it has the advantage over textbooks of including recent information.

The encyclopedia is available either online from LexisNexis Butterworths (**2–4**), or as 60 print volumes. The fourth edition was completed in 1987 and forms the basis of both the online and print versions. There is an ongoing programme to update the encyclopedia. The online version features update sections and the print volumes which have been most affected by changes in the law are reissued.

Whether online or in print, *Halsbury's Laws* provides an effective statement of the whole of the law of England and Wales. The print volumes are arranged alphabetically by subject, from "Administrative Law" to "Wills" and these divisions are also present in the *Halsbury's Laws* database. Each print volume covers between one and seven subjects. The subjects are in turn divided into numbered paragraphs and each paragraph gives a description of the law relating to a particular topic, together with copious footnote references to relevant statutes and cases. Remember that *Halsbury's Laws* gives a useful summary of the law: you will need to go to other works to find the actual text of an Act of Parliament or law report.

How to use Halsbury's Laws online

Select the "Commentary" databases from the LexisNexis Butterworths home page (**2–4**), to **7–4** check if your library has a subscription to *Halsbury's Laws of England. Halsbury's Laws* can be found using the "Select Sources" drop-down menu. If your library has subscriptions to other LexisNexis Butterworths works providing commentary on the law, their titles are displayed on the same menu. These might include *Hall and Morison on Children*, for example, or the *Encyclopedia of Forms and Precedents* noted in **7–7**.

If you are sure of the area of law you wish to research, one approach is to use the "Browse" tab available under the commentary heading. The subject headings found in the print volumes of *Halsbury's Laws* are then displayed alphabetically. Within each heading, contents listings can be used to work through the hierarchy of sub-headings used in the encyclopedia, until the full text of a particular section is reached. The "British Nationality, Immigration and Asylum" heading might be selected, for example, followed by "Immigration", then further subheadings, in order to reach sections on the law relating to deportation.

However, the subject heading to choose may not be obvious. In this case, a more effective way of using the *Halsbury's Laws* is to search the full text of the entire encyclopedia using the "Enter Search Terms" section displayed on the commentary search page. As this is a full text database it is important to consider the different ways in which subject you are interested in might be described, in order to be sure that you have adequately explored the database (see **2–11** for more on database searching). Suppose, for example, you wish to discover the current law on bomb hoaxes.

> ### SEARCH TIP
>
> Be as specific as you can when searching *Halsbury's Laws* using keywords. Use single words and short phrases and combine them with "AND".

How should you phrase your search? Fortunately, the Butterworths LexisNexis commentary databases can be searched using the same proximity limiters that operate in LexisNexis Professional. This means that you can specify how close you wish terms to be found in the text of the encyclopedia in order to ensure that all potentially relevant results are found. Searching for "bomb w/6 hoax", for example, specifies that the two words should be between six words of each other. This means that text including the phrase "bomb hoax" is found, but also text including the phrase "hoax bomb call", or "hoax call suggesting that a bomb", etc. A further refinement of the search would be to use "hoax*", where the asterisk ensures that all words beginning "hoax" are found, e.g. "hoax" and "hoaxes". Using proximity searches in this way ensures that you are not defeated by the variety of natural language.

In this particular case, searching *Halsbury's Laws* for matches to "bomb w/6 hoax*" finds two relevant sections in the encyclopedia. One can be found under the "Criminal Law" heading, on "Sending indecent, obscene or false messages by telephone etc", the other, on

"Criminal liability for public nuisance", can be found under the "Nuisance" heading. The print index (see **6–9**) only lists the first section.

Example results page from Halsbury's Laws online

484. Bomb hoaxes.

Any person who (1) places any article[1] in any place whatever, or dispatches any article by post, rail or any other means whatever of sending things from one place to another, with the intention, in either case, of inducing in some other person a belief that it is likely to explode or ignite and thereby cause personal injury or damage to property[2]; or (2) communicates any information which he knows or believes to be false to another person with the intention of inducing in him or any other person a false belief that a bomb or other thing liable to explode or ignite is present in any place or location whatever[3], is guilty of an offence and liable on conviction on indictment to imprisonment for a term not exceeding five years, or on summary conviction to imprisonment for a term not exceeding three months or a fine not exceeding the prescribed sum, or to both[4].

For a person to be guilty of an offence under heads (1) or (2) above, it is not necessary for him to have any particular person in mind as the person in whom he intends to induce the belief there mentioned[5].

[1]   For these purposes, 'article' includes substance: Criminal Law Act 1977 s.51(1).
[2]   Ibid s.51(1).
[3]   Ibid s.51(2).
[4]   Ibid s.51(4) (amended by the Magistrates' Courts Act 1980 s.32(2)). For the meaning of 'the prescribed sum' see para 807 post.
[5]   Criminal Law Act 1977 s.51(3). As to threatening to contaminate or interfere with goods see para 193 ante; and as to threatening to destroy or damage property see para 595 post.

UPDATE

484 Bomb hoaxes

TEXT AND NOTE 4—Maximum terms of imprisonment increased to seven years and six months respectively: Criminal Justice Act 1991 s.26(4).
NOTE 4—As to sentence for delivering a package containing an inert hand grenade, see *R v Bosworth* [1998] 1 Cr App Rep (S) 356, CA.

Once you have found the encyclopedia's description of the law on a subject, it is important to check the update section at the end of the main text. The main text entry is that found in the original volume of the fourth edition and updates need to be checked even for relatively old changes in the law. The update to the section on bomb hoaxes includes a note that maximum terms of imprisonment have been increased by the Criminal Justice Act 1991 s.26(4). Recent updates are also included, so that in 2005, for example, updates included the Prevention of Terrorism Act 2005.

How to use Halsbury's Laws in print

To use *Halsbury's Laws* in print, start by looking up the subject that interests you in the   **7–5**
Consolidated Index (Volumes 55 and 56). The entry refers you to the appropriate *volume*
number (in **bold** type) and *paragraph* number (not page number). The presence of "n" followed by a small number indicates that you are being referred to one of the footnotes at the
end of the appropriate paragraph number. For information on the law related to bomb
hoaxes, you would turn to Volume 11(1), paragraph 484. Paragraph 484 gives a statement of
the law relating to bomb hoaxes, together with footnotes which refer you to relevant statutes.
Halsbury's Laws also refers you to cases and other sources of information, as appropriate.

   Remember that it is possible that the information in the volumes is out of date. New legislation, or other changes in the law, could have made the information incomplete or inaccurate.
To find out if there have been any changes in the law since the volumes were published, make
a note of the relevant volume and paragraph numbers, and turn to the *Cumulative Supplement*.
For example, the information on bomb hoaxes was contained in Volume 11(1), paragraph 484.
If you turn to the latest *Cumulative Supplement* (only the latest Supplement should be used)
and look up the entry for Volume 11(1), paragraph 484, you can check to see if there have been
changes in the law since Volume 11(1) was written. It is therefore important to read the information in the *Cumulative Supplement* in conjunction with that found in the main volume.

   These two volumes bring the information up to date to the end of last year. But have there
been changes in the law since then? To find out, turn to the looseleaf *Noter-Up* in Binder 2.
The *Noter-Up* is arranged in the same way as the *Cumulative Supplement*, in volume and
paragraph number.

Summary: How to use Halsbury's Laws in Print

1. Look up the subject in the *Consolidated Index*. This tells you the number of the *volume*
   and *paragraph* which contains the information.
2. Find the relevant volume and paragraph number in the main work.
3. To make sure the information is up to date, consult:
   (a) the *Cumulative Supplement*, and
   (b) the *Noter-Up* in Binder 2, under the relevant volume and paragraph number.

Remember there are four steps in using *Halsbury's Laws*:

   Consolidated Index;
   Main Work;
   Cumulative Supplement;
   Noter-Up.

   At the back of each volume of the main work, there are separate indexes to each of the
subject areas dealt with in the volume.

   The last two volumes of *Halsbury's Laws* (Volumes 51 and 52) are devoted to the law of the
European Communities, and its effect upon UK law. A similar but more sophisticated system

of paragraph numbers is used in these two volumes and footnote references refer you to the relevant Directives, Decisions and Regulations of the European Communities. Volume 52 contains a useful glossary of technical terms, as well as a detailed index to both volumes. The information is kept up to date by the information in the *Cumulative Supplement* and *Noter-Up*.

The *Monthly Reviews* (published as booklets and filed in Binder 1) can be used as a general means of keeping up with new developments in subjects you are studying since they give, under subject headings, recent changes in the law with summaries of cases, statutes, statutory instruments and other materials. The *Monthly Reviews* are not arranged in the same volume and paragraph order as the main volumes, so in order to find relevant information you will need to look up the subject again in the Cumulative Index to the Reviews at the back of the Binder. The *Monthly Reviews* are replaced by an *Annual Abridgment,* which summarises all the changes in the law during a particular year (commencing in 1974 when the first *Abridgment* appeared). At the beginning of the volume, a section headed "In brief" summarises the major development in the law of each subject during the year. At the beginning of each subject, there is a reference to the main volume of *Halsbury's Laws* which deals with that subject and there is a highly selective list of journal articles written on the subject during the year.

Specialised encyclopedias

7–6   There are a number of specialised encyclopedias which can provide you with an up-to-date statement of the law in particular subject areas. Many of these are issued in looseleaf format, so that the information can be updated by the insertion of replacement pages whenever there is a change in the law. Most of them are also available online or on CD-ROM. The *Encyclopedia of Planning Law and Practice*, published by Sweet & Maxwell, is an example of a title available on CD-ROM (the CD-ROM is called *Sweet & Maxwell's Planning Law Service*); other looseleafs and CD-ROM's cover topics such as housing, environmental law and health and safety at work. LexisNexis Butterworths have issued similar works covering, for example, education law, family law and landlord and tenant. Some are available online from LexisNexis Butterworths as "Commentary" databases (see **2–4**). Specialised encyclopedias are particularly useful in subjects such as taxation, where the law changes very rapidly. When using the looseleaf version of a specialised encyclopedia, you should check the pages near the beginning of the volume which tell you how recent the information is. This will enable you to be certain that the latest supplementary pages have all been inserted. Specialised encyclopedias usually contain an explanation of the law, together with the up-to-date versions of the relevant statutes, statutory instruments and government circulars, and notes of relevant cases. Publishers are now issuing some books for practitioners, such as *Ruoff & Roper*: *Registered Conveyancing*, in looseleaf format, so that the text can be kept up to date. This is a development of the long-established practice of issuing cumulative supplements in between editions, to update the last edition.

Precedent books and rule books

7–7   These are principally intended for the practitioner. The basic object of precedent books is to provide specimens of wills, conveyances, tenancy agreements or other forms of legal documents which solicitors are called upon to draw up. In addition, there are some precedent books which provide specimens of the types of forms that will be required whenever a case is taken to court. Rule books contain the rules that govern procedure in court, and specimen copies of the various orders and forms used by the courts and by the parties to litigation.

The multi-volume *Encyclopaedia of Forms and Precedents* aims to provide a form for every transaction likely to be encountered by practitioners, except for court forms. The Encyclopedia is also available from LexisNexis Butterworths (**2–4**). The entries are arranged by subject, e.g. "Animals", "Mortgages". Some idea of the wide scope of the work can be obtained by glancing through the subject headings. For instance, the section on animals covers such diverse topics as the sale and leasing of animals, applications for a licence to keep mink or to keep an animals' boarding establishment, a veterinary surgeon's certificate for the destruction of an animal and the relevant documents prohibiting movement of animals during an outbreak of disease. If you are using the print version, the looseleaf service volume keeps the information up to date. The *Cumulative Index* refers you to the *volume* (in **bold** type) and *paragraph* number that you require. Each individual volume also has its own index. References in the index to paragraph numbers in square brackets refer to precedents: paragraph numbers not enclosed in brackets refer to the preliminary notes. Checklists of procedures to be followed are provided under some subject headings.

Atkins Court Forms is a complementary publication, covering the procedure in civil courts and tribunals. Again, the volume is available from LexisNexis Butterworths. The print volume on divorce, for instance, contains all the necessary documents needed during the court action, together with a detailed list of the steps to be taken and the forms required at each stage. The volumes are reissued from time to time to incorporate new material. An annual supplement keeps the information up to date. The *Consolidated Index* is also published yearly.

There are many precedent books dealing with specific areas of the law, e.g. the looseleaf *Jackson & Powell*: *Professional Liability Precedents*. In addition, some textbooks designed for practitioners will include precedents.

The rules and procedures governing various courts are set out in a number of places. Sweet & Maxwell's *White Book* service and Bullen & Leek & Jacob's *Precedents of Pleading* are available online from Westlaw UK (**2–5**). Select the "Directory" link from the home page and search for "civil procedure". *Archbold: Criminal Pleading*, *Evidence and Practice* is used by those engaged in criminal work. It is also available from Westlaw UK. Search for "Archbold" on the Directory search page.

The coloured pages in each issue of the *Law Society Gazette* are of particular interest to practitioners. These often include specimen forms and precedents, and details of Home Office circulars and practice directions. Practice directions are also published in the major series of law reports, e.g. the *All England Law Reports* and the *Weekly Law Reports*.

Tracing Cases on a Subject

Cases on a particular subject can be traced by consulting the following sources.   **7–8**

The Westlaw UK *Case Locator* database (**7–9**);
Full-text case law databases (**7–10**);

Databases of recent judgments (**7–11**);
Current Law (**7–12** and **7–13**);
The Digest (**7–14** and **7–15**);
Halsbury's Laws of England (**7–4**);
Indexes to individual series of law reports (**7–16**);
Updates on recent cases (**7–17**);
Indexes to articles in Legal Journals (**5–5**);
Relevant textbooks (**7–29**).

How to use the Westlaw UK Case Locators

7–9   The Westlaw UK *Case Locators* database contains abstracts of almost all England and Wales cases reported since 1947. Standard keywords are also added to the abstracts. This makes the database ideal for subject searching. Suppose, for example, that you wish to find cases that might concern privacy and human rights (you might already have found some relevant journal articles using the *Legal Journals Index* as suggested in **5–6**). If you were to use keyword search terms such as "privacy" and "human rights" in a full text database of case law (see **7–10**), your results list would contain numerous minor and incidental mentions of the search words, making it difficult to find relevant cases. The inclusion of both "human rights" and "privacy" in a brief abstract of a case, on the other hand, means that the case is much more likely to be of interest.

To use the *Case Locators* database for subject searching, select the "Case Locators" shortcut from the Westlaw UK home page to display the full range of search options. Then enter your search words using either the "Terms" search box, or "Subject, Keyword, Catchphrase". If you use the "Terms" search, your search seeks a match for your keywords in the full text of the abstract as well as the additional keywords. As was the case with the *Legal Journals Index*, restricting your search to the "Subject, Keyword, Catchphrase" search is probably best done after you have searched using the more inclusive "Terms" option. Potentially relevant keywords and catchphrases can then be noted and a new search made using the more limited "Subject, Keyword, Catchphrase" search. Keywords and subject entries are standard for the database, so that searching using words found in these sections means that you do not need to worry about the variations of language found in the text of abstracts.

> **SEARCH TIP**
>
> Only search using "Subject, Keyword, Catchphrase" in the *Case Locators* database when you have already identified standard subject and keyword terms for a subject.

To continue with the privacy and human rights example, an initial "Terms" search on "human rights and privacy" will generate too many results to be particularly useful (more than 300 references are found). Having made the initial search, it would make more sense to add additional keywords to refine your search, taking into account particular aspects of human rights law and privacy that might be of interest to you, e.g. "privacy and human rights and media". This produces just over 50 references. Such a search finds the case *Campbell v Mirror Group Newspapers Ltd* for example, and *Douglas v Hello (no.6)* which applied the ruling made in *Campbell v Mirror Group Newspapers Ltd*. If you wanted to find other similar cases, you could then use some of keywords used in the *Case Locator* entries, such as "Breach of Confidence" or "Celebrities" in a further, more focused, search. Other cases found in the "privacy and human rights and media" search might suggest different aspects of human rights law and privacy issues, which could also be pursued. The case, *Carr v News Group Newspapers Ltd*, might suggest further searches using "Anonymity" for example, and "right to respect for private and family life" as possible areas for research.

Using the *Case Locator* in this way allows you to explore subject areas and find relevant cases, many of which can then be found in full text on Westlaw UK (see **3–15**).

Using full-text databases to find case law by subject

The full text databases of case law found in LexisNexis Professional (**2–3**) and Westlaw UK **7–10** (**2–5**) provide the largest archives of law reports and judgments available for subject searching. Your library may also have particular series of law reports available from either LexisNexis Butterworths (**2–4**) or Justis (**2–7**), constituting additional potential sources of case law. If you wish to include the widest possible range of relatively recent judgments, the databases on the BAILII website (**2–13**) should also not be ignored. Though the nature of law reporting means that a particular judgment is likely to appear in more than one of these databases, there remain specialist law reports whose judgments only appear online in one of these sources. As a result, a comprehensive approach subject searching using full text sources of case law requires that you repeat your search on all of the databases to which you have access.

For all of these databases, the process of searching is straightforward. They all have some form of free text search box in which you can enter your search words and they accept the search syntax described in **2–11**, in particular the use of "AND", "OR" etc. to combine search words. Some form of

> **SEARCH TIP**
>
> Use textbooks or *Halsbury's Laws* to clarify the keywords you should use when searching full text databases of case law.

proximity searching will also be available, ensuring that your search words must occur close together in the text being searched.

If you are using a full text database of case law, the most important thing to remember is that you must be as specific as possible in your choice of search words. As noted in **2–11**, if you enter general terms such as "copyright" or even "copyright AND software", you will obtain as a search result, either a list of the many thousands of cases in which the word "copyright" appears on its own, or the many hundreds of cases in which both the word "copyright" and the word "software" appear, but not necessarily in any proximity to each other. Most databases halt a search which would retrieve a very large number of cases. A corollary is that you need a good understanding of what it is you are researching in order to be able to home in on the important keywords. It makes sense to use full text databases as the last stage in your subject searching. Try looking at likely textbooks before you make your search, in order to select key terms to use. *Halsbury's Laws of England* (**7–3**), either online or in print, can also help you in the initial stages of a subject search, clarifying terminology and listing key cases.

You should think of different ways your topic is likely to be discussed in a judgment. For the most part you are only searching the text of the words used in the judgment and you will need to think about the different ways the same basic issue can be expressed. Ensure also that you use the symbol or "search operator" for the database that specifies that your key-words must be found close to each other in the long text of a judgment. Many databases allow "NEAR" to specify a standard proximity, LexisNexis Professional uses "w/" so that "w/6" specifies within 6 words. The "w/" proximity operator can also be used in Westlaw UK. Once you have considered various possibilities and tried different searches, the time will come to read the law reports you have found and see which cases they have cited.

How to use databases of recent judgments

7–11   The sources of recent judgments described in 3–20 provide a means of searching for judg-ments from a range of UK courts. BAILII, Casetrack and Lawtel all allow the full text of judgments to be searched using keywords. The need to decide your key search words and think of alternative ways in which the same idea can be expressed applies to these databases just as much as it does to the databases noted in 7–10. Keywords and phrases can be com-bined and "proximity" searches are possible. Check the search and help screens of the data-bases you are using for further information on how to combine search words.

How to use the Current Law Monthly Digest

7–12   *Current Law* is published monthly under the title *Current Law Monthly Digest*. The main part is arranged by subject and under each subject heading is given a summary of recent cases on the subject, new statutes and statutory instruments, government reports and recent books and journal articles on that subject. Full details are given to enable you to trace the cases and other materials mentioned in your own library. A page from the *Monthly Digest* is shown on page 121. On this page alone, an article is mentioned (item 359), a case is sum-marised (item 356) and a statutory instrument is outlined (item 357).

At the back of each issue is a Table of Cases which contains a list of all the cases which have been reported during the current year. It is therefore only necessary to look at the Table of Cases in the *latest* issue of the *Current Law Monthly Digest* to trace a case reported at any time during the year. (This list of cases brings the information in the *Current Law Case Citators* up to date (3–16).)

The *Current Law Monthly Digest* also contains a subject index. Again it is cumulative, so it is only necessary to consult the index in the latest month's issue. This enables you to trace any development in the law during the current year. The reference given, e.g. Feb 80, is to the appropriate monthly issue (in this example, the February issue) and the item number in the issue, i.e. item 80. If the reference is followed by an S (e.g. Jan 821S), the item contains Scottish material.

The Table of Cases provides a list of reports of cases. Suppose, however, that you know that there has been a recent case on the subject but you do not know the name of the parties. In this instance, you can trace the cases on the subject during the current year by looking in the cumulative Subject Index in the latest issue of the *Current Law Monthly Digest*. The Subject Index can also help when you have spelt the name of the parties incorrectly or have an incomplete reference.

Example Page from Current Law Monthly Digest

UK, England & Wales & EU

LEGAL ADVICE AND FUNDING

356. CLS funding–funding–third parties–entitlement to costs where assisted litigant in receipt of private funding

[Civil Legal Aid (General) Regulations 1989 (SI 1989) Reg.64.]

The appellant (S) appealed against a refusal to make a costs order in his favour in respect of the hearing of a preliminary issue decided in S's favour. S had had the benefit of a civil legal aid certificate but had received private funds from a third party (M) to fund the proceedings on the preliminary issue, as he believed the legal aid certificate did not cover those proceedings. The judge had found that the legal aid certificate did cover the proceedings; thus the receipt of private funds was contrary to the Civil Legal Aid (General) Regulations 1989 Reg.64. The judge then refused to make a costs order in S's favour because any costs ordered to be paid by the respondent (P) would in turn be paid out to M since the Legal Services Commission had incurred no liability to S's solicitors. S contended that the fact that a third party had agreed to fund a litigant's costs was irrelevant to any question of costs provided that the successful litigant remained liable to pay those costs.

Held, allowing the appeal, that the judge had been wrong to decide that any costs which P was ordered to pay would be paid to M. The finding that the legal aid certificate covered the proceedings led inevitably to a conclusion that S's solicitors would have to pay any costs they received from P to the Legal Aid Board. Furthermore, a breach of Reg.64 did not automatically preclude S from being awarded his costs. Although the appeal court should be slow to interfere with the exercise of a discretion not to award costs, where that exercise had been erroneously conducted the decision could not stand. Given the fact that the breach of Reg.64 was not conscious or deliberate, the refusal to award S costs was neither just nor proportionate.

STACY v. PLAYER; *sub nom*. STACEY v. PLAYER, [2004] EWCA Civ 241, [2004] 4 Costs L.R. 585, Lord Phillips of Worth Matravers, M.R., CA.

357. Legal services–asylum and immigration appeals–appellants costs

COMMUNITY LEGAL SERVICE (ASYLUM AND IMMIGRATION APPEALS) REGULATIONS 2005, SI 2005 966; made under the Nationality, Immigration and Asylum Act 2002 s.103D. In force: April 4, 2005; £3.00.

These Regulations make provision about the exercise of powers in the Nationality, Immigration and Asylum Act 2002 s.103D (1) (3) for the High Court or the Asylum and Immigration Tribunal to order payment of an appellant's costs out of the Community Legal Service Fund. These Regulations give effect to a special legal aid scheme for applications under s.103A of the 2002 Act by an appellant for a review of the Tribunal's decision on an asylum or immigration appeal, and proceedings for the reconsideration by the Tribunal of its decision following an order made on such an application, under which the High Court or the Tribunal decides when it determines an application or reconsiders an appeal whether to order the payment out of the Fund of costs incurred by the appellant's legal representative.

358. Legal services–Community Legal Service–persons subject to control orders

COMMUNITY LEGAL SERVICE (FINANCIAL) (AMENDMENT NO.2) REGULATIONS 2005, SI 2005 1097; made under the Access to Justice Act 1999 s.7. In force: in accordance with Reg.1; £3.00.

These Regulations amend the Community Legal Service (Financial) Regulations 2000 (SI 2000 516) to make legal help and representation under the Community Legal Service available to a person subject to a control order under the Prevention of Terrorism Act 2005 without reference to the person's financial resources.

359. Articles

At breaking point *(Rohan, Paula)*: L.S.G. 2005, 102(18), 16-18. Examines the opposition by legal aid firms to competitive tendering in crime work, in light of

How to use the Current Law Year Books

7–13   The issues of the *Current Law Monthly Digest* are replaced by an annual volume, the *Current Law Year Book.*

The *Year Book* is arranged by subject, in the same way as the *Monthly Digest,* and contains a summary of all the cases, legislation and other developments in that subject during the year. Lists of journal articles and books written on a subject during the year are printed at the back of the volume. (The 1956 *Year Book* contains a list of journal articles published between 1947 and 1956.)

Since 1991, the *Current Law Year Book* contains Scottish material as well as that from England. Before then, there was a separate Scottish version, called the *Scottish Current Law Year Book,* Despite the name, this included all the English material, plus a separate section at the back of the volume containing Scottish developments during the year. The Scottish section remains separate from the English material in the *Current Law Year Book* and there are separate indexes to the two sections.

At the back of the 1976 *Year Book,* there is a Subject Index to all the entries in all the *Year Books* from 1947 to 1976. Entries give the last two digits of the year, and a reference to the individual item number within that year's volume, e.g. 69/3260 is a reference to item 3260 in the 1969 *Year Book.* Entries which have no year in front of them will be found in the *Current Law Consolidation 1947–1951.* Cumulative indexes were also published in the 1986 and 1989 *Year Books.* These indexes, together with the *Year Books* since 1989 and the latest *Current Law Monthly Digest,* provide complete coverage of any developments in the law of that subject since 1947.

Master Volumes were published in the 1956, 1961, 1966 and 1971 *Year Books.* These volumes contain, under the usual subject headings, detailed entries for all developments during the year in which they were published, together with a summary of the developments during the previous four years. References are given to enable you to trace the full details in the appropriate *Current Law Year Book.* Thus it is possible, by using the *Master Volumes* and the *Current Law Consolidation 1947–1951,* to see at a glance a summary of every entry that has appeared in *Current Law* on a particular subject over a five-year period.

Summary: How to Use Current Law in Print

(1) If you know the name of a case and want to find out where it has been reported and whether the case has subsequently been judicially considered, consult:
the *Current Law Case Citator* volumes (see **3–16**); and
the Table of Cases in the latest *Current Law Monthly Digest.*
(2) To trace any developments (cases, statutes, etc.) on a particular subject, consult:
The Cumulative Index covering 1947–1976 at the back of the 1976 *Current Law Year Book*;
the Cumulative Index at the back of the 1986 *Year Book* covering the years 1972–1986;
the Cumulative Index at the back of the 1989 *Year Book* covering the years 1987–1989;

the Indexes in the back of the *Year Books* since 1989; and

the Subject Index in the latest issue of the *Current Law Monthly Digest*.

(3) To obtain a general view of developments in a topic over a number of years, consult:

the *Current Law Consolidation 1947–1951*;

the *Master Volumes* (1956, 1961, 1966, 1971 *Year Books*);

all the *Year Books* published since the last *Master Volume* was issued; and

all the issues of the *Current Law Monthly Digest* for this year.

(4) To trace books and journal articles on a subject, look in the back of the 1956 *Year Book* and each subsequent *Year Book* and in the *Current Law Monthly Digests* under the appropriate subject heading. There are, however, quicker and more comprehensive sources for tracing journals (**5–5**) and books (**7–29** *et seq.*).

Remember that *Current Law* only contains information on cases reported or mentioned in court since 1947 and other developments in the law since 1947. To trace earlier cases, use *The Digest*.

The Digest

The Digest (formerly known as the *English and Empire Digest*) contains summaries of cases that have appeared in law reports from the thirteenth century to the present day, arranged in subject order. It enables you to trace cases of any date that deal with your particular subject. In addition to English cases, reports of Irish, Scottish and many Commonwealth cases are included, together with cases on European Communities law. These are printed in smaller type to enable them to be easily distinguishable from English cases.   **7–14**

For each case, a summary of the decision is given, followed by the name of the case, and a list of places where the case is reported. The subsequent judicial history of the case is also shown, in the annotations section. A list of the abbreviations used for law reports will be found in the front of Volume 1 and also in the front of the *Cumulative Supplement*.

How to use The Digest to trace cases on a subject

7–15

To find cases on a particular subject using *The Digest*, start by looking at the multi-volume *Index*. This is re-issued every year. The *Index* includes both broad subject categories and highly specific entries for particular subjects. These can take you directly to a summary of the judgment in a particular case. Suppose you are interested in the evidence needed to force a local authority to review a decision on the existence of a public right of way. Try looking under "footpath". In the *Index* you will find a reference to "Footpath—public—new evidence justifying a review" (see the illustration on page 124). The reference gives a volume number, notes the relevant subject heading within the volume, and adds a case number, e.g.

26(2) *Hghys* [i.e. Highways] 1392.

The reference could also have been found under "Public path".

Example Page from The Digest Index

Example Page from The Digest, Volume 26(2)

6 PUBLIC PATHS   Case **1393**

1389 Deletion of footpath from definitive map — Evidence

The Wildlife and Countryside Act 1981 s 53(5)*(c)*(iii) provides that as regards every definitive map and statement, the surveying authority must make such modifications to the map and statement as appear to be requisite in consequence of the discovery by the authority of evidence which, when considered with all other evidence available to it, shows that there is no public right of way over land shown on the map and statement as a highway of any description.

A footpath on the applicant's farm had been included as a public right of way on the definitive map compiled under the National Parks and Access to the Countryside Act 1949. The only evidence relating to the inclusion of the footpath on the map was the surveyor's record card which gave a detailed description of the footpath, but said nothing under the heading "Evidence of Right of Way". Some years later, the applicant applied to the council under the Wildlife and Countryside Act 1981 s 53(5) for the deletion of the footpath from the map. The application was refused and the National Assembly for Wales dismissed the applicant's appeal. On an application for judicial review of that decision: *Held* the National Assembly had erred in placing weight on the initial inclusion of the footpath on the definitive map, and on the absence of objection by the landowners through the years. The correct approach was to consider the evidence. Since s 53(5) specifically referred to evidence, there was no room for any assumptions or presumptions, and the question was therefore whether the evidence, assessed on the balance of probabilities, showed that there was no public right of way over the relevant land. On the facts of the instant case, the witness evidence was determinative and it had been shown, on the balance of probabilities, that the footpath was not a public right of way at the relevant date. The application would be allowed, accordingly.

R v National Assembly for Wales, Ex p Robinson (2000) 80 P & CR 348

1390 Byways — Reclassification by surveying authority — Quality of objections

It has been held that a surveying authority is not entitled to ignore an objection to its own order reclassifying a path under the Wildlife and Countryside Act 1981 s 54 on the grounds that the objection was based on legally irrelevant factors. Once an objection has been duly made a surveying authority has to submit the order to the Secretary of State for confirmation.

Lasham Parish Meeting v Hampshire County Council (1992) 91 LGR 209; 65 P & CR 331; [1993] COD 42; [1993] JPL 841; (1992) Times, 7 September

1391 Footpaths — Reclassification by surveying authority — Duties when modifying the definitive map

A surveying authority reclassified three footpaths as byways open to all traffic. On appeal against the order the appellant contended that the surveying authority had ignored the byways' unsuitability for vehicular traffic: *Held* in deciding whether to reclassify a footpath as a byway open to all traffic, under the Wildlife and Countryside Act 1981, a surveying authority was entitled to consider only whether vehicular rights existed along a footpath and were not obliged to consider the desirability or suitability of such a reclassification. A surveying authority's duty under the 1981 Act was solely to ascertain public rights of way and to modify the definitive map so that it correctly defined those rights. Accordingly, the appeal would be dismissed.

Mayhew v Secretary of State for the Environment (1992) 65 P & CR 344; [1993] COD 45; [1993] JPL 831; (1992) Times, 17 September

1392 Public path — New evidence justifying review   ◄——

The Wildlife and Countryside Act 1981 s 53(3)*(c)*(i) states that a local authority must make modifications to its definitive map and statement when it discovers evidence which shows that a right of way subsists.

The applicants applied for judicial review of the Secretary of State's decisions refusing to order their respective local authorities to modify their definitive maps so as to add, respectively, a public footpath, and a byway open to all traffic: *Held* it was for the local authority, in the first instance, and then the Secretary of State to decide whether it was reasonable for a claimant to allege that a right of way existed. The Secretary of State's decision was final, subject to common law principles of unreasonableness. The evidence necessary to establish that a right of way was reasonably alleged to subsist was less than that necessary to establish that such a right did, in fact, subsist. Once such a finding had been made, it was always possible for some form of further inquiry to take place to confirm or overrule that finding. Accordingly, the applications would be granted.

R v Secretary of State for the Environment, Ex p Bagshaw; R v Same, Ex p Norton (1994) 68 P & CR 402; (1994) Times, 6 May

1393 Public path — Reclassification as byway open to all traffic — Consideration of hardship — New evidence justifying review

A track was classified in the local definitive map in one section as a "road used as a public path" and in another as a bridleway. The authority proposed to reclassify both sections as a byway open to all traffic. At the inquiry, objectors to the reclassification con-

In the main volumes, cases are listed in number order for the volume under appropriate subject headings (see the illustration on page 125 for the entry for case 1392). Scots, Irish and Commonwealth cases are grouped together at the end of each section within the volume.

One consequence of putting the cases in number order is that case numbers change when a volume is reissued. This is because additional cases have been inserted into the sequence. In the back of each volume of *The Digest* is a Reference Adaptor. Wherever you find a cross-reference to a volume which has been reissued very recently, you need to look in the volume's Reference Adaptor to convert the reference. The Reference Adaptor consists of a long list of all the case numbers in the old volume, alongside the number which replaces it in the reissued volume.

After finding the relevant cases on your subject in the main volumes, you should check to see if there have been more recent cases on the subject since the volume was written. To do this update, you must consult the *Cumulative Supplement*. Make a note of the volume number, subject heading and case number(s) in the main volumes which contain relevant information. Now turn to the *Cumulative Supplement* and look to see if there is an entry for that volume, subject heading and case number. If there is an entry, this will provide information on a later case, in which the case you were consulting in the main works has been referred to, considered, overruled, etc. (A full list of the abbreviations used and their meanings appears at the front of the *Cumulative Supplement*, under the heading "Meaning of the terms used in classifying annotating cases.") The following entry is found for case 1392:

> 1392 Consd Todd and another v Secretary of State for the Environment
> [2004] 4 All ER 497.

This means that case 1392 in the main volumes has subsequently been considered in the 2004 case of *Todd and another v Secretary of State for the Environment* (see p. 127).

The *Cumulative Supplement* also includes references to new cases and a summary is provided. The system of numbering the new cases in the *Cumulative Supplement* corresponds to that in the main volumes. The small letter after the number shows that the case follows on naturally from the similarly numbered case in the volumes.

The *Cumulative Supplement* is revised annually; the front cover tells you how recent the information is. If you are looking for new cases on a particular subject, within the last few months, then *The Digest* is not sufficiently up to date and you should use online sources (7–8) or print publications, such as *Current Law*, the latest *Pink Index* to the *Law Reports* or the *Monthly Reviews* in *Halsbury's Laws of England*.

Summary: Tracing Cases on a Subject in The Digest

1. Look up the subject in the *Index*. This will refer you to the volume, subject heading and case numbers where cases on that subject can be found.
2. To see if there have been any more recent cases on the same subject, look in the *Cumulative Supplement* under the relevant volume, subject heading and case number. This will provide you with up-to-date information.

Example Page from the Digest Cumulative Supplement

Vol 26(2) — HIGHWAYS, STREETS AND BRIDGES   168

(2) The existence of the broad public duty in s 39 of the 1988 Act did not generate a common law duty of care and thus a private law right of action. A common law duty to act could not be imposed upon a local authority based solely on the existence of a broad public law duty. It was in the public interest that local authorities should take steps to promote road safety, but that did not require a private law duty to a careless driver or to any other road user. Accordingly, the appeal would be dismissed.

Gorringe v Calderdale Metropolitan Borough Council [2004] UKHL 15; [2004] 2 All ER 326; [2004] 1 WLR 1057; [2004] RTR 443; 148 Sol Jo LB 419; [2004] All ER (D) 06 (Apr); (2004) Times, 2 April, HL

906 Apld Gorringe v Calderdale Metropolitan Borough Council [2004] 2 All ER 326

1022 Apld Gorringe v Calderdale Metropolitan Borough Council [2004] 2 All ER 326

Part 6 — PUBLIC PATHS

1379 Consd Todd and another v Secretary of State for the Environment, Food and Rural Affairs [2004] 4 All ER 497

1380 Apld (dictum Sullivan J) R (on the appln of Godmanchester Town Council) v Secretary of State for Environment, Food and Rural Affairs; R (on the appln of Drain) v Secretary of State for Environment, Food and Rural Affairs [2004] 4 All ER 342

1392 Consd Todd and another v Secretary of State for the Environment, Food and Rural Affairs [2004] 4 All ER 497

Part 7 — IMPROVEMENT OF HIGHWAYS

1429 Critsd (dictum Lord Woolf CJ) Gorringe v Calderdale Metropolitan Borough Council [2004] 2 All ER 326

Part 8 — PROTECTION OF HIGHWAYS

1821 Apld Gorringe v Calderdale Metropolitan Borough Council [2004] 2 All ER 326

1855 Overd Bakewell Management Ltd v Brandwood and others [2004] 2 All ER 305

Part 9 — STATUTORY WORKS IN HIGHWAYS

2 Street works under the New Roads and Street Works Act 1991

A1980 Street works — Execution of works by highway authority affecting apparatus of utility undertaker — Costs of measures needing to be taken in relation to apparatus in consequence of works — What costs allowable

The defendant local authority proposed to undertake major bridge works which potentially involved moving part of the claimant utility undertaker's apparatus. In such circumstances s 84(1) of the New Roads and Street Works Act 1991 imposed a duty on the authority and the undertaker inter alia to take such steps as were reasonably required to identify any measures needing to be taken in relation to the apparatus in consequence of the execution of the authority's works, and to settle a specification of the necessary measures. Section 85(1) of the 1991 Act provided that the 'allowable costs' of measures needing to be taken in relation to the undertaker's apparatus affected by major works were to be borne by the authority and the undertaker in such manner as might be prescribed, and reg 2(2) of the Street Works (Sharing of Costs of Works) Regulations 1992 defined 'allowable costs' as all the reasonable costs of the measures needed to be taken for the purpose specified in s 84(1) of the 1991 Act, except costs incurred 'in preparing the initial set of plans and estimates in relation to those measures (but not in preparing any further plans and estimates which the authority may require)'. In the procedures for the necessary measures in relation to the undertaker's apparatus, the parties followed the code of practice approved by the relevant Secretaries of State under the 1991 Act. Appendix C of the code of practice identified seven basic stages in the procedures for necessary measures in relation to undertakers' apparatus. Stage C2 was preliminary inquiries. Stage C3 dealt with draft schemes and budget estimates and stage C4 dealt with the final detailed scheme and detailed estimates. At stage C3 the authority wrote to the undertaker with copies of the draft scheme plans and sought preliminary details of the effect on the undertaker's apparatus and budget estimates. Those the undertaker provided. The authority then produced its final detailed scheme and detailed estimates, stated to be pursuant to C4, and the undertaker produced its stage C4 'detailed client estimate'. It also sent its invoice for the preparation of the C4 estimate, but the authority refused to pay its share, on the basis that the cost of the estimate was not an allowable cost under reg 2(2) of the 1992 regulations, being still part of the preliminary planning and liaison stages. The undertaker was successful in proceedings it brought against the authority in the county court and the authority appealed, contending, inter alia, that 'allowable costs' related only

How to use individual indexes to series of Law Reports to trace cases on a subject

7–16   If the facilities in your library are limited, you may need to use the indexes to individual series of law reports to trace relevant cases on a subject. The most useful is the *Law Reports Index* (**3–18**) because it covers a number of other important series in addition to the *Law Reports*. Indexes are available covering each 10-year period since 1951 and supplementary indexes (an annual *Red Index* and the latest *Pink Index*: **3–18**) bring the information up to date to within a few weeks. The *Law Reports Index* is easier to use than *The Digest*, but remember that it covers fewer series of English law reports and no foreign cases.

In addition to the *Law Reports Index* (and the series of *Digests*, which preceded it, going back to 1865) there are indexes to other series, such as the *All England Law Reports*, which have a *Consolidated Tables and Index* in three volumes, covering 1937–1992. This is kept up to date by supplements (**3–18**). In addition, there is an *Index* volume to the *All England Law Reports Reprint*, which includes a subject index to selected cases from 1558–1935.

Finding updates on recent cases by subject

7–17   Summaries of recent cases by subject can be found using the updating services described in **3–22**. The *All England Reporter* database provides summaries of a wide range of recent judgments under legal practice subject headings ("Banking", "Civil Procedure" etc.). Only some are later reported in the *All England Law Reports*. The *WLR Daily* service uses similar subject headings, but is more selective. Summaries are only provided of judgments that will later be reported in the *Weekly Law Reports*.

The Westlaw UK *Case Locators* database (**3–15**) can be used to find updates on recent reported cases. Searches can be limited to recent cases and subject keywords entered. These are the updates on reported cases found in print in the *Current Law Monthly Digest* (**7–12**).

Newspaper reports of recent cases in a particular subject area can be found using the current awareness databases provided by both LexisNexis Professional and Westlaw UK (see **5–22**). The full text of newspaper law reports (and other legal news items) can be found using the "My Practice Areas" section of the LexisNexis Professional current awareness page. Notes of newspaper reports, along with notes of press releases and other legal news items, can be found in the "Browse by Legal Subject" section of the Westlaw UK current awareness page.

Tracing the Subsequent Judicial History of a Case

7–18   Judges often rely on earlier cases to support the reasons they have given for a decision, and from time to time a judge will review the case law in an attempt to explain the principles stated in earlier cases, or to use them as a springboard to create a new application of the principles. Occasionally a case will be "distinguished" in order that the judge will not feel obliged to follow it. Less frequently, a superior court will state that an earlier case was wrongly decided, and will overrule it, so that the principles laid down in the case will not be followed thereafter.

The treatment a case receives when it is subsequently judicially considered has a direct bearing on its importance and reliability. For example, if in an essay you cited as an authority the common law rules laid down in a particular case, you would be embarrassed to discover that the rules were later abolished by statute. Similarly, you should check that a particular case you have referred to, e.g. *Gillick v West Norfolk and Wisbech AHA* [1984] 1 All E.R. 365, was not later reversed on appeal to the House of Lords, as happened in *Gillick v West Norfolk and Wisbech AHA* [1985] 1 All E.R. 533. Consequently, you must be alert to the need to trace the full judicial history of a particular case.

The simplest way to do this is to use the Westlaw UK *Case Locators* database (**3–15**). The well-known old case *Carlill v Carbolic Smoke Ball Co.*, for example, can be found in the *Case Locators* database because it has been considered several times since 1947 (the case itself dates from 1893). The "History of the Case" section of the *Case Locators* results page for *Carlill v Carbolic Smoke Ball Co.* shows that the decision in the case has been most recently applied by *Bowerman v Association of British Travel Agents Ltd* [1996] C.L.C. 451. It was also distinguished in *Pharmaceutical Society of Great Britain v Boots Cash Chemist (Southern) Ltd* [1952] 2 Q.B. 795. The most recent case to consider *Carlill* was *Bardissy v D'Souza* [2003] W.T.L.R. 929. The "History of the Case" links suggests, in other words, that the case is still of relevance. The *Case Locators* result also gives a citation for a 2005 journal article in "Case Comments" which discusses the case in the context of in-house lawyers, marketing and misleading advertising.

If you were using the print volumes of the *Current Law Case Citator* the same information could be traced by checking first the volume covering 1947 to 1976. This gives page and volume numbers to entries in the *Current Law Year Book* after the case citations. These enable you to check the *Year Book* summaries for cases which have applied, approved, distinguished or considered the *Carlill* case between 1947 and 1976. Subsequent volumes of the *Current Law Case Citator* then need to be checked in order to discover *Year Book* summaries of the 1996 and 2003 cases mentioned earlier.

How to Find Words and Phrases Judicially Considered

The meaning of words is of great importance to lawyers. The interpretation of statutes and **7–19** documents may hinge upon the meaning of a single word. For example, does "day" in banking terms mean 24 hours, or does it end at the close of working hours? How should the words "on a road" be interpreted in the Road Traffic Act 1988?

Two specialised dictionaries record the courts' decisions on problems such as these. *Stroud's Judicial Dictionary* provides the meaning of words as defined in the case law and in statutes. *Words and Phrases Legally Defined* is a similar publication; both are kept up to date by supplements.

The *Law Reports Index* includes a heading "Words and Phrases", in which full details of cases defining a particular word or phrase are given (see the figure on p. 130).

Example Page of Entries under "Words and Phrases" in the Law Reports Cumulative Index—the "Pink Index"

The Weekly Law Reports   29 April 2005

Subject Matter

45

WORDS AND PHRASES—*continued*

"Application for membership"—Disability Discrimination Act 1995, s 13(1)(b)
Higham v Horton, CA [2005] ICR 292

"Been declared bankrupt, been the subject of bankruptcy proceedings or made any arrangement with creditors"—Insurance proposal form
Doheny v New India Assurance Co Ltd, CA [2005] 1 All ER (Comm) 382

"Bill of lading or any similar document of title"—Carriage of Goods by Sea Act 1971, s 1(4)
J I MacWilliam Co Inc v Mediterranean Shipping Co SA, HL(E) [2005] 2 WLR 554

"Conduct"—Extradition Act 2003, s 65
Office of the King's Prosecutor, Brussels v Cando Armas, DC [2005] 1 WLR 1389

"Confession"—Police and Criminal Evidence Act 1984, s 82(1)
R v Z, HL(E) [2005] 2 WLR 709

"Deliberately"—Exclusion clause
Tektrol Ltd (formerly Atto Power Controls Ltd) v International Insurance Co of Hanover Ltd, [2005] 1 All ER (Comm) 132

"Designated by conflicts rules"—Recognition of Trusts Act 1987, Sch, art 15
C v C (Ancillary Relief: Nuptial Settlement), CA [2005] Fam 250; [2005] 2 WLR 241

"Determination . . . of civil rights and obligations"—Human Rights Act 1998, Sch 1, Pt I, art 6(1)
R (West) v Parole Board, HL(E) [2005] 1 WLR 350

"Determination . . . of . . . criminal charge"—Human Rights Act 1998, Sch 1, Pt I, art 6(1)
R (West) v Parole Board, HL(E) [2005] 1 WLR 350

"Disclose"—Social Security Administration Act 1992, s 71(1)
Hinchy v Secretary of State for Work and Pensions, HL(E) [2005] 1 WLR 967

"Dismissing"—Disability Discrimination Act 1995, s 4(2)(d)
Meikle v Nottinghamshire County Council, CA [2005] ICR 1

"Earnings"—Child Support (Maintenance Assessments and Special Cases) Regulations 1992, Sch 1, para 2A (as inserted)
Smith v Smith, CA [2005] 1 WLR 1318

"Enumerated"—Carriage of Goods by Sea Act 1991, Sch 1A (as inserted), art 4, r 5(c) (Australia)
El Greco (Australia) Pty Ltd v Mediterranean Shipping Co SA, Federal Court of Australia [2004] 2 Lloyd's Rep 537

"Establishment"—Care Standards Act 2000, s 3
R (Moore) v Care Standards Tribunal, Mitting J [2005] LGR 179

"Family life"—Human Rights Act 1998, Sch 1, Pt I, art 8(1)
Pawandeep Singh v Entry Clearance Officer, New Delhi, CA [2005] 2 WLR 325

"For any and all other amounts . . . alleged to be for charterers' account"—Charterparty
Odfjfell Seachem A/S v Continentale des Petroles et d'Investissements, Nigel Teare QC [2005] 1 All ER (Comm) 421; [2005] 1 Lloyd's Rep 275

"For the benefit"—Children Act 1989, Sch 1, para 1(2)
In re S (A Child) (Financial Provision), CA [2005] 2 WLR 895

"Good faith"—Employment Rights Act 1996, s 43G(1)(a) (as inserted)
Street v Derbyshire Unemployed Workers' Centre, CA [2005] ICR 97

"Gross amount of the total sales"—Lease
Debenhams Retail plc v Sun Alliance & London Assurance Co Ltd, Etherton J [2005] STC 171

"Grounds for mitigating the normal consequences of the conviction"—Road Traffic Offenders Act 1988, s 35(1)
Miller v Director of Public Prosecutions, Richards J [2005] RTR 44

"Held by the insured in trust for which the insured is responsible"—Insurance policy
Ramco (UK) Ltd v International Insurance Co of Hanover Ltd, CA [2004] 2 All ER (Comm) 866; [2004] 2 Lloyd's Rep 595

"In accordance with law"—Human Rights Act 1998, Sch 1, Pt I, art 8(2)
R (Kent Pharmaceuticals Ltd) v Director of the Serious Fraud Office, CA [2005] 1 WLR 1302

"Incidental transactions"—Council Directive 77/388/EEC, art 19(2)
Empresa de Desenvolvimento Mineiro SGPS SA (EDM) v Fazenda Pública (Ministério Público intervening), ECJ [2005] STC 65

"Judgment"—Civil Liability (Contribution) Act 1978, s 1(5)
Moy v Pettman Smith, HL(E) [2005] 1 WLR 581

"Judgment"—Convention on Jurisdiction and the Enforcement of Judgments in Civil and Commercial Matters 1968 (as amended), art 25
Mærsk Olie & Gas A/S v Firma M de Haan (Case C-39/02), ECJ [2005] 1 Lloyd's Rep 210

"Modify"—Pensions Act 1995, s 67
Aon Trust Corpn v KPMG, Sir Andrew Morritt V-C [2005] 1 WLR 995

"Money purchase scheme"—Pensions Act 1995, s 56(2)(a)
Aon Trust Corpn v KPMG, Sir Andrew Morritt V-C [2005] 1 WLR 995

"Necessarily incurred"—Child Support (Maintenance Assessments and Special Cases) Regulations 1992, Sch 3, para 4(1)(a)
Pabari v Secretary of State for Work and Pensions, CA [2005] 1 All ER 287

"Of . . . individual concern"—EC Treaty, art 230 EC
Jégo-Quéré & Cie SA v Commission of the European Communities (Case C-263/02P), ECJ [2005] QB 237; [2005] 2 WLR 179

"On a road"—Road Traffic Act 1988, ss 5(1)(a), 103(1) (as substituted)
Brewer v Director of Public Prosecutions, DC [2005] RTR 66

"Orders"—Employment Tribunals (Constitution and Rules of Procedure) Regulations 2004, Sch 1, r 10
Onwuka v Spherion Technology UK Ltd, EAT [2005] ICR 567

"Overthrowing lawful authority"—Prison Security Act 1992, s 1(2)
R v Mason, CA [2005] 1 Cr App R 145

(Reproduced by permission of the Incorporated Council of Law Reporting for England and Wales.)

The *Current Law Monthly Digests* and *Year Books* also include an entry "Words and Phrases" and the *Index* to the *All England Law Reports* and the *Consolidated Index* to *Halsbury's Laws* have a similar heading.

How to Trace Statutes on a Subject

Full-text databases (**7–21**);   **7–20**
Other online sources (**7–22**);
Halsbury's Statutes of England (**7–23**);
Current Law (**7–24**).

How to use full-text databases of legislation

The LexisNexis Butterworths *UK Parliament Acts* database (**4–13**), the LexisNexis   **7–21**
Professional *UK Legislation* database (**4–14**) and the *UK Legislation* database from Westlaw UK (**4–15**) can all be used to trace statutes in force by subject. The Justis *UK Statutes* database (**4–9**) adds the ability to search for statutes no longer in force.

Subject searching these databases works best, however, when you already know the wording of a section of an Act, or of a phrase unique to a piece of legislation; there are no added keywords or subject links that might help guide you to a piece of legislation. As a result the advice given in section **7–10**, on keyword searching full text case law databases, remains valid when searching the legislation databases. It makes sense to turn to textbooks and other secondary searches first if you are taking a subject approach to legislation, in order to have a firm grasp of the key terms before you make use of legislation databases.

SEARCH TIP

Place phrases in quotation marks when searching Westlaw UK, otherwise your search will find sections of Acts in which the search words appear, but not necessarily next to each other. LexisNexis databases treat consecutive words as phrases.

Suppose, for example, you are reviewing the legislation in force on an aspect of insolvency law. Simply typing "insolvency" into the search box of a legislation database will lead—if the database allows this—to pages and pages of "hits" being displayed on your results screen. Remember that these databases list their results section by section, so all the sections of Acts that feature the word "insolvency" will be displayed.

However, you may have clarified in advance that it is administration orders that interest you, and more specifically, how they are made. In this case, if you are using the LexisNexis Professional *UK Legislation* database for example, put "insolvency" in the title search box (this searches Acts with "insolvency" in the title) and combine this with the words "administration order" in the "Text" search box. The entry in the "Source" box can also be changed so that only statutes are searched and not both statutes and statutory instruments. Your search then finds 17 separate sections of two different insolvency acts which contain the words "administration orders". Most are drawn from the Insolvency Act 1986, some from later amending legislation (the Insolvency Act 2000). Scrolling down the results list, you come across Part II, section 9 "Application for an Order". Following the relevant link allows you to view the full amended text of the section, incorporating, as it does, amendments from the Access to Justice Act 1999 and other legislation.

A similar search can be made using the *UK Legislation* database on Westlaw UK. Enter "administration order" in the "Terms" search box and "insolvency" in the "Act or SI Name" box. It is important when using Westlaw UK to enclose the search phrase ("administration order") in quotes, to ensure that the database search treats the two words as a phrase. Considerably more results hits are found using Westlaw UK, as the *UK Legislation* quick search does not allow statutes to be specified as a source. It searches both statutes and statutory instruments. Limiting the search to statutes requires the use of the Westlaw UK directory pages to specify a source directory.

If you do not have access to a subscription database of legislation, the statutes held on the OPSI website (**4–6**) provide an alternative source of legislation for subject keyword searching. Remember, that the database only covers legislation from 1988 onwards, and that Acts appear in their original unamended form. Keyword searching is possible using the "Advanced Search" available on the legislation pages (at *www.opsi.gov.uk/legislation*). Your search can be restricted to Acts and both insolvency and administration orders can be entered as keywords. The relevance ranking used by the OPSI advanced search places legislation in which the keywords are close together at the top of the results list. A particular problem for the search on insolvency legislation, however, is that Northern Ireland legislation is included in the OPSI Acts search. This means that search results are dominated by references to the Insolvency (Northern Ireland) Order 1989. Over 200 results are found in total. References to the Insolvency Act 2000 will be found, amending the Insolvency Act 1986, but the 1986 Act will not be included, as it predates the 1988 start date of the database.

The BAILII databases (at *www.bailii.org*) allows more conventional database searching from its UK Legislation pages, but coverage does not extend beyond that of the OPSI website. Again, legislation is provided in its unamended form. The BAILII website does, though, allow a search to be restricted to UK statutes.

Other online sources for tracing legislation by subject

7–22   Catalogues of official publications offer an alternative to full text databases of legislation for tracing legislation by subject. The TSO bookshop catalogue (**6–15**) enables statutes to be searched by title keyword and the "Advanced Search" allows searches to be restricted to Acts. Using the *UKOP* database (**6–16**) "Flexible Search" widens the range of subject searching, as the *UKOP* thesaurus enables results to be found using both the search words you have entered and alternative, closely related, terms.

Another approach to legislation searching using Westlaw UK, is to select the *UK Legislation Locators* database (**4–18**). This is not a full text database, and searches are only made on the titles of Acts and sections of Acts. Despite the name, however, the strength of the database lies in its ability to track changes to legislation and provide links to related case law. It is of less use when searching for legislation using keywords. Similar considerations apply to search for statutes using Lawtel (**2–6**).

Halsbury's Statutes of England

Halsbury's Statutes provides the amended text of legislation which is still in force, along   **7–23**
with annotations detailing, for example, statutory instruments made under the Act, case
law, judicial interpretation of words and phrases and references to relevant sections of
Halsbury's Laws.

The 50 volumes of the main work are arranged alphabetically by broad subject areas. Acts
dealing with agriculture, for example, are found in Volume 1, whereas statutes on the subject
of wills are found in Volume 50.

The annual *Table of Statutes and General Index* provides a comprehensive subject
index to the volumes to enable you to find statutes on a particular topic. The Index will refer
you to the appropriate *volume* and *page* number. In the *Table of Statutes and General
Index* volume there is a separate subject index to the *Current Statutes Service*, which
contains those Acts that were passed after the main volumes were issued. If you are
looking for the latest Acts on a particular subject, look also in the subject index at the front
of the looseleaf Volume 1 of the *Current Statutes Service*. This indexes the material that
has been added to the *Service* since the annual *Table of Statutes and General Index* was
published.

Once you have identified those Acts which are of relevance to you, it is essential to consult
both the *Cumulative Supplement* and the *Noter-Up* to see if there have been any changes in
the law. An explanation of how to do this, along with further details of *Halsbury's Statutes*,
can be found at **4–17**.

Other print sources for tracing legislation on a subject

Halsbury's Laws (**7–3**) contains references to relevant statutes, although the text of the   **7–24**
Acts is not printed. The *Current Law Monthly Digests* and *Year Books* (**7–12** and **7–13**)
are arranged by subject and include entries for new statutes and statutory instruments as
well as for cases on a subject. A brief summary appears under the appropriate subject
heading.

How to Trace Statutory Instruments on a Subject

Statutory instruments on a particular subject can be traced by consulting: **7–25**

Online sources (**7–26**);
Halsbury's Statutory Instruments (**7–27**).

For an explanation of the nature and purpose of statutory instruments, refer back to **4–26**.

Online sources for tracing statutory instruments

7–26   The full-text databases of legislation noted in **7–21** all provide access to statutory instruments. The considerations relevant to searching for statutory instruments are consequently much the same. The LexisNexis Professional *UK Legislation* database (**4–14**) is a useful starting point for searching for statutory instruments, as the database source can be limited so that only statutory instruments are searched. In Westlaw UK, the standard *UK Legislation* database search includes both statutes and statutory instruments (see **4–15**). Both LexisNexis Professional and Westlaw UK contain statutory instruments in force. The Justis *UK Statutory Instruments* database contains the full text of all statutory instruments from 1987 onwards, and a further archive database contains statutory instruments published between 1671 and 1986. However, only a few libraries are likely to subscribe to the archive.

The OPSI website "Advanced Search" can be used to provide an alternative approach to searching for statutory instruments and key search considerations are as noted in **7–21**. The search can be found from the legislation page (at *www.opsi.gov.uk/legislation*). Coverage begins in 1987 and searches can be restricted so that only statutory instruments are retrieved. The BAILII database (at *www.bailii.org*) provides an additional non-subscription source.

Halsbury's Statutory Instruments

7–27   *Halsbury's Statutory Instruments* is a series which covers every statutory instrument of general application in force in England and Wales. It reproduces the text of a selected number and provides summaries of others. The series is arranged alphabetically by subject and is kept up to date by a *Service* binder containing notes of changes in the law and the text of selected new instruments. A full description of the work can be found in **4–29**.

If you are looking for statutory instruments dealing with a particular subject, you should start by looking up your subject in the *Consolidated Index*. This paperback volume is issued annually and indexes the contents of all the main volumes. The entries give you the volume number (in **bold** type) and page number in the main work and the number of the statutory instrument (in brackets).

Occasionally you will find that the volume to which you are referred has been reissued since the latest *Consolidated Index* was published. The references from the *Consolidated Index* will no longer be correct and in this case you will need to refer to the subject index at the back of the new volume.

Once you have traced the relevant statutory instruments on your subject in the main volumes, it is important to turn to the *Service* binder to find out if the information you have traced is still up to date. To do this, turn to the *Monthly Survey* section of the *Service* binder and look up the relevant subject title. This shows new statutory instruments which have appeared since the main volume was compiled. It tells you which statutory instruments printed in the main volumes are no longer law and provides you with a page-by-page guide to changes made since the main volume was published.

Summary: How to Use Halsbury's Statutory Instruments to Find Information on a Subject

1. Consult the *Consolidated Index*. This tells you the volume, page number and statutory instrument numbers you require.
2. To check if there have been any changes in the law, look in the *Monthly Survey* pages of the *Service* binder.

Tracing recent statutory instruments

The OPSI legislation site (at *www.opsi.gov.uk/legislation*) lists statutory instruments in   **7–28** number order making it possible to check for the most recent statutory instruments added to the site. If you suspect that a statutory instrument is very recent, it might also be convenient to check entries in the TSO *Daily List* (**6–15**), available both online and in print. The print *Current Law Monthly Digest* has the advantage of listing relatively recent statutory instruments under subject headings.

All draft statutory instruments awaiting approval are also published in full text on the OPSI legislation website and they remain on the site until they are superseded by a statutory instrument, or, in some cases, until they are withdrawn.

Finding Books on a Subject

Your first task is to find out what suitable books are available in your own library. Start with   **7–29** your library catalogue. All catalogues allow you to search for keywords in the titles of books. This means you can search for title words that match your subject. A keyword search on "negligence", for example, picks up the titles "Introduction to negligence", "The law of negligence" and so on. If you do not find books on your subject, try some alternative headings or look under a more general, or a more specific subject. Negligence, for instance, is part of the law of torts and there will be a chapter on negligence in all general textbooks on the law of torts.

Many library catalogues also have a subject search. This acts as an index to the classification scheme. If you enter the word "negligence" using a subject search you are shown the classification number (or classmark) for books on negligence. The catalogue then links you to a list of books sharing that classmark. Such a subject search is a more systematic approach to searching the catalogue, as the books listed represent all the books in the library which share a common subject. If you searched on "negligence", you see a list of the general works on negligence, whether or not they have the word negligence in the title. Using a subject search is of particular help if you want to find books on a specific aspect of a subject, and are not sure where the classification scheme places the books on the library shelves. For medical negligence, for example, a subject search of this kind leads you to a classification which places books on medical negligence with other books on medical law, often some distance away from the general textbooks on negligence.

If your library catalogue does not have a subject search of this kind, an alternative approach is to search for keywords in book titles and note the classmark of a book that matches your subject interest, even if that book might be hopelessly out of date. Most computerised catalogues enable you to search by classmark. You can then find a list of the books on a subject, usually showing the most recent first.

Remember also that footnotes and bibliographies (lists of books) in textbooks and journal articles refer you to other books, journals and cases on a subject. Check in the library catalogue to find out if these are available in your library. Government reports on a subject may not be entered, and you need to make use of other catalogues and indexes to trace these publications (see **6–15** and **6–18**).

You are not restricted to your own catalogue, if you wish to trace books on a subject. The online catalogues of all of the UK universities, along with the British Library, can be searched. COPAC (at *www.copac.ac.uk*) provides a particularly useful starting point for UK academic research libraries as it provides access to the merged catalogues of the largest research libraries in the UK and Ireland. This means that a single catalogue search can find details of a book held by, among others, the Cambridge University Library, the Bodleian Library, Trinity College Dublin and the Institute of Advanced Legal Studies. The Institute of Advanced Legal Studies collections can by searched via the Institute's own library pages (at *ials.sas.ac.uk/library.htm*). The British Library catalogue (at *blpc.bl.uk*) includes both the main reference and document supply collections.

Many universities also have subscriptions to the OCLC FirstSearch service which contains the WorldCat database, the largest online catalogue available. It has records which are based largely, though not exclusively, on US university holdings. The Library of Congress catalogue (at *catalog.loc.gov*) provides another starting point for US publications.

Legal bibliographies

7–30   Bibliographies list books that have been published on a subject, both in this country and abroad. A number of possible sources are given below. All of them are print volumes that list books under legal subject headings. Not all of them may be available in your library. However, you will only need one or two of them to trace relevant books.

D. Raistrick—Lawyer's Law Books

7–31   Now somewhat out of date, *Lawyers' Law Books* (3rd ed. 1995) is the only convenient single-volume bibliography listing textbooks by subject. However, as many of the textbooks listed can be found in current editions the bibliography is still of some value. At the beginning of each subject heading, there are references to alternative headings and a list of the major legal reference works and journals that contain information on that topic.

Current Law

At the back of each *Current Law Monthly Digest* is a list of new books published during that month (mainly British, with a few foreign works in English). When the *Monthly Digests* are replaced by the *Current Law Year Book*, a list of books published during the year is printed at the back of the *Year Book*.   **7–32**

Current Publications in Legal and Related Fields

Current Publications in Legal and Related Fields (published by the American publisher Hein) is issued in looseleaf parts which are replaced by annual volumes. There are entries under authors and titles in the looseleaf volume.   **7–33**

In the annual volume, a detailed subject index at the front of the volume guides you to relevant entries in the main (alphabetically arranged) part of the work. Each item has its own individual number. The bibliography includes UK published works.

Law Books 1876–1981

The first three volumes of *Law Books 1876–1981* are arranged by subject and cover books published mainly in the US, although some British and other countries' publications are also included. The fourth volume contains some entries under authors, titles and serials. Rather than update the original work, the publishers, Bowker, now publish *Bowker's Law Books and Serials in Print: a Multimedia Sourcebook*, in three annual volumes (see **7–37**).   **7–34**

Other Legal Bibliographies

Sweet & Maxwell's *Legal Bibliography of the British Commonwealth* is especially useful for tracing older British Books. C. Szladits, *Biliography on Foreign and Comparative Law* is a detailed bibliography covering books and articles on foreign and comparative law published in English.   **7–35**

Many other specialist legal bibliographies have also been published, e.g. P. O'Higgens and M. Partington, *Social Security Law in Britain and Ireland: a Bibliography* (1986); E. Beyerly, *Public International Law: a Guide to Information Sources* (1991); and R. W. M. Dias, *Bibliography of Jurisprudence* (1979). As you can see from their publication dates, such bibliographies do not always provide a guide to recent publications, but this does not exhaust their usefulness. Raistrick's *Lawyers' Law Books* (**7–31**) contains list of more specialised legal bibliographies, under the heading "Bibliographies".

Library staff will help you to trace recent bibliographies. Remember too, that many textbooks will also contain a bibliography on their subject.

The British National Bibliography

The main source of information for British books which have been published since 1950 is the *British National Bibliography* (BNB). This is published weekly and the last issue of each month contains an index to books published that month. At the end of the year, an annual volume is produced containing details of British books published that year. Entries are   **7–36** arranged by subject in a classification scheme. You will first need to look up your subject in the Subject Index, which refers you to the classification number under which the books can be found. Entries for law books are at the numbers 340–349.

The BNB is also available on CD-ROM, from the publishers, the British Library. Unlike the print version, the CD-ROM enables you to make highly specific searches using title keywords and author names.

Sources for books in print

7–37
A number of sources enable you to search for the titles of books in print. Among the electronic sources, the commercial books in print databases allow subject searching using keywords, and these have been supplemented by the catalogues of the Internet booksellers. Publishers' websites also list current and forthcoming publications and many organise their titles by subject.

If you want to search the web pages of the major law publishers there are Internet gateway sites (**2–15**) which provide a current listing. Sarah Carter's *Lawlinks* site for example (at *library.kent.ac.uk/library/lawlinks*) lists UK legal publishers. Many law school sites provide similar listings. *Findlaw* (at *www.findlaw.com*) lists UK and American publishers, as does *Hieros Gamos* (at *www.hg.org*).

The Amazon website (at *www.amazon.co.uk*) should not be overlooked as a useful source for information for books in print, as most publishers supply the site with title information. The American site (at *www.amazon.com*) is also worth searching. Contents pages are often available for viewing online. Some libraries may be able to check titles for you, using the *BookWise* service from Nielson BookData, the major commercial source for information on UK books in print. Access may also be offered to book supplier databases, such as *enterBooks.com* from Dawson Books.

Law Books in Print, from the American publishers Oceana, is available online and covers UK titles alongside American publications. Searches are possible by subject, author, title and publisher. Another American publication, *Books in Print*, is also available online from a number of sources. The publishers, Bowker, have in addition launched *booksinprint.com* and *globalbooksinprint.com* as internet services directly available from their website (at *www. bowker.com*). As these are subscription sources, you need to check if your library can provide access. The print issues of another Bowker publication, *Law Books and Serials in Print*, may also be of use for American titles. Check your library reference holdings for availability.

Theses

7–38
If you are undertaking a comprehensive piece of research, you may need to find out if any theses have already been written on that subject. The *Index to Theses*, more fully, the *Index to Theses Accepted for Higher Degrees by the Universities of Great Britain and Ireland*, is, as the title suggests, the major source for tracing British and Irish theses. Coverage is extensive, but it does rely on universities to submit theses information. The *Index* is available online but this is a subscription database, so you will need to check if your library can provide

access. Online coverage begins in 1970. The print version dates back to 1950. Another print source of information for UK law theses, *Legal Research in the United Kingdom, 1905–1984*, was published by the Institute of Advanced Legal Studies, and updated until 1988 by the *List of Current Legal Research Topics*. Publication has now ceased.

Details of the vast majority of North American theses can be found in *Dissertation Abstracts International*, which also includes some non-North American theses. Abstracts are available from 1980. The publishers, UMI, have made the *Dissertation Abstracts International* database available to a number of online database providers. The Proquest Digital Dissertations link on the UMI website (at *www.umi.com*) offers free access to the most recent three months of the database.

Theses which have been completed at your own institution are normally available for consultation in the library. It is usually possible for the library staff to borrow, on inter-library loan, copies of theses completed in other universities in this country and abroad.

8 European Community law

Introduction

8–1   European Community law is as much part of the law of this country as the laws passed by the UK Parliament. For this reason, UK legal sources should, and often will, include references to the relevant EC rules. However, because this is not always so, and because EC law is organised in a different way from English law, students also need to become familiar with the sources of EC law.

The use of the term "EC law" in this chapter needs to be explained at the outset. The Treaty of Maastricht, or Treaty on European Union, which came into force in 1993, made what were then three European Communities the first "pillar" of the European Union. These were the European Community, the European Coal and Steel Community (until its expiry in 2002) and the European Atomic Energy Community. This chapter is concerned with the body of law based around these Communities; hence the term "EC law". Before Maastricht, the European Community was referred to as the European Economic Community (EEC).

Some textbooks and articles discuss "European Union law". The term "European Union" (EU) is used in this chapter to refer to the institutional framework of the European Union. The European Commission for example, is an institution of the EU. Many of the sources of information you will be using when studying EC law have been provided by the institutions of the EU.

The sources of EC law, along with a great deal of other information, are made available both online and in print by the EU. Online access is provided from the Europa website (**8–2**), the main source for official EU information. EC treaties, legislation and case law are available from the EUR-Lex web pages (**8–3**). There is no subscription charge for access.

Most, if not all, of the printed sources will also be available in your law library, especially if it is a designated European Documentation Centre (E.D.C.). E.D.C.'s are part of the European Information Relay Network and receive copies of publicly available documents from the European Commission. Details of the UK E.D.C.s and other sources of EU information are found on the website of the European Commission Representation office in the UK (at *www.cec.org.uk*).

Europa

The Europa website (at *europa.eu.int*) is the main EU website, providing a wealth of infor-   **8–2**
mation from the EU institutions. The home page carries recent news items from the EU
and links can be followed under "All the news" to the press releases from the RAPID database (**8–27**). Further information is grouped under four major headings: "Activities",
"Institutions", "Documents" and "Services". All four headings provide useful approaches
to finding legal information.

A subject approach to legal information is possible using the "Activities" heading on the
website. A number of major subject areas are listed, e.g. "Employment and Social Affairs",
"Enlargement", and "Environment". Within each heading, links are then available to summaries of key legislation in that area. Further links go to the relevant full text. The "Key
sites" section for each subject area provides links to important bodies within the major institutions. If the "Environment" heading is selected, for example, a link is provided to the
Committee on the Environment, Public Health and Food Safety page within the European
Parliament site. Additional links are provided for subject-specific entries in the *Bulletin of
the European Union* and the *General Report on the Activities of the European Union* (**8–26**).
Press releases can also be viewed for the subject area chosen.

The "Institutions" heading is a useful heading if you wish to find further information on the
activities of any of the major institutions: the European Parliament, the Council of the
European Union, the European Commission and the Court of Justice of the European Communities. There are also links to other significant bodies, such as the Office for Official Publications of the European Communities (the Publications Office), the EU's official publisher.

The "Documents" heading of the Europa site provides a direct link to the EUR-Lex site
(**8–3**), along with additional links for preparatory legislation and case law. This is the site to
use if you wish to search the primary sources of EC law in their entirety.

Europa's "Services" heading provides a link to Eurostat, the EU's statistical information
service, under the "Statistics" heading, also a link to the European Commission's Central
Library and its catalogue (ECLAS), a useful source of information for books and journal
articles relevant to the EU (**8–25**).

The "Advanced Search" page of the Europa website's search engine allows searches to be
restricted by subject area. However, if you are searching for legislation or case law by subject,
a better approach is to use the keyword search facilities provided in the EUR-Lex web pages.

EUR-Lex

The EUR-Lex website (at *europa.eu.int/eur-lex/en*), provides access to both legislation and   **8–3**
case law. It contains the full text of the following:

Treaties as currently amended;
Legislation in force—adopted legislation and the consolidated texts of secondary
legislation;

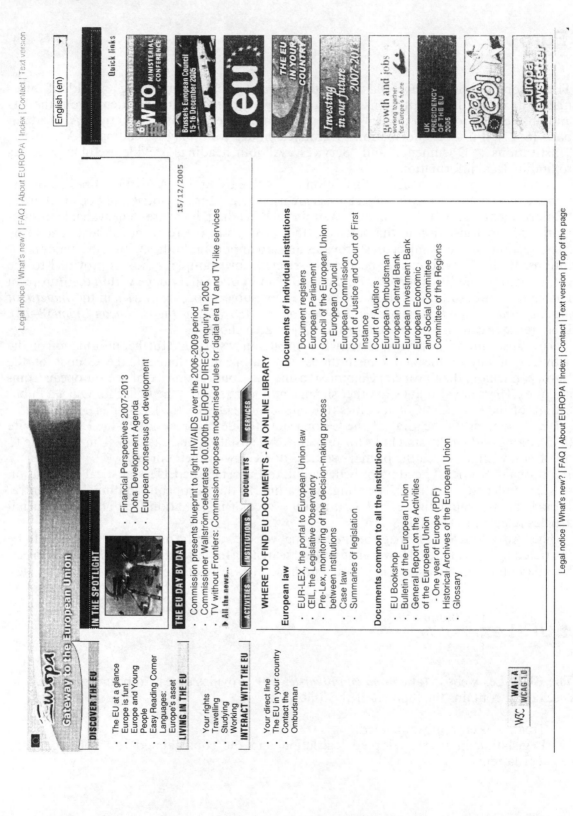

Proposed legislation;
Case-law
Parliamentary questions

The full text of the *Official Journal C* and *L Series* is also available **(8–4)**.

In 2005 the information on the EUR-Lex site was merged with information from the EU's *CELEX* database. Until the end of 2004, *CELEX* had been the EU's official legal database. An accompanying redesign of the EUR-Lex web pages was carried out to ensure that the full range of database searches available on *CELEX* was also available when searching for legislation and case law on EUR-Lex.

The Official Journal

The *Official Journal of the European Communities* is issued in print and online by the   **8–4**
Publications Office of the European Union and is the official and authoritative source of legislation. It carries the text of proposed and enacted legislation, as well as official announcements and information on the activities of the EU's institutions.

Print editions of the *Official Journal* are published about six times a week carrying the latest legislation and announcements. The issues are also placed online in the same format on the EUR-Lex site (at *europa.eu.int/eur-lex/en*). Your library may no longer take the print issues. The *Journal* is published in two sequences:

1. *L series (Legislation)*: this consists of the texts of enacted legislation, divided into a further two sequences.

   (a) acts whose publication is obligatory (primarily regulations, directives addressed to all member states);
   (b) acts whose publication is not obligatory (all other legislation).

2. *C series (Information and Notices)*: this is arranged in three parts, as follows:

   (a) Part I, *Information* from the various Community institutions including:

      (i) *Commission*—EURO exchange rates, communications and notices concerning Community policy and notifications from companies and governments applying Community law;
      (ii) *Court of Justice*—a list of new cases brought before this court and the Court of the First Instance, summaries of judgments of the Court of Justice and the Court of First Instance;
      (iii) *European Parliament*—minutes of the plenary sessions and written questions from members of the European Parliament;
      (iv) *Economic and Social Committee*—Opinions;

   (b) Part II, Preparatory Acts: the texts of proposed legislation;
   (c) Part III, *Notices* of invitation to tender for commercial and research contracts and notices of staff vacancies in Community institutions;

Eurlex - Microsoft Internet Explorer

File   Edit   View   Favorites   Tools   Help

Back   Search   Favorites   Media

Address http://europa.eu.int/eur-lex/lex/en/index.htm   Go   Links »

EUR-Lex

EUROPA > EUR-Lex

Important legal notice

Site map | LexAlert | FAQ | Help | Contact | Links

ES CS DA DE ET EL EN FR LV LT HU MT NL PL PT SK SL FI SV

The access to European Union law

OFFICIAL JOURNAL

SIMPLE SEARCH

ADVANCED SEARCH

COLLECTIONS
Treaties
International agreements
Legislation in force
Preparatory acts
Case-law
Parliamentary questions

QUICK LINKS
Budget of the European Union
The institutions' registers

ABOUT EU LAW
Process and players
Legislative drafting

Welcome

EUR-Lex provides direct free access to European Union law. The system makes it possible to consult the Official Journal of the European Union and it includes inter alia the treaties, legislation, case-law and legislative proposals. It offers extensive search facilities. »

News

▶ **Newsletter 05/12/2005**   de   en   fr
National implementing measures: »

▶ **Selection of new documents**
13/12/2005: JUDGMENT OF THE COURT (Grand Chamber) 13 December 2005 In Case C-446/03, Marks & Spencer plc ▶ **html**

▶ **Dossiers by topics**
07/10/2005: Air safety : »

Enlargement

▶ **Enlargement: Community legislation in force on 1 May 2004**

▶ **Treaty concerning the accession of the Republic of Bulgaria and Romania to the European Union**   bg   ro

Official Journal

Latest issues

My profile

User ID:
User ID
Password:
Password
Registration

Buy the OJ on CD-ROM

OJ L and C
OJ S – Public procurement

EU Bookshop

Managed by the Publications Office

Internet

Official Journal
of the European Union

ISSN 1725-2555

L 273
Volume 48
19 October 2005

English edition   Legislation

Contents

I *Acts whose publication is obligatory*

An *Official Journal: annex—debates of the European Parliament* was published in print until 2000 and has been published on CD-ROM since 2000 by the Publications Office.

An S Series publishing details of public contracts open to competitive tender has been published on CD-ROM since 1997. *Tenders Electronic Daily (TED)* (at *ted.eur-op.eu.int*) is the EU's internet version of the S Series. TED is updated daily and provides an archive of the last five years of the S Series.

The Publications Office has issued a monthly CD-ROM version of the *Official Journal C* and *L* series since 1999 which should be available in E.D.C. libraries. An *Official Journal C E* edition was also launched in 1999. It contains the text of preparatory acts and is only available on the EUR-Lex website or as part of the monthly *Official Journal* CD-ROM. The full text of legislative proposals no longer appears in the printed *Official Journal* C Series.

The full text of the *Official Journal* C is also available online from Westlaw UK (**2–5**) under the "EU Materials (General)" shortcut. LexisNexis Professional (**2–4**) includes all *Official Journal* material in its "EU Legislation" search.

The citation of references to the *Official Journal* is not standardised. The most common forms are O.J. No. L271 15.10.2005, p.14; [2005] O.J. L271/14; and O.J. 2005, L271/14.

The Community Treaties

8–5   The principle source of Community law is the EC Treaty (The Treaty Establishing European Union). However, there are many other related treaties, including:

The ECSC Treaty, 1951;
The EURATOM Treaty, 1957;
The Single European Act, 1986;
The Treaty on European Union, 1992;
The Treaty of Amsterdam, 1997;
The Treaty of Nice, 2001.

The current form of the EC Treaty is the result of changes made by the Single European Act, the Treaty on European Union (the Maastricht Treaty), the Treaty of Amsterdam and the Treaty of Nice. These amended the text of the original EEC Treaty, 1957. The Treaty on European Union was responsible for the change in name from EEC Treaty to EC Treaty.

The EC Treaty performs two main tasks. The first is that it represents a system of substantive rules which are binding on the member states, and whose aim is to foster social and economic integration among the member states. Secondly, and equally importantly, the treaty creates a set of institutions and a procedural framework through which these institutions can create secondary Community legislation and take other measures which have a legally binding effect.

One of the amendments made by the Treaty of Amsterdam you should be aware of is the renumbering of the provisions of the EC Treaty (and the Treaty on European Union). For example, Article 119 EC of the EC Treaty is now Article 141 EC. A number of textbooks provide conversion tables listing the old and revised Article numbers.

The consolidated text of the founding treaties can be found on the EUR-Lex website (at *europa.eu.int/eur-lex/en*). EUR-Lex has also added the text of the Treaty Establishing a Constitution for Europe (December 16, 2004), which will amend the existing Treaties if ratified by member states.

Primary legislation is published in the *Official Journal* (**8–4**). The Treaty Establishing a Constitution for Europe, for example, was published in *Official Journal* C Series, in issue C310 of December 16, 2004. It can usually also be located in the form of separately published documents, or even as United Kingdom Command Papers. The Treaty Establishing a Constitution for Europe was published as Command Paper Cm. 6309.

In addition to these official sources, many of the important texts of primary materials are published in student textbooks. *Blackstone's Statutes on EC Legislation*, for example, edited by Nigel Foster, and currently revised annually (16th edition 2005–2006). The *Encyclopedia of European Union Laws*, a loose-leaf publication, also contains the texts of the treaties.

Secondary Legislation

Secondary legislation is that which is created by the institutions of the European **8–6** Communities in implementing the powers granted to them in the Community treaties. There are different types of legislative acts, and these are given different names depending on whether they are made under the EC and EURATOM Treaties, or the former ECSC Treaty. You will be most concerned with the different kinds of act made under the EC Treaty. These are explained in Article 249 (previously Article 189) of the Treaty and are as follows:

Regulations
Directives
Decisions
Recommendations
Opinions

The legislative process of the EU is very different from that of the UK. Draft legislation or proposals are put forward by the Commission and the final versions are published as *Commission Documents* (known as *COM Docs*). They are also published in the *Official Journal* C *Series*. Proposals are then considered by the European Parliament and the European Economic and Social Committee (EESC) or the Committee of the Regions (CoR), which publish *Reports* or *Opinions*. The European Parliament may also initiate proposals for legislation.

Consultative documents from the relevant bodies are available online from EU sources, though the websites involved are not always easy to navigate. *COM Docs* are included on EUR-Lex under "Preparatory Acts". EESC and CoR *Opinions* are published in the *Official Journal* C *Series*. Recent EESC *Opinions* are available on their website (at *www.esc.eu.int*). Committee of the Regions *Opinions* are available from the Committee website (at *www.cor.eu.int*). Resolutions of the European Parliament (but not the full report) are published in the *Official Journal* C *Series*. The full text of the *Reports of Proceedings*, along with Committee opinions and other relevant documents, is available on the European Parliament website (at *www.europarl.eu.int*).

Once the various suggestions from these bodies have been considered, and the original proposals amended if necessary, the Council will adopt a directive or regulation and the text is published in the *Official Journal* L *Series*. Directives must then be implemented in the law of the Member States.

Citation of EC legislative acts

8–7   The formal citation of a European Communities legislative act is made up of the following elements:

1. The institutional origin of the act (Commission or Council).
2. The form of the act (regulation, directive, decision, etc.).
3. An act number.
4. The year of the enactment.
5. The institutional treaty basis (EC, ECSC, EURATOM).
6. The date the act was passed.

Regulation numbers are written with the number first and the year following. Decisions and directives are written the other way round, with the year first and the number following. All indexes will therefore always list regulations first and decisions and directives afterwards. Two examples follow:

1. Commission Regulation (EC) No. 1699/2005 of 18 October establishing the standard import values for determining the entry price of certain fruit and vegetables. (This can be abbreviated to Reg. (EC) 1699/2005.)
2. Directive 2003/88/EC of the European Parliament and of the Council of 4 November concerning certain aspects of the organisation of working time. (This can be abbreviated to Dir. 2003/88/EC.)

Between 1958 and 1967, this citation form varied. The variations are laid out in *Halsbury's Statutes* (4th ed.), Vol. 50, pp. 211–212. From 1992, directives and decisions were given separate numerical sequences, with the consequence that a directive and a decision can both be given the same number. Thus there exist both Dir. 2005/12/EC and Dec. 2005/12/EC.

A legislative act is given a date of enactment but this does not indicate the date when the act is published in the *Official Journal*: this can be up to several months later.

How to trace the text of an EC regulation or directive

8–8   Suppose you wish to look for the current text of Directive 2003/88/EC on the organisation of working time. How should you set about finding it? The best approach is to use the EUR-Lex website (at *europa.eu.int/eur-lex*).

To begin, select the "Simple Search" from the EUR-Lex home page. Then select the "Natural number" search option under the "Search by document number" heading. A search form can then be used to specify that you wish to search for a directive ("Regulation" or "Decision" could also be specified at this point). A year and document number also need to be entered for the directive. The year is derived from the start of the standard abbreviation and is entered as a 4 digit number (i.e. 2003). The document number is 88. Once these details have been entered,

SEARCH TIP

Always check the "bibliographic notice" when tracing the text of a directive on the EUR-Lex site. Links are provided to amending legislation, consolidated texts and important cases.

your search will display a results screen with the full title and *Official Journal* reference for the directive. Select the "Bibliographic + Text" option to see all the available text.

The bibliographic notice lists any amendments or repeals for a directive and provides links to the full text of the related legislation. For Directive 2003/88/EC, which repeals an earlier working time directive (93/104/EC), the bibliographic notice lists the directive repealed. If a directive has been amended a number of times, the bibliographic notice provides a link to a consolidated version of the text, incorporating all the amendments made. The full text displayed in your search result is the original text of the directive.

Text of Directive 2003/88/EC from the EUR-Lex website

32003L0088

Directive 2003/88/EC of the European Parliament and of the Council of 4 November 2003 concerning certain aspects of the organisation of working time

Official Journal L 299, 18/11/2003 P. 0009 - 0019

Directive 2003/88/EC of the European Parliament and of the Council
of 4 November 2003
concerning certain aspects of the organisation of working time
THE EUROPEAN PARLIAMENT AND THE COUNCIL OF THE EUROPEAN UNION,
Having regard to the Treaty establishing the European Community, and in particular Article 137(2) thereof,
Having regard to the proposal from the Commission,
Having regard to the opinion of the European Economic and Social Committee(1),
Having consulted the Committee of the Regions,
Acting in accordance with the procedure referred to in Article 251 of the Treaty(2),
Whereas:

(1) Council Directive 93/104/EC of 23 November 1993, concerning certain aspects of the organisation of working time(3), which lays down minimum safety and health requirements for the organisation of working time, in respect of periods of daily rest, breaks, weekly rest, maximum weekly working time, annual leave and aspects of night work, shift work and patterns of work, has been significantly amended. In order to clarify matters, a codification of the provisions in question should be drawn up.

(2) Article 137 of the Treaty provides that the Community is to support and complement the activities of the Member States with a view to improving the working environment to protect workers' health and safety. Directives adopted on the basis of that Article are to avoid imposing administrative, financial and legal constraints in a way which would hold back the creation and development of small and medium-sized undertakings.

(3) The provisions of Council Directive 89/391/EEC of 12 June 1989 on the introduction of measures to encourage improvements in the safety and health of workers at work(4) remain fully applicable to the areas covered by this Directive without prejudice to more stringent and/or specific provisions contained herein.

(4) The improvement of workers' safety, hygiene and health at work is an objective which should not be subordinated to purely economic considerations.

(5) All workers should have adequate rest periods. The concept of "rest" must be expressed in units of time, i.e. in days, hours and/or fractions thereof. Community workers must be granted minimum daily, weekly and annual periods of rest and adequate breaks. It is also necessary in this context to place a maximum limit on weekly working hours.

(6) Account should be taken of the principles of the International Labour Organisation with regard to the organisation of working time, including those relating to night work.

(7) Research has shown that the human body is more sensitive at night to environmental disturbances and also to certain burdensome forms of work organisation and that long periods of night work can be detrimental to the health of workers and can endanger safety at the workplace.

(8) There is a need to limit the duration of periods of night work, including overtime, and to provide for employers who regularly use night workers to bring this information to the attention of the competent authorities if they so request.

Directives can also be found using the EC Legislation searches of either Westlaw UK (**2–5**) or LexisNexis Professional (**2–4**). To find a directive, use the standard abbreviation for a directive in a citation search, e.g. "2003/88/EC". However, there is no equivalent in either database of the bibliographic notice.

How to trace EC legislation on a subject without a reference

8–9 If you have been told, for example, that there is a directive on part-time working or parental leave, but you do not have a number or a date, you will need to use a subject approach. In most cases, choosing the correct terminology is the first problem you will encounter. Directives are commonly given colloquial titles such as the "Part-Time Working Directive" or the "Parental Leave Directive", but these are not official titles. The "Parental Leave Directive" has the official title "Council Directive 96/34/EC of 3 June 1996 on the framework agreement on parental leave concluded by UNICE, CEEP and the ETUC". However, the colloquial titles used for directives usually contain the keywords needed to search an online database. A search for directives containing the words "parental leave" using EUR-Lex, Westlaw UK or LexisNexis Professional finds the relevant directive.

Because of the advantages provided by the bibliographic notices for legislation noted in **8–8**, the EUR-Lex website provides the best starting point for searching for a directive using keywords. Use the "Simple Search" option and select "Legislation" under "Search by file category". This means that your keyword searches will only find legislation and not all categories of material found on EUR-Lex. "Directives" can be specified as legislation type on the next screen with "search terms" as the search option. A search on "parental leave" then finds two directives: Directive 96/34/EC on parental leave and Directive 97/34/EC amending the original directive and extending it to the UK. The bibliographic note for 96/34/EC includes a link to a consolidated text for 96/34/EC incorporating the amending directive.

More complex searches can be carried out using search terms such as "with" or "except". These are explained on the "Search using search terms" screen. Searches can also be extended to include the full text of legislation, along with the title.

If you are not sure of the keywords to use in searching for a directive, an alternative approach is to use the "Classification headings" search available under the EUR-Lex "Simple Search". A standard EU analytical table of headings is displayed, enabling the Parental Leave directive to be found, for example, under the following string of headings: "05 Freedom of movement for workers and social policy"; "Social Policy"; "Employment and unemployment"; and "Protection of workers". As can be seen from this example, some familiarity with the analytical structure of the headings is required before you can find the most likely path to legislation that might interest you.

The loose-leaf service, Vaughan, *Law of the European Union* (Richmond Law & Tax) provides a print approach to finding EC legislation by subject.

How to check if EC legislation is in force

If you have used EUR-Lex to find a directive or regulation as described in **8–8**, the accompanying bibliographic note will confirm whether it is still in force. An analytical overview of all legislation in force can also be found if you select the "Legislation in force" link from the EUR-Lex home page (at *europa.eu.int/eur-lex*). The overview uses the standard EU classification scheme noted in **8–9** and links are provided to the full text of legislation listed under each heading. Consolidated versions of legislation are provided where relevant.   **8–10**

If you are searching EUR-Lex by subject keyword (see **8–9**) a tick box can be used when specifying the type of search you wish to make, restricting the search to legislation in force. This can save possible confusion. If you search for directives using the keywords "working time" and tick the "Restrict your search to acts in force" box, only the current in-force directives are retrieved. You do not see Directive 93/104/EC and its various amending directives. Both the older Directive 93/104/EC and the current Directive 2003/88/EC are directives "concerning certain aspects of the organisation of working time".

How to trace proposals for legislation

In the UK, draft legislation is introduced into Parliament and becomes law during the same parliamentary session. This is not the case with EC legislation, which may take years to either become law or ultimately fail to become law. How would you know if legislation has been proposed on a particular subject?   **8–11**

The *Bulletin of the European Union* is a useful starting point for updates on recent proposals. This can be accessed by subject area if you start from the "Activities" section of the EUROPA website (see **8–2**). Searching under "Activities" and "Environment" in 2005 finds an entry in the *Bulletin*, for example, on a proposed directive on the protection of groundwater against pollution. Links are provided for the *Bulletin* entry to the *Official Journal* entries for the original Commission proposal, and also to opinions from the Committee of the Regions, the Economic and Social Committee and the European Parliament. There are links to the full text of the original proposal (COM 2003 550) and an amended Commission proposal (COM 2005 282). The text of the COM documents is provided from the *Prelex* database (see below).

A more systematic search for proposals can be undertaken from the EUR-Lex website. The "Preparatory acts" heading on the EUR-Lex home page provides a link to a "Search in preparatory acts" option which allows searches to be made for preparatory acts using keywords, date limits or classification headings. A keyword search for "groundwater" with "pollution", for example, finds the two COM documents mentioned above. Again there are links to entries made for the proposal in the *Prelex* database. These can be found in the bibliographic notice that accompanies the full text of the amended Commission proposal COM 2005 282. There is also a link to the entry for the proposal made in the *Legislative Observatory* (*OEIL*) database of the European Parliament.

The *PreLex* database (at *europa.eu.intl/prelex*) was launched by the European Commission in 2000. It provides database entries following all Commission proposals and communications from the Council or European Parliament through to adoption or rejection. It provides detailed tracking of a proposal through all the stages at which it is considered and provides links to the relevant full text.

The *Legislative Observatory* (*OEIL*) database (at *www.europarl.eu.intl/oeil*) is a database provided by the European Parliament which contains the details of all procedures or proposals still ongoing, along with those concluded since the beginning of the fourth legislative term in July 1994. The *OEIL* entry for proposed legislation provides access to *Legislative Opinions* of the European Parliament and the full text of relevant committee reports. It is possible to search both *PreLex* and *OEIL* using keywords and document reference numbers.

The loose-leaf print service, Vaughan, *Law of the European Union*, also includes proposed legislation.

How to trace whether a directive has been implemented in the United Kingdom

8–12   Directives, once adopted by the Council of the European Union, must be implemented by Member States by the most appropriate method for each country. In the UK, this is generally done by passing an Act of Parliament or issuing a statutory instrument. Member States are given a set period of time in which to do this. Tracing UK legislation implementing a directive can be problematic.

It the text of a directive is found using either Westlaw UK or LexisNexis Professional, notes of the implementing legislation for Member States derived from the no longer updated *CELEX* database can be found. However, this information is often either missing or incomplete. The European Commission is developing a new database, NAT-Lex, which is to provide details of all national implementing measures. Until NAT-Lex becomes available, the only online route to UK legislation implementing directives is to use the UK legislation searches of Westlaw UK, LexisNexis Professional, or LexisNexis Butterworths. To use these databases, follow the approach outlined for searching for legislation by subject in **7–21**.

> **SEARCH TIP**
>
> The *EC Legislation Implementor* volume of *Halsbury's Statutory Instruments* provides a convenient quick reference source for UK implementing legislation. The full text can then be found online using UK legislation databases.

To search for legislation implementing the Parental Leave directive, for example, use a keyword search to find references to "96/34/EC". An explanatory paragraph is found for the Maternity and Parental Leave etc. Regulations 1999/3312 which includes the statement that "provisions relating to parental leave implement Council Directive 96/34/EC on the framework agreement on parental leave (OJ No.L145, 19.6.96, p.4)". The Maternity and Parental Leave (Amendment) Regulations 2001/4010 and the Maternity and Parental Leave (Amendment) Regulations 2002/2789 are also found.

A convenient print alternative for tracing implementing legislation is provided by the *EC Legislation Implementator* volume of *Halsbury's Statutory Instruments* (**7–28**). If you have already discovered the reference for a directive, a chronological listing of directives enables you to look up the implementing UK legislation. All three statutory instruments noted above for Directive 96/34/EC can be traced from the entry for the directive. The *EC Legislation Implementator* is revised annually.

Case Law

There are two courts which interpret and enforce EC law. The first, the European Court of **8–13** Justice (ECJ), has been in existence since the Communities were founded. The second, the Court of the First Instance (CFI), gave its first judgments in 1990. The ECJ hears all types of cases, including appeals from the CFI, but the CFI only hears competition, anti-dumping and staff cases. The case law of both courts has assumed a position of great importance.

The *Official Journal* C *Series* carries notices of cases pending before the courts. Brief details only of the nature of the proceedings and the judgment are provided.

European Court Reports

The official source of European Court judgments is the *Reports of Cases before the Court*. **8–14** These are more commonly known as the *European Court Reports* (abbreviated to E.C.R.). In this series, the opinion of the Advocate General is given alongside the judgment. This is an important stage in the proceedings before the European Court of Justice. The Advocate General's opinion is not binding on the court, but it is of great use to students of Community law in that it will include a thorough analysis of the facts and legal arguments in the case. There is an English language set of the *Reports* covering the judgments of the courts since 1954. Since 1990, the *Reports* have been split into two parts in each issue. Part I contains ECJ cases and Part II contains CFI cases. Since 1994 staff cases are being published in a separate series known as *Reports of European Community Staff Cases* (ECS-SC), and are not all translated into other languages.

Although the E.C.R. is the official series, it suffers from major delays in publication. Precise and accurate translation into the various Community languages results in delays of up to two years which makes it impossible to use it for recent cases. However, both opinions of the Advocate General and judgments of the European Court of Justice are available online from the Court website (at *curia.eu.int/en*). Opinions and judgments for 1989 onwards can also be searched from the EUR-Lex website (at *europa.eu.int/eur-lex/en*). These sites provide the official online source of all opinions and judgments from the European Court of Justice. As with all EU websites, there is no subscription charge for access. (See **8–18** to **8–22** for more on searching using these sites).

Citation of European Court of Justice and Court of First Instance cases

8–15   The case citation is made up as follows:

1. case number;
2. year;
3. name of parties;
4. citation: indicating where the case can be found in the *European Court Reports* (E.C.R.):

> E.g. Case C–59/89 *Commission* v *Germany* [1991] E.C.R. I–2607 Case T–12/90 *Bayer* v *Commission* [1991] E.C.R. II–219.

Alternatively the citations for the European Court Reports can be written as follows:

> [1991] I E.C.R. 2067 and [1991] II E.C.R. 219.

Note that each case after 1990 is preceded by the letter C (European Court of Justice) or the letter T (Court of First Instance). Also note that a case with a reference ... /03, for example, means that the application or reference to the court was made in 2003. The judgment was not given in that year. This means that you cannot automatically go to the E.C.R. for the year 2003 to find the judgment.

Other sources of EC case law

8–16   A number of UK published law reports publish reports of European Court of Justice cases. The *Common Market Law Reports* (C.M.L.R) provides the main alternative to the *European Court Reports*. It is published by Sweet & Maxwell and also covers the cases with an EC dimension in national courts. C.M.L.R. appears sooner than the *European Court Reports* with a full, if not official, report. Both the Advocate General's opinion and the judgment made in a case are included in the reports. Whilst it does not report all cases, it does report all cases of significance. The reports are available online from Westlaw UK (**2–5**).

The *All England Reporter (European Cases)*—All E.R. (EC)—has published decisions from the Court of Justice and the Court of First Instance since 1995. The reports are available online from LexisNexis Professional (**2–3**) and from LexisNexis Butterworths (**2–4**). *European Community Cases* (C.E.C) is another source of case law. Only very important cases are covered. Specialist law report series such as *Fleet Street Reports* or *Industrial Relations Law Reports* also include relevant EC case law.

Both Westlaw UK and LexisNexis Professional can also be used to search for judgments online as noted in the following sections.

How to find a Court of Justice judgment or opinion if you have the reference

Suppose you are given the following case reference: Case C-336/03 *easyCar Ltd v Office of*   **8–17**
Fair Trading. How do you find it?

Both the Court of Justice website (at *curia.eu.int/en*) and the EUR-Lex website (at *europa.eu.int/eur-lex/en*) provide free public access to the full text of judgments and opinions. Whichever route you choose, the final text is the same. Direct access to judgments from the Court of Justice site is possible using the "Numerical access to case-law" link under the Case-law heading. Coverage is from 1953 onwards and pending cases are also listed. Recent judgments and opinions (from 1997 onwards) can be found using the site's search form. The *easyCar* case can then be found using either the case number or the "Names of parties" search. The Advocate General's opinion and the judgment are found as separate entries in the database along with links to the *Official Journal* notices for the case.

> ### SEARCH TIP
>
> Use either Westlaw UK or LexisNexis Professional to search for pre-1987 Court of Justice cases using keywords.

Numerical access to case law is also possible under the "Case-law" link on the EUR-Lex home page. Links for the most recent judgment or opinions are provided at the top of the page, followed by a drop-down menu which allows either judgments or opinions to be selected by year and case number. For the period 1954 to 1997 access is by year only. Database searching for cases is possible (for 1997 onwards) using the "Simple Search" link from the home page. The search by "Natural number" option can then be chosen and a case law search specified.

Court of Justice cases can be found on LexisNexis Professional using the "EU Case Law" shortcut and searching by case number or party name. Both the opinion and the judgment are found for *easyCar Ltd v Office of Fair Trading*. A search for the case using the "EU Cases" shortcut on Westlaw UK also finds the full text of both the opinion and the judgment in the case. However a further link is also provided in the results list to the full text of the report found in the *Common Market Law Reports* [2005] 2 C.M.L.R. 2. The text of both opinion and judgment can be found with additional explanatory material.

How to find a judgment of the Court of Justice on a subject

What can you do if you want to find cases on, for instance, the Common Customs Tariff?   **8–18**

Both the Court of Justice website and the EUR-Lex websites allow the full text of judgments and opinions to be searched from 1997 onwards. Keywords can be entered using the Court of Justice search form found under "Case-law" (at *curia.eu.int/en*). Using EUR-Lex, select the "Simple Search" option from the home page (at *europa.eu.int/eur-lex/en*) and choose the Case-law file category, before selecting the option enabling a search using search terms. The phrase "Common Customs Tariff" can then be entered to find relevant cases.

Searches can also be made using the "EU Case Law" shortcut in LexisNexis Professional (**2–4**) or the Westlaw UK "EU Cases" shortcut (**2–5**). The advice given in **7–10** on searching full-text databases of UK case law holds equally well for searches of EU case law. Unless you are only interested in very recent cases, for example, your first concern, if searching for cases on the Common Customs Tariff, will be to find a way of further restricting your search

Example page from a European Court of Justice judgment on the Curia website

JUDGMENT OF THE COURT (First Chamber)
10 March 2005 **(1)**

(Protection of consumers in respect of distance contracts—Directive 97/7/EC—Contracts for the provision of transport services—Meaning—Contracts for car hire)

In Case C-336/03,

REFERENCE to the Court under Article 234 EC by the High Court of Justice of England and Wales, Chancery Division (United Kingdom), 21 July 2003, received at the Court on 30 July 2003, for a preliminary ruling in the proceedings

easyCar (UK) Ltd

v

Office of Fair Trading,

THE COURT (First Chamber),

composed of P. Jann, President of the Chamber, K. Lenaerts, J.N. Cunha Rodrigues, K. Schiemann and M. Ilešič (Rapporteur), Judges,

Advocate General: C. Stix-Hackl,
Registrar: K. Sztranc, Administrator,

having regard to the written procedure and further to the hearing on 29 September 2004,

after considering the observations submitted on behalf of:

– easyCar (UK) Ltd, by D. Anderson QC, K. Bacon, Barrister, and D. Burnside, Solicitor,

– the United Kingdom Government, by C. Jackson, acting as Agent, and M. Hoskins, Barrister,

– the Spanish Government, by S. Ortiz Vaamonde, acting as Agent,

– the French Government, by R. Loosli-Surrans, acting as Agent,

– the Commission of the European Communities, by N. Yerrell and M.-J. Jonczy, acting as Agents,

after hearing the Opinion of the Advocate General at the sitting on 11 November 2004, gives the following

Judgment

1. The reference for a preliminary ruling concerns the interpretation of Article 3(2) of Directive 97/7/EC of the European Parliament and of the Council of 20 May 1997 on the protection of consumers in respect of distance contracts (OJ 1997 L 144, p. 19, hereinafter "the directive").

so that a manageable list of results can be found. Are you for instance interested in cases where issues of nomenclature are important? Or is it another aspect of cases discussing the Commons Customs Tariff that interests you?

The print volumes of *The Digest* (**7–14**) provide a more selective approach to finding Court of Justice cases by subject. Volume 21 contains the main collection of cases on EC law, with alphabetical and case number indexes. You can update it by referring to the *Cumulative Supplement.*

How to trace further information on a case

If a case has been reported in a UK published law report, the Westlaw UK *Case Locators*   **8–19**
database (**3–15**), is a useful source of case summaries and further information. The *easyCar Ltd v Office of Fair Trading* mentioned in **8–17**, for example, can be found in the *Case Locator* along with citations to the *Common Market Law Reports* and the *All England Law Reports (European Cases)*. Legislation cited in the case is noted, along with a list of journal articles discussing the case.

The *Case Locators* database can be particularly useful tracing information on key cases that have had a significant impact on EC law. A search for "Factortame", for example, under "Search by Party Name(s)" finds details of joined cases C-46/93 and C-48–93 *Brasserie du Pecheur SA v Germany* and *R. v Secretary of State for Transport Ex p. Factortame Ltd*. The "History of the Case" section of the *Case* Locator results page lists reported cases which have applied, followed, or considered *Factortame*, both in the European Court of Justice and in UK domestic courts. Citations for case comment in journal articles are also given.

How to trace cases which have interpreted EC legislation

Commonly in research, there is a need to trace cases which are concerned with the inter-   **8–20**
pretation of the provisions of EC law. For example, how do you find Court of Justice cases which have interpreted Directive 93/104/EC on the organisation of working time?

The best approach is to search for the directive using EUR-Lex as described in **8–8**. Once the directive has been found, the accompanying bibliographic notice provides links to any cases providing interpretation. A number of cases are listed for Directive 93/104/EC, including C-84/94 *United Kingdom v Council of the European Union*, which declared the directive void.

An alternative approach is to use the Westlaw UK *Case Locators* database (**3–15**) to search for UK reported cases which have interpreted the directive. Results will include Court of Justice cases reported in reports such as the *Common Market Law Reports* along with UK domestic reported cases. Search using "93/104" as a search term.

How to trace recent judgments

If you wish to go directly to the full text of a judgment (or opinion) which you know to be   **8–21**
very recent, the EUR-Lex website (at *europa.eu.int/eur-lex*) provides a convenient list of recent judgments under the "Case-law" section of the website.

A complete listing of judicial proceedings is available from the "News" section of the European Court of Justice website (at *curia.eu.int/en*). Brief notes of recent judgments are available along with notes of opinions and new cases brought before the court. A link is provided for each case to the Court's case law database.

The Court press releases on cases can also be found from the "News" section of the website. These can often help identify the key issues considered in recent judgments.

Legal Encyclopedias

8–22   *Vaughan: Law of the European Union* provides coverage of EC Law by subject. The *Encyclopedia of European Union Laws* also provides coverage of all EC constitutional texts. There are four sections: the Treaties, the Institutions, Ancillary texts, and the Union Pillars.

Halsbury's Laws of England (7–3) is also a potential source of information on EC Law. If you are using the online version from LexisNexis Butterworths, a search on Directive 2003/88 on working time, for example, finds a section summarising EC requirements and noting UK implementation. Relevant Court of Justice cases are also noted and the update section cites a 2004 judgment relating to the directive (Joined Cases 397/01 to 403/01).

Books

8–23   The European Commission publishes a wide range of material providing introductions, overviews and summaries of topics. All these will be available to you if your library is a European Documentation Centre (see 8–1). The library catalogue will help you locate them.

The library catalogue can also help you find relevant textbooks. These may include books on political and economic aspects of European integration found outside the law section of your library. Remember that books in almost any area of law can provide discussion of EC law. Though there will be a specific section on EC law within your library, the textbooks found there are not the only ones that can help you understand EC law.

ECLAS, the European Commission's own library catalogue (at *europa.eu.int/eclas*) can provide an effective means of tracing details of books of all kinds on EC law and wider EU related issues. Select "General document" and "English" to find books in English on a subject, e.g. competition law.

Journals

8–24   Many legal journals cover EU topics in a selective manner. Major English language journals that specialise in the subject include the *Common Market Law Review*, the *European Law Review*, the *European Business Law Review*, the *European Competition Law Review*,

International and Comparative Law Quarterly and the *Yearbook of European Law*. Your library may be able to provide access to recent issues both in print and online (see **5–2**).

How to find articles on EC law

If you are looking for recent articles on EC law the best source for coverage in UK law jour-   **8–25**
nals is the Legal Journals Index. See **5–6** for further information on searching the index using keywords. Citations for Court of Justice cases and EC legislation can also be used to trace articles.

The European Commission's ECLAS catalogue (at *europa.eu.int/eclas*) can also help trace journal articles on EC law. Limit the catalogue search to "Article" and "English" to find details of English language journal articles on a subject, e.g. "Common Customs Tariff".

The Bulletin of the European Union and General Report

The "Documents" section of the Europa website (at *europa.eu.int*) provides a link to the   **8–26**
current issue of the *Bulletin of the European Union*, a monthly review of the Union's work. The EU's standard headings are used and news items are listed for each subject area. These include notes of new legislation. Earlier issues can also be accessed.

The *General Report on the Activities of the European Union* can also be accessed from Europa's "Documents" page. The *General Review* is an annual review, summarising key developments in particular areas. EU actions can be reviewed under standard subject headings, e.g. "Environment", for the previous year. If you turn to previous issues of the *General Review* a picture can be built up of the development of EU policy in an area.

Current Information

Recent EU developments can be traced using the EU News section of the Europa website.   **8–27**
Access is provided from the "All the news" link on the home page. The latest press releases are available along with a list of upcoming events. The EU News page also has a link to the EU's database of press releases (RAPID), which provides access to press releases from 1985 onwards. The database search can be restricted to search for press releases from particular EU institutions, e.g. the Court of Justice.

If your library has a subscription to the news database provided by LexisNexis Executive, you can also access the full text news coverage of European newspapers.

Appendix I Online Sources of Scots and Northern Ireland Law

A1–1 Scots Law

Case Law

A1–2 Westlaw UK (**2–5**) provides access to the two major series of Scottish law reports:
Session Cases
   cited, e.g. *Mowbray v Valentine* 2004 S.C. 21
Scots Law Times
   cited, e.g. *Brogan v O'Rourke Ltd* 2005 S.L.T. 29
LexisNexis Butterworths (**2–4**) provides access to the Law Society of Scotland's *Scottish Criminal Case Reports* and *Scottish Civil Law Reports*. Access is also provided to *Butterworths Scottish Case Digests*.

   Judgments are available from the Scottish Court Service (at *www.scotcourts.gov.uk*); also from the BAILII website (at *www.bailii.org*).

Acts of the Scottish Parliament

A1–3 Acts of the Scottish Parliament (ASPs) are cited, e.g. as
   Transport (Scotland) Act 2005 asp 12
The official version of the text is provided by Queen's Printer for Scotland (at *www.oqps.gov.uk*). BAILII (at *www.bailii.org*) provides alternative non-subscription access. Justis *UK Statutes* (**2–7**) and Lawtel (**2–6**) also provide access to the original unamended text. Links are provided to amending legislation.

   LexisNexis Butterworths (**2–4**) and Westlaw UK (**2–5**) provide access to the amended text of Acts in force.

Scottish Statutory Instruments

Scottish Statutory Instruments are cited, e.g. as   **A1–4**
   The Dissolution of Funding Councils (Scotland) Order 2005 S.S.I. 2005/437
The official version of the text is provided by Queen's Printer for Scotland (at
www.oqps.gov.uk). BAILII (at *www.bailii.org*) provides alternative non-subscription access.
The unamended text is also contained in Justis *UK Statutes* (**2–7**).
   LexisNexis Butterworths (**2–4**) and Westlaw UK (**2–5**) provide access to the amended text
of Acts in force. LexisNexis Butterworths provides links to statutory instruments made
under the Scotland Act 1998.

The Scottish Parliament

The *Official Report* of the Scottish Parliament can be found on the Parliament   **A1–5**
website (*www.scottishparliament.uk*). The "Current Business" section of the website provides links to the full text of Bills, Committee web pages, research briefings and fact
sheets.

The Scottish Executive

Papers from the Scottish Executive can be found on its website (at *www.scotland. gov.uk*).   **A1–6**

Official Publications

Official Publications can be traced using the TSO Scotland section of the TSO bookshop   **A1–7**
Parliamentary and Legal pages (at *www.tso.co.uk/parliament*); other official publications can
be traced using the UKOP database (**6–16**).

Encyclopedias

The *Laws of Scotland: Stair Memorial Encyclopedia* is available from LexisNexis   **A1–8**
Butterworths (**2–4**). *Laws of Scotland* provides a comprehensive statement of the law of
Scotland, comparable to that provided for England and Wales by *Halsbury's Laws of
England* (**7–3**).
   Westlaw UK (**2–5**) provides access to the full text of *Renton and Brown Criminal
Procedure* (6th edition) and *Renton and Brown Criminal Procedure Legislation*.

A1–9   Northern Ireland law

Case law

A1–10   LexisNexis Professional provides full text access to the two major series of Northern Ireland law reports:
Northern Ireland Reports
   cited, e.g. *Re Jordan's Applications for Judicial Review* [2005] N.I. 144
Northern Ireland Judgments Bulletin
   cited, e.g. *Belfast Fashions v Wellworth Properties Ltd* [2005] N.I.J.B. 95
   Judgments are available from the Northern Ireland Court Service (at *www.courtsni.gov.uk*); also from the BAILII website (at *www.bailii.org*).

Northern Ireland Statutes

A1–11   The full updated text of Northern Ireland Statutes from 1922 to 2004 can be found on the Northern Ireland Legislation page on the OPSI legislation website (at *www.opsi. gov.uk/legislation*).
   The unamended text of all primary legislation for Northern Ireland from 1987 onwards can be found on both the OPSI legislation website and the BAILII website (at *www. bailii.org*). This includes:
Acts of the Northern Ireland Assembly
   cited, e.g. Social Security (Northern Ireland) Act 2002 c.10
Orders in Council
   cited, e.g. Pensions (Northern Ireland) Order 2005
Orders in council are also cited as UK statutory instruments, e.g. S.I. 2005/255 (N.I. 1).

Statutory Rules of Northern Ireland

A1–12   The unamended text of all primary legislation for Northern Ireland from 1996 onwards can be found on both the OPSI legislation website (at *www.opsi.gov.uk/legislation*) and the BAILII website (at *www.bailii.org*). A selection of Statutory Rules is available for 1991–1995.

Northern Ireland Assembly

A1–13   The Official Report of debates is available for 1998–2003 from the Northern Ireland Assembly website (at *www.niassembly.gov.uk*). Assembly and Committee Reports (published as Northern Ireland Assembly Papers) are available for 1999–2003.

Northern Ireland Office

The Northern Ireland Office (NIO) (at *www.nio.gov.uk*) has a "Publications" link for   **A1–14**
Northern Ireland Office Papers. There are also links to Northern Ireland government
departments. If devolution is restored, many of the functions of the NIO pass to the
Northern Ireland Executive (at *www.nics.gov.uk*).

Official Publications

Official Publications can be traced using the TSO Ireland section of the TSO bookshop   **A1–15**
Parliamentary and Legal pages (at *www.tso.co.uk/parliament*); other official publications can
be traced using the UKOP database (**6–16**).

Bulletin of Northern Ireland Law

The *Bulletin of Northern Ireland Law* provides updates on legal developments in Northern   **A1–16**
Ireland. Online access is available for SLS Publications (at *www.sls.qub.ac.uk*). This is a subscription service.

Appendix II Abbreviations of Reports, Series and Journals

A2–1 This alphabetical list contains a selection of the more commonly used abbreviations in the UK, the EC and the Commonwealth. It is not exhaustive and further information can be found in D. Raistrick, *Index to Legal Citations and Abbreviations* and in the I.A.L.S. *Manual of Legal Citations*, Vols. I and II, the *Index to Legal Periodicals*, the *Legal Journals Index. The Digest (Cumulative Supplement)* and the *Current Law Citators* also contain lists of abbreviations, at the front.

A.C.—Law Reports Appeal Cases 1891–
A.J.—Acts Juridica
A.J.I.L.—American Journal of International Law
A.L.J.—Australian Law Journal
A.L.R.—American Law Reports Annotated
A.L.R.—Australian Law Reports, formerly Argus Law Reports
All E.R.—All England Law Reports 1936–
All E.R. Rep.—All England Law Reports Reprint 1558–1935
Am. J. Comp. L.—American Journal of Comparative Law
Anglo-Am. L.R.—Anglo-American Law Review
Ann. Dig.—Annual Digest of Public International Law Cases (1919–1949). (From 1950 this series has been published as the International Law Reports—I.L.R.)
App. Cas.—Law Reports Appeal Cases 1875—1890

B.C.L.C.—Butterworths Company Law Cases
B.D.I.L.—British Digest of International Law
B.F.S.P.—British and Foreign State Papers
B.I.L.C.—British International Law Cases
B.J.A.L.—British Journal of Administrative Law
B.J. Crim.—British Journal of Criminology
B.J.L.S.—British Journal of Law and Society
B.L.R.—Building Law Reports
B.L.R.—Business Law Review
B.N.I.L.—Bulletin of Northern Ireland Law
B.T.R.—British Tax Review

B.Y.I.L.—British Yearbook of International Law
Bull. E.C.—Bulletin of the European Communities
Business L.R.—Business Law Review

C.A.R.—Criminal Appeal Reports
C.A.T.—Court of Appeal Transcript (unpublished)
C.B.R.—Canadian Bar Review
C.D.E.—Cahiers de Droit Européen
C.J.Q.—Civil Justice Quarterly
C.L.—Current Law
C.L.J.—Cambridge Law Journal
C.L.P.—Current Legal Problems
C.L.R.—Commonwealth Law Reports (Australia)
C.M.L.R.—Common Market Law Reports
C.M.L. Rev.—Common Market Law Review
C.P.D.—Law Reports Common Pleas Division 1875–1880
C.T.S.—Consolidated Treaty Series
Calif. L. Rev.—California Law Review
Camb. L.J.—Cambridge Law Journal
Can. B.R.—Canadian Bar Review
Ch.—Law Reports Chancery Division 1891–
Ch.D.—Law Reports Chancery Division 1875–1890
Co. Law.—Company Lawyer
Colum. L. Rev.—Columbia Law Review
Com. Cas.—Commercial Cases 1895–1941
Constr. L.J.—Construction Law Journal
Conv.; Conv.—N.S.—Conveyancer and Property Lawyer
Cox C.C.—Cox's Criminal Law Cases
Cr. App. R.; Cr. App. Rep.—Criminal Appeal Reports
Cr.App.R.(S.)—Criminal Appeal Reports (Sentencing)
Crim. L.R.—Criminal Law Review

D.L.R.—Dominion Law Reports (Canada)
D.U.L.J.—Dublin University Law Journal

E.C.R.—European Court Reports
E.G.—Estates Gazette
E.G.L.R.—Estates Gazette Law Reports
E.H.R.R.—European Human Rights Reports
E.I.P.R.—European Intellectual Property Review
E.L. Rev.—European Law Review
E.R.—English Reports
Eng. Rep.—English Reports
Eur. Comm. H.R. D.R.—European Commission for Human Rights Decisions and Reports
Eur. Court H.R. Series A/Series B—European Court of Human Rights Series A & B
Euro C.L.—European Current Law
Ex.D.—Law Reports Exchequer Division 1875–1880

F.L.R.—Family Law Reports
F.L.R.—Federal Law Reports
F.S.R.—Fleet Street Reports
F.T.—Financial Times
Fam.—Law Reports Family Division 1972—
Fam. Law—Family Law

Grotius Trans.—Transactions of the Grotius Society

H.L.R.—Housing Law Reports
Harv. L. Rev.—Harvard Law Review

I.C.J. Rep.—International Court of Justice Reports
I.C.J.Y.B.—International Court of Justice Yearbook
I.C.L.Q.—International and Comparative Law Quarterly
I.C.R.—Industrial Cases Reports 1975–
I.C.R.—Industrial Court Reports 1972–1974
I.J.; Ir. Jur.—Irish Jurist
I.L.J.—Industrial Law Journal
I.L.M.—International Legal Materials
I.L.Q.—International Law Quarterly
I.L.R.—International Law Reports
I.L.R.M.—Irish Law Reports Monthly
I.L.T.; Ir.L.T.—Irish Law Times
I.R.—Irish Reports
I.R.L.R.—Industrial Relations Law Reports
I.R.R.R.—Industrial Relations Review & Reports
Imm.A.R.—Immigration Appeal Reports
Ir. Jur.—Irish Jurist
I.T.R.—Industrial Tribunal Reports

J.B.L.—Journal of Business Law
J.C.—Session Cases: Justiciary Cases (Scotland)
J.C.L.—Journal of Criminal Law
J.C.M.S.—Journal of Common Market Studies
J.I.S.E.L.—Journal of the Irish Society for European Law
J.I.S.L.L.—Journal of the Irish Society for Labour Law
J.L.S.—Journal of Law and Society
J.L.S.—Journal of the Law Society of Scotland
J. Legal Ed.—Journal of Legal Education
J.O.—Journal Officiel des Communautés Européennes
J.P.—Justice of the Peace Reports (*also* Justice of the Peace (journal))
J.P.I.L.—Journal of Personal Injury Litigation
J.P.L.—Journal of Planning and Environment Law
J.R.—Juridical Review
J.S.P.T.L.—Journal of the Society of Public Teachers of Law
J.S.W.L.—Journal of Social Welfare Law

K.B.—Law Reports: King's Bench Division 1901–1952
K.I.R.—Knight's Industrial Reports

L.A.G. Bul.—Legal Action Group Bulletin
L.G.C.—Local Government Chronicle
L.G.R.—Knight's Local Government Reports
L.J.—Law Journal 1866–1965 (newspaper)
L.J. Adm.—Law Journal: Admiralty N.S. 1865–1875
L.J. Bcy.—Law Journal: Bankruptcy N.S. 1832–1880
L.J.C.C.R.—Law Journal: County Courts Reports 1912–1933
L.J.C.P.—Law Journal: Common Pleas N.S. 1831–1875
L.J. Ch.—Law Journal: Chancery N.S. 1831–1946
L.J. Eccl.—Law Journal: Ecclesiastical Cases N.S. 1866–1875
L.J. Eq.—Law Journal: Equity N.S. 1831–1946
L.J. Ex.—Law Journal: Exchequer N.S. 1831–1875
L.J. Ex. Eq.—Law Journal: Exchequer in Equity 1835–1841
L.J.K.B. (or Q.B.)—Law Journal: King's (or Queen's) Bench N.S. 1831–1946
L.J.M.C.—Law Journal: Magistrates' Cases N.S. 1831–1896
L.J.N.C.—Law Journal: Notes of Cases 1866–1892
L.J.N.C.C.R.—Law Journal Newspaper: County Court Reports 1934–1947
L.J.O.S.—Law Journal (Old Series) 1822–1831
L.J.P.—Law Journal: Probate, Divorce and Admiralty N.S. 1875–1946
L.J.P.D. & A.—Law Journal: Probate, Divorce and Admiralty N.S. 1875–1946
L.J.P. & M. — Law Journal: Probate and Matrimonial Cases N.S. 1858–1859, 1866–1875
L.J.P.C.—Law Journal: Privy Council N.S. 1865–1946
L.J.P.M. & A.—Law Journal: Probate, Matrimonial and Admiralty N.S. 1860–1865
L.J.R.—Law Journal Reports 1947–1949
L. Lib.J.—Law Library Journal
L.M.C.L.Q.—Lloyd's Maritime and Commercial Law Quarterly
L.N.T.S.—League of Nations Treaty Series
L.Q.R.—Law Quarterly Review
L.R.A. & E.—Law Reports: Admiralty and Ecclesiastical Cases 1865–1875
L.R.C.C.R.—Law Reports: Crown Cases Reserved 1865–1875
L.R. C.P.—Law Reports: Common Pleas Cases 1865–1875
L.R. Ch. App.—Law Reports: Chancery Appeal Cases 1865–1875
L.R. Eq.—Law Reports: Equity Cases 1866–1875
L.R. Ex.—Law Reports: Exchequer Cases 1865–1875
L.R.H.L.—Law Reports: English and Irish Appeals 1866–1875
L.R. P. & D.—Law Reports: Probate and Divorce Cases 1865–1875
L.R.P.C.—Law Reports: Privy Council Appeals 1865–1875
L.R.Q.B.—Law Reports: Queen's Bench 1865–1875
L.R.R.P.; L.R. R.P.C.—Law Reports: Restrictive Practices Cases 1957–1973
L.S.—Legal Studies
L.S. Gaz.—Law Society Gazette
L.T.—Law Times
L.T.R.; L.T. Rep.—Law Times Reports (New Series) 1859–1947
L.T.Jo.—Law Times (newspaper) 1843–1965

L.T.O.S.—Law Times Reports (Old Series) 1843–1860
L. Teach.—Law Teacher
Law & Contemp. Prob.—Law and Contemporary Problems
Lit.—Litigation
Liverpool L.R.—Liverpool Law Review
Ll. L.L.R.; Ll.L.R.; LL.L. Rep.—Lloyd's List Law Reports *later* Lloyd's Law Reports
Lloyd's L.R.; Lloyd's Rep.—Lloyd's List Law Reports *later* Lloyd's Law Reports

M.L.J.—Malayan Law Journal
M.L.R.—Modern Law Review
Man. Law—Managerial Law
Med. Sci. & Law—Medicine, Science & the Law
Mich. L. Rev.—Michigan Law Review

N.I.—Northern Ireland Law Reports
N.I.J.B.—Northern Ireland Law Reports Bulletin of Judgments
N.I.L.Q.—Northern Ireland Legal Quarterly
N.I.L.R.—Northern Ireland Law Reports
N.L.J.—New Law Journal
N.Y.U.L. Rev.—New York University Law Review
N.Z.L.R.—New Zealand Law Reports
New L.J.—New Law Journal

O.J.—Official Journal of the European Communities
O.J.C.—Official Journal of the European Communities: Information and Notices
O.J.L.—Official Journal of the European Communities: Legislation, e.g. 1972, L139/28
O.J.L.S.—Oxford Journal of Legal Studies

P.—Law Reports: Probate, Divorce and Admiralty 1891–1971
P. & C.R.—Planning (Property from 1968) and Compensation Reports
P.C.I.J.—Permanent Court of International Justice Reports of Judgments
P.D.—Law Reports: Probate Division 1875–1890
P.L.—Public Law
P.N.—Professional Negligence

Q.B.—Law Reports: Queen's Bench Division 1891–1901, 1952–
Q.B.D.—Law Reports: Queen's Bench Division 1875–1890

R.D.E.—Rivista di Diritto Europeo
R.G.D.I.P.—Revue Générale de Droit International Public
R.M.C.—Revue du Marché Commun
R.P.C.—Reports of Patent, Design & Trade Mark Cases
R.R.—Revised Reports
R.R.C.—Ryde's Rating Cases
R.T.R.—Road Traffic Reports
R.V.R.—Rating & Valuation Reporter
Rec.—Recueil des Cours
Rec.—Recueil de la Jurisprudence de la Cour (Court of Justice of the European Communities)

S.A.—South African Law Reports
S.C.—Session Cases (Scotland)
S.C. (H.L.)—Session Cases: House of Lords (Scotland)
S.C.(J.)—Session Cases: Justiciary Cases (Scotland)
S.C.C.R.—Scottish Criminal Case Reports
S.I.—Statutory Instruments
S.J.—Solicitors Journal
S.L.R.—Law Reporter/Scottish Law Review
S.L.T.—Scots Law Times
S.R.—Statutory Rules (Northern Ireland)
S.R. & O.—Statutory Rules and Orders
S.T.C.—Simon's Tax Cases
Scolag.—Bulletin of the Scottish Legal Action Group
Sol. Jo.—Solicitors Journal
St. Tr.; State Tr.—State Trials 1163–1820
Stat.L.R.—Statute Law Review
State Tr. N.S.—State Trials (New Series) 1820–1858

T.C.—Reports of Tax Cases
T.L.R.—Times Law Reports
TSO—The Stationery Office, 1996–
Tax Cas.—Reports of Tax Cases
Tul. L. Rev.—Tulane Law Review

U. Chi. L. Rev.—University of Chicago Law Review
U.K.T.S.—United Kingdom Treaty Series
U.N.T.S.—United Nations Treaty Series
U.N.J.Y.—United Nations Juridical Yearbook
U.N.Y.B.—Yearbook of the United Nations
U. Pa. L. Rev.—University of Pennsylvania Law Review
U.S. —United States Supreme Court Reports
U.S.T.S.—United States Treaty Series

V.A.T.T.R.—Value Added Tax Tribunal Reports
V.L.R.—Victorian Law Reports (Australia)

W.I.R.—West Indian Reports
W.L.R.—Weekly Law Reports
W.N.—Weekly Notes
W.W.R.—Western Weekly Reporter

Y.B.—Yearbook (old law report), e.g. (1466) Y.B.Mich. (the term) 6 Edw. 4, pl. 18, fol.7
(plea, folio)
Y.B.W.A.—Yearbook of World Affairs
Yale L.J.—Yale Law Journal
Yearbook E.C.H.R.—Yearbook of the European Convention on Human Rights

Appendix III How Do I Find?
A Summary of Sources for
English Law

Abbreviations (3–5)

A3–1 *Cardiff Index to Legal Abbreviations*
D. Raistrick, *Index to Legal Citations and Abbreviations*.
The front pages of: *Current Law Case Citator; The Digest*, Vol. 1 and the *Cumulative Supplement*; *Halsbury's Laws of England*, Vol. 1.

A3–2 ## Books

Tracing Books on a Subject

Use the library catalogue (**7–29**).
Consult bibliographies (see below).

Tracing Books by Author or Title

Use the library catalogue (**7–29**).
Consult bibliographies (see below).

Bibliographies

D. Raistrick, *Lawyers' Law Books* (**7–31**).   A3–3
Current Publications in Legal and Related Fields (authors, titles and subjects) (**7–33**).
Legal Bibliography of the British Commonwealth (useful for older books) (**7–35**).
Bibliography on Foreign and Comparative Law (**7–35**).
British National Bibliography (**7–36**).
Law Books 1876–1981 (**7–34**).
Specialist legal bibliographies (**7–35**)—ask the library staff for advice.
The catalogues of large specialist and national libraries (**7–29**).
Sources for books in print (**7–37**).

Finding Cases

If you Know the Name of the Case (Summary: after **3–20**)   A3–4
Westlaw UK *Case Locators* (**3–15**).
Current Law Case Citators (**3–16**).
Online databases of case law (**2–2, 3–8**).
The Digest (**3–15**).
English Reports (for English cases *before* 1865) (**3–10**).
For Recent Law Reports
Westlaw UK *Case Locators* (**3–15**).
Current Law (**3–16**).
Cases in recent issues of *The Times* and other newspapers (**5–22**).
For Very Recent Unreported Cases (**3–17**)
Online updates on recent cases (**3–22**).
Daily Law Notes (**3–22**).
Full-text databases of judgments (**3–19** and **3–20**).

Tracing Cases on a Subject
Westlaw UK *Case Locators* (**7–9**).
Current Law (**7–12** and **7–13**).
The Digest (**7–14**).
Full-text case law databases (**7–10**).
Halsbury's Laws of England (**7–4**).
Databases providing updates to recent cases (**3–22**).

Tracing the Subsequent Judicial History of a Case (**7–18**)
Westlaw UK *Case Locators* (**7–9**).
Current Law (**7–12** and **7–13**).
The Digest (**7–14**).
Full-text case law databases (**7–10**).
Law Reports Index (table of cases judicially considered) (**7–16**).

Are there any Journal Articles on this Case?
Latest issue of *Current Law Monthly* (entries in the Cumulative Table of Cases).
Lawtel *Journals Index* (**5–8**).
Legal Journals Index (**5–6**).
Indexes to individual journals, e.g. *Modern Law Review; Law Quarterly Review*.

General Statements of The Law

A3–5   Textbooks (**7–29**).
Halsbury's Laws of England (**7–3**).
Specialised legal encyclopedias (**7–6**).

Government Publications

A3–6   **Tracing Government Publications**
BOPCRIS database (pre-1995 publications) (**6–16**).
General Index to Accounts and Papers (**6–16**).
Subject Catalogue of House of Commons Parliamentary Papers (or *Index to House of Commons Papers* on CD-ROM) (**6–16**).
TSO *Daily Lists* and catalogues (HMSO pre-1996) (**6–15**).
UKOP database (**6–16**).

A3–7   # Journal Articles

Articles on a Subject

Legal Journals Index (**5–6**).
Lawtel *Journals Index* (**5–8**).
Index to Legal Periodicals (**5–7**).
Index to Foreign Legal Periodicals (**5–9**).
Current Law Monthly Digests (under appropriate subject heading) (**7–12**) and *Current Law Year Books* (at the back of the volumes) (**7–13**).
Other non-legal journal indexes (**5–12** *et seq.*)

Articles on a Case

Latest issue of *Current Law Monthly* (entries in the Cumulative Table of Cases).
Legal Journals Index (**5–6**).
Lawtel *Journals Index* (**5–8**).
Indexes to individual journals, e.g. *Modern Law Review; Law Quarterly Review.*

Articles on an Act

Legal Journals Index (**5–6**).
Westlaw UK *UK Legislation Locators* (**4–18**).
Current Law Legislation Citators (**4–19**).
Indexes to journals (under the appropriate subject heading).

Tracing Journals

Consult the library's periodicals catalogue (**1–8**).
If the journal is not available in your library, use other catalogues as for books (**7–29**)—ask
  the library staff for advice.

Statutes

Collections of the Statutes   A3–8

Older statutes
Statutes of the Realm (**4–22**).
Statutes at Large (various editions) (**4–23**).
Acts and Ordinances of the Interregnum (**4–24**).

Modern statutes
BAILII United Kingdom Statutes (**4–8**).
Justis *UK Statutes* (**4–9**).
Current Law Statutes (**4–11**).
LexisNexis Butterworths *UK Parliament Acts* (**4–13**).
LexisNexis Professional *UK Legislation* (**4–14**).
Westlaw UK *UK Legislation* (**4–15**).
Halsbury's Statutes (**4–16**).

Collections of Acts by subject
Halsbury's Statutes (**4–16, 7–23**).

Annotated editions of statutes
Current Law Statutes (**4–11**).
Halsbury's Statutes (**4–16, 7–23**).

Statutes in force
Halsbury's Statutes (**4–16, 7–23**).
Westlaw UK *UK Legislation Locators* (**4–18**).
LexisNexis Butterworths *UK Parliament Acts* (**4–13**).
LexisNexis Professional *UK Legislation* (**4–14**).
Westlaw UK *UK Legislation* (**4–15**).
Chronological Table of the Statutes (**4–20**).
Current Law Legislation Citators (**4–19**).
Is It In Force? (**4–17**).

Tracing Statutes on a Subject
Halsbury's Statutes (**4–17, 7–23**).
Full-text databases of legislation (**7–21**) (other online sources **7–22**).
Halsbury's Laws (**7–3**).

Indexes to the Statutes
Chronological Table of the Statutes (shows whether Acts of any date are still in force) (**4–20**).
Is It In Force? (**4–17**).
Halsbury's Statutes (alphabetically arranged by subject. Consult alphabetical list of statutes, then look in the *Cumulative Supplement* and *Noter-Up* service to check if an Act is still in force) (**7–23**).
Public General Acts: Tables and Index (annual—brings the information in the *Chronological Table of Statutes* up to date) (**4–6**).

Local and Personal Acts—Indexes
Index to Local and Personal Acts 1801–1947 (**4–25**).
Supplementary Index to the Local and Personal Acts 1948–1966 (**4–25**).
Local and Personal Acts; Tables and Index (annual) (**4–25**).

Is this Act Still in Force? Has it Been Amended?
Is It In Force? (shows whether Acts passed since 1961 are still in force) (**4–17**).
Chronological Table of the Statutes (indicates if an Act of any date is in force) (**4–20**).
Westlaw UK Legislation Locators (**4–18**).
Current Law Legislation Citators (**4–19**).
Full-text databases of legislation in force (**4–12**).
Public General Acts: Tables and Index (annual—brings the information in the *Chronological Table* up to date—see the table "Effects of Legislation") (**4–6**).
Halsbury's Statutes (consult the main volumes, the *Cumulative Supplement and* the looseleaf *Service* volume) (**4–16**).

What Cases Have there Been on the Interpretation of this Act?
Westlaw UK *Legislation Locators* (**4–18**).
Current Law Legislation Citators (**4–19**).
Halsbury's Statutes (**7–23**).

What Statutory Instruments Have Been Made under this Act?
Westlaw UK *Legislation Locators* (**4–18**).
Current Law Legislation Citators (**4–19**).
Halsbury's Statutes (**4–16**).

Have any Journal Articles Been Written about this Act?
Westlaw UK *Legislation Locators* (**4–18**).
Current Law Legislation Citators (**4–19**).
Legal Journals Index (**5–6**).
Other indexes to journal articles (see heading "Journal Articles", above).

Has this Act Been Brought into Force by a Statutory Instrument?
Halsbury's Statutes (**4–16**).
Westlaw UK *Legislation Locators* (**4–18**).
Current Law Legislation Citators (**4–19**).

Statutory Instruments

Collections of Statutory Instruments   A3–9

Statutory Rules and Orders and Statutory Instruments Revised (all statutory instruments in
    force in 1948) (**4–26**).
Statutory Instruments (annual volumes—subject index in last volume of each year) (**4–26**).
Halsbury's Statutory Instruments (selective—arranged by subject) (**4–29**).
Justis *UK Statutory Instruments* database (**4–26**).
Full-text databases of legislation (**4–12**).

Is this Statutory Instrument in Force? Has it Been Amended?

Halsbury's Statutory Instruments (**4–29**).
Full-text databases of legislation in force (**4–12**).

What Statutory Instruments Have been Made under this Act?

Westlaw UK *Legislation Locators* (**4–18**).
Current Law Legislation Citator (**4–19**).
Halsbury's Statutes (**4–16**).

Has this Act Been Brought into Force by a Statutory Instrument?

Is It in Force? (**4–17**).
Westlaw UK *Legislation Locators* (**4–18**).
Current Law Legislation Citators (**4–19**).

Indexes to Statutory Instruments

Halsbury's Statutory Instruments (chronological, alphabetical and by subject) (**4–29, 7–27**).
TSO Daily Lists (includes all new Instruments as they are published) (**6–15**).

Theses

A3–10   *Index to Theses* (**7–38**).
Dissertation Abstracts (**7–38**).

Words And Phrases

A3–11   For the meaning of words and phrases, use legal dictionaries (**1–10**).
For Latin phrases, use legal dictionaries and Broom's *Legal Maxims* (**1–10**).

Judicial and Statutory Definitions of Words and Phrases
Words and Phrases Legally Defined (**7–19**).
Stroud's Judicial Dictionary.
The entry "Words and Phrases" in: *Law Reports: Consolidated Index; Current Law Monthly Digests* and *Current Law Year Books*; and indexes to the *All England Law Reports, Halsbury's Laws*, and *The Digest*.

Index

(all references are to paragraph number)